Vocabulary Workshop Answer Keys

Introductory Through Sixth Courses

FOR

- **Vocabulary Workshop**
- **Vocabulary Workshop Tests**

HOLT, RINEHART AND WINSTON

A Harcourt Classroom Education Company

Austin · New York · Orlando · Atlanta · San Francisco · Boston · Dallas · Toronto · London

STAFF CREDITS

EDITORIAL

Director
Mescal Evler

Manager of Editorial Operations
Bill Wahlgren

Executive Editor
Emily G. Shenk

Project Editor
Cheryl L. Christian

Writer and Editor
Janis D. Russell

Copyediting
Michael Neibergall, *Copyediting Manager;* Mary Malone, *Senior Copyeditor;* Joel Bourgeois, Elizabeth Dickson, Gabrielle Field, Jane Kominek, Julie A. Mills, Millicent Ondras, Theresa Reding, Dennis Scharnberg, Kathleen Scheiner, Laurie Schlesinger, *Copyeditors*

Project Administration
Marie Price, *Managing Editor;* Lori De La Garza, *Editorial Operations Coordinator;* Thomas Browne, Heather Cheyne, Diane Hardin, Mark Holland, Marcus Johnson, Jill O'Neal, Joyce Rector, Janet Riley, Kelly Tankersley, *Project Administration;* Gail Coupland, Ruth Hooker, Margaret Sanchez, *Word Processing*

Editorial Permissions
Janet Harrington, *Permissions Editor*

ART, DESIGN AND PHOTO

Graphic Services
Kristen Darby, *Manager*

Image Acquisitions
Joe London, *Director;* Tim Taylor, *Photo Research Supervisor;* Rick Benavides, *Assistant Photo Researcher;* Elaine Tate, *Supervisor;* Erin Cone, *Art Buyer*

Cover Design
Sunday Patterson

PRODUCTION
Belinda Barbosa Lopez, *Senior Production Coordinator;* Simira Davis, *Supervisor;* Nancy Hargis, *Media Production Supervisor;* Joan Lindsay, *Production Coordinator;* Beth Prevelige, *Prepress Manager*

ELECTRONIC PUBLISHING
Carol Martin, *Senior Electronic Publishing Manager;* Robert Franklin, *Electronic Publishing Manager;* Indira Konanur, *Project Coordinator;* JoAnn Brown, Richard Chavez, Jim Gaile, Heather Jernt, Lana Kaupp, Christopher Lucas, Nanda Patel, *EP staff;* Anne Johnson, Katelijne Lefevere, Sally Williams, *Quality Control Coordinators*

MANUFACTURING
Michael Roche, *Senior Manufacturing Coordinator*

Printed in the United States of America

ISBN 0-03-057416-1

8 9 054 05 04

Table of Contents

Table of Contents *(continued)*

Using *Vocabulary Workshop*

The Design of
Vocabulary Workshop

Vocabulary instruction works best in an interactive, student-centered model. Instead of providing students with alphabetized lists of words to memorize, *Vocabulary Workshop* presents words in groups, in the context of meaningful subject matter.

Each *Vocabulary Workshop* book is based on a list of three hundred words. Because students learn and remember new vocabulary best when the words are introduced in small groups, each *Vocabulary Workshop* book divides the word list into three broad context areas of one hundred words each. For example, in the Introductory Course, the three one-hundred-word groups are titled "Amazing Nature," "People and Places," and "Ecology and Environment." These three groupings are further separated into clusters of either ten or twenty words.

The exercises in *Vocabulary Workshop* are designed to reflect the latest testing practices. Making New Words Your Own, Understanding New Words and Their Uses, and Reading New Words in Context in the Introductory, First, and Second Courses reflect the kind of items students will encounter in the Metropolitan Achievement Tests, the Stanford Achievement Test, and the Comprehensive Test of Basic Skills. Reading New Words in Context in the Third through Sixth Courses has been influenced by the SAT. Connecting New Words and Patterns is designed to introduce students to the kind of analogies they may also encounter on the SAT.

Vocabulary Workshop:
Text Organization

Making New Words Your Own introduces students to each Vocabulary Word through Wordbusting and Context Clues items. Ten Vocabulary Words are introduced in each of the thirty lessons in Making New Words Your Own. In Wordbusting, students figure out the meaning of a new word by examining the context in which it is used, analyzing the structure of the word, determining what the word sounds like, and looking up its definition. In Context Clues, students read the Vocabulary Word in another context and match the word to its correct definition. In the Introductory, First, and Second Courses, students also identify synonyms and antonyms in Like Meanings and Opposite Meanings items. In the Third, Fourth, Fifth, and Sixth Courses, students work Sentence Completion items, using the Vocabulary Words in context.

Understanding New Words and Their Uses in the Introductory, First, and Second Courses includes exercises in Multimeaning and Word Analysis. In the Multimeaning exercise, students compare sentences that use different meanings of the same word. In Word Analysis, students identify a word's meaning by using prefixes, suffixes, and word origins.

Using *Vocabulary Workshop*

Each of the fifteen lessons in Connecting New Words and Patterns allows students to build logic skills through practice with analogies. In the Introductory, First, and Second Courses, students identify the relationship of the pair of words in the stem and in the answer options. They then match the appropriate relationships. In the Third, Fourth, Fifth, and Sixth Courses, students choose the pair of words that expresses the same relationship as the stem words.

In Reading New Words in Context, the Vocabulary Words are used in fifteen reading passages. Students answer twenty multiple-choice items in each lesson, using the passage to determine the meaning of each Vocabulary Word. In the Third, Fourth, Fifth, and Sixth Courses, students also provide synonyms for each of the twenty words in a lesson by referring to the passage.

Vocabulary Workshop Tests

Vocabulary Workshop Tests assess students' mastery of the words presented in *Vocabulary Workshop*, using both formative and summative tests.

Each formative test asks students to choose synonyms for the ten Vocabulary Words that correspond to one lesson in Making New Words Your Own, the first section of *Vocabulary Workshop*.

The three elaborate summative tests are modeled on state and national tests and use the same subject matter covered in the accompanying *Vocabulary Workshop* lessons. Each test covers one hundred words used in ten lessons of Making New Words Your Own.

Vocabulary Workshop Answer Key

Vocabulary Workshop

The answers for every item in the the seven courses of *Vocabulary Workshop* are included in the *Vocabulary Workshop Answer Key*. The answers for the exercises in Connecting New Words and Patterns also contain an explanation of the correct analogy.

Vocabulary Workshop Tests

The answers for each test are also included in the answer key. The point scoring for each test is included in the directions for the test. The score for each test totals 100 points.

Using *Vocabulary Workshop*

Sequence of the Lessons and Tests | The following chart shows how the various sections of *Vocabulary Workshop* interrelate and how the *Vocabulary Workshop Tests* assess the Vocabulary Words used in the first of the three broad context areas.

How *Vocabulary Workshop* and *Vocabulary Workshop Tests* Interrelate

CONTEXT: Amazing Nature					
Book Title		*Vocabulary Workshop*	*Vocabulary Workshop Tests*	*Vocabulary Workshop*	*Vocabulary Workshop Tests*
Section Title in *Vocabulary Workshop* or *Vocabulary Workshop Tests*	**Vocabulary Words**	**Making New Words Your Own**	**Formative Assessment**	**Understanding New Words and Their Uses (Introductory, First, and Second Courses only)** + **Connecting New Words and Patterns** + **Reading New Words in Context**	**Summative Assessment**
Lesson or Test	1st set of 10 words from the list	Lesson 1	Test 1	Lesson 1 (first 20 words)	Test 1
	2nd set of 10 words from the list	Lesson 2	Test 2		
	3rd set of 10 words from the list	Lesson 3	Test 3	Lesson 2 (second 20 words)	
	4th set of 10 words from the list	Lesson 4	Test 4		
	5th set of 10 words from the list	Lesson 5	Test 5	Lesson 3 (third 20 words)	
	6th set of 10 words from the list	Lesson 6	Test 6		
	7th set of 10 words from the list	Lesson 7	Test 7	Lesson 4 (fourth 20 words)	
	8th set of 10 words from the list	Lesson 8	Test 8		
	9th set of 10 words from the list	Lesson 9	Test 9	Lesson 5 (fifth 20 words)	
	10th set of 10 words from the list	Lesson 10	Test 10		

Using *Vocabulary Workshop*

Using *Vocabulary Workshop* in the Classroom

You may wish to work with this innovative series in one of the following ways.

Option 1

- Working with twenty words at a time, begin by teaching two lessons in Making New Words Your Own. For example, for the Introductory, First, and Second Courses, work through Lessons 1 and 2 of Making New Words Your Own, then proceed directly to Lesson 1 of Understanding New Words and Their Uses, Lesson 1 of Connecting New Words and Patterns, and Lesson 1 of Reading New Words in Contest. Then, administer the accompanying Formative Assessment Tests 1 and 2.

- After completing ten lessons in Making New Words Your Own and each of the corresponding lessons in the remaining sections of *Vocabulary Workshop,* administer the accompanying Summative Assessment in *Vocabulary Workshop Tests.*

Option 2

- Proceed through each of the thirty lessons in Making New Words Your Own. In this way, you will introduce students to the entire three-hundred-word list, ten words at a time. After students complete each lesson in Making New Words Your Own, administer the accompanying formative test.

- If the mean score on these tests is eighty percent or above, you may not find it necessary to work through the remaining *Vocabulary Workshop* sections.

- If the mean score is below eighty percent, or if your goal is to prepare students for standardized tests, you may wish to assign Connecting New Words and Patterns, Reading New Words in Context, and, for the Introductory, First, and Second Courses, Understanding New Words and Their Uses.

- After working through ten lessons of Making New Words Your Own and the corresponding lessons in each of the remaining sections of *Vocabulary Workshop,* administer the accompanying Summative Test in *Vocabulary Workshop Tests.*

Making New Words Your Own

Lesson 1

p. 3 | Exercise 1: Wordbusting

> **NOTES**
> - For each Vocabulary Word, students should fill in at least one of the **context, structure,** and **sound** boxes.
> - Check that students vary the boxes they use throughout the exercise.
> - Make sure students look up each word in the dictionary and fill in the dictionary box; answers will vary depending on the dictionary used.

p. 5 | Exercise 2: Context Clues

11. B	majority	16. E	vivid
12. D	definite	17. H	deny
13. I	symbol	18. C	twilight
14. G	doubtful	19. A	descendant
15. J	navigator	20. F	reliable

p. 6 | Exercise 3: Like Meanings and Opposite Meanings

21. B	26. C
22. A	27. B
23. D	28. C
24. C	29. A
25. B	30. D

Lesson 2

p. 7 | Exercise 1: Wordbusting

> **NOTES**
> - For each Vocabulary Word, students should fill in at least one of the **context, structure,** and **sound** boxes.
> - Check that students vary the boxes they use throughout the exercise.
> - Make sure students look up each word in the dictionary and fill in the dictionary box; answers will vary depending on the dictionary used.

p. 9 | Exercise 2: Context Clues

11. G	astonish	16. B	innumerable
12. A	legend	17. I	conference
13. D	interview	18. F	journalism
14. J	unexpectedly	19. H	session
15. E	quote	20. C	summarize

p. 10 | Exercise 3: Like Meanings and Opposite Meanings

21. B	26. C
22. A	27. B
23. D	28. C
24. A	29. A
25. C	30. A

Lesson 3

p. 11 | Exercise 1: Wordbusting

> **NOTES**
> - For each Vocabulary Word, students should fill in at least one of the **context, structure,** and **sound** boxes.
> - Check that students vary the boxes they use throughout the exercise.
> - Make sure students look up each word in the dictionary and fill in the dictionary box; answers will vary depending on the dictionary used.

p. 13 | Exercise 2: Context Clues

11. J	rash	16. D	predict
12. A	foundation	17. E	incident
13. B	disastrous	18. I	collapse
14. C	nuisance	19. G	fatal
15. F	collide	20. H	complex

p. 14 | Exercise 3: Like Meanings and Opposite Meanings

21. D	26. B
22. A	27. A
23. B	28. D
24. C	29. D
25. D	30. A

Lesson 4

p. 15 | Exercise 1: Wordbusting

> **NOTES**
> - For each Vocabulary Word, students should fill in at least one of the **context, structure,** and **sound** boxes.
> - Check that students vary the boxes they use throughout the exercise.
> - Make sure students look up each word in the dictionary and fill in the dictionary box; answers will vary depending on the dictionary used.

p. 17 | Exercise 2: Context Clues

11. I aviation	17. J exception
12. G disturb	18. C demonstra-
13. F miraculous	tion
14. A locally	19. D detect
15. E instinct	20. B departure
16. H unfavorable	

p. 18 | Exercise 3: Like Meanings and Opposite Meanings

21. D	26. B
22. A	27. A
23. C	28. A
24. D	29. D
25. B	30. C

Lesson 5

p. 19 | Exercise 1: Wordbusting

> **NOTES**
> - For each Vocabulary Word, students should fill in at least one of the **context, structure,** and **sound** boxes.
> - Check that students vary the boxes they use throughout the exercise.
> - Make sure students look up each word in the dictionary and fill in the dictionary box; answers will vary depending on the dictionary used.

p. 21 | Exercise 2: Context Clues

11. G gratitude	16. C heroic
12. E caution	17. J generation
13. H involve	18. I separation
14. D error	19. B dread
15. F congratulate	20. A previous

p. 22 | Exercise 3: Like Meanings and Opposite Meanings

21. A	26. C
22. C	27. A
23. B	28. D
24. D	29. A
25. C	30. C

Lesson 6

p. 23 | Exercise 1: Wordbusting

> **NOTES**
> - For each Vocabulary Word, students should fill in at least one of the **context, structure,** and **sound** boxes.
> - Check that students vary the boxes they use throughout the exercise.
> - Make sure students look up each word in the dictionary and fill in the dictionary box; answers will vary depending on the dictionary used.

p. 25 | Exercise 2: Context Clues

11. F abdomen	16. G foe
12. B hoist	17. E flexible
13. A escort	18. C paralysis
14. D mobile	19. I maximum
15. H commotion	20. J competition

p. 26 | Exercise 3: Like Meanings and Opposite Meanings

21. D	26. B
22. B	27. B
23. A	28. D
24. C	29. A
25. B	30. B

Lesson 7

p. 27 | Exercise 1: Wordbusting

NOTES
- For each Vocabulary Word, students should fill in at least one of the **context, structure,** and **sound** boxes.
- Check that students vary the boxes they use throughout the exercise.
- Make sure students look up each word in the dictionary and fill in the dictionary box; answers will vary depending on the dictionary used.

p. 29 | Exercise 2: Context Clues

11. D linger
12. H discomfort
13. C vault
14. I inhale
15. E earnest
16. G discourage
17. A requirement
18. B dainty
19. F vacuum
20. J regulate

p. 30 | Exercise 3: Like Meanings and Opposite Meanings

21. A
22. D
23. C
24. D
25. B
26. C
27. A
28. C
29. D
30. C

Lesson 8

p. 31 | Exercise 1: Wordbusting

NOTES
- For each Vocabulary Word, students should fill in at least one of the **context, structure,** and **sound** boxes.
- Check that students vary the boxes they use throughout the exercise.
- Make sure students look up each word in the dictionary and fill in the dictionary box; answers will vary depending on the dictionary used.

p. 33 | Exercise 2: Context Clues

11. G gasp
12. F acquire
13. H portion
14. E imposter
15. A terminal
16. J disguise
17. I hibernate
18. C conceal
19. B reference
20. D imitate

p. 34 | Exercise 3: Like Meanings and Opposite Meanings

21. C
22. A
23. A
24. B
25. D
26. A
27. C
28. C
29. A
30. D

Lesson 9

p. 35 | Exercise 1: Wordbusting

NOTES
- For each Vocabulary Word, students should fill in at least one of the **context, structure,** and **sound** boxes.
- Check that students vary the boxes they use throughout the exercise.
- Make sure students look up each word in the dictionary and fill in the dictionary box; answers will vary depending on the dictionary used.

p. 37 | Exercise 2: Context Clues

11. E pierce
12. A surgery
13. H bureau
14. D receipt
15. F resign
16. J particle
17. G bombard
18. C static
19. B pharmacy
20. I lunar

p. 38 | Exercise 3: Like Meanings and Opposite Meanings

21. B
22. B
23. D
24. C
25. A
26. A
27. A
28. D
29. A
30. B

Workshop Answer Key *(continued)*

Lesson 10

p. 39 | Exercise 1: Wordbusting

> **NOTES**
> - For each Vocabulary Word, students should fill in at least one of the **context, structure,** and **sound** boxes.
> - Check that students vary the boxes they use throughout the exercise.
> - Make sure students look up each word in the dictionary and fill in the dictionary box; answers will vary depending on the dictionary used.

p. 41 | Exercise 2: Context Clues

11. G stray		**16.** F suspicion
12. C jeopardy		**17.** I conviction
13. E toll		**18.** H gossip
14. A license		**19.** J ransom
15. D pry		**20.** B flammable

p. 42 | Exercise 3: Like Meanings and Opposite Meanings

21. B	**26.** B
22. A	**27.** A
23. C	**28.** B
24. C	**29.** D
25. B	**30.** A

Lesson 11

p. 43 | Exercise 1: Wordbusting

> **NOTES**
> - For each Vocabulary Word, students should fill in at least one of the **context, structure,** and **sound** boxes.
> - Check that students vary the boxes they use throughout the exercise.
> - Make sure students look up each word in the dictionary and fill in the dictionary box; answers will vary depending on the dictionary used.

p. 45 | Exercise 2: Context Clues

11. A essential	**16.** E reaction
12. G thorough	**17.** H document
13. I publicity	**18.** D career
14. J debate	**19.** F offspring
15. B identical	**20.** C analyze

p. 46 | Exercise 3: Like Meanings and Opposite Meanings

21. B	**26.** C
22. B	**27.** A
23. C	**28.** C
24. A	**29.** B
25. D	**30.** D

Lesson 12

p. 47 | Exercise 1: Wordbusting

> **NOTES**
> - For each Vocabulary Word, students should fill in at least one of the **context, structure,** and **sound** boxes.
> - Check that students vary the boxes they use throughout the exercise.
> - Make sure students look up each word in the dictionary and fill in the dictionary box; answers will vary depending on the dictionary used.

p. 49 | Exercise 2: Context Clues

11. A notion	**16.** D generous
12. H self-confidence	**17.** G destination
13. B determination	**18.** F profession
14. C respectable	**19.** I scholar
15. J biography	**20.** E routine

p. 50 | Exercise 3: Like Meanings and Opposite Meanings

21. D	**26.** A
22. C	**27.** C
23. A	**28.** A
24. D	**29.** B
25. B	**30.** C

Lesson 13

p. 51 | Exercise 1: Wordbusting

> **NOTES**
> - For each Vocabulary Word, students should fill in at least one of the **context, structure,** and **sound** boxes.
> - Check that students vary the boxes they use throughout the exercise.
> - Make sure students look up each word in the dictionary and fill in the dictionary box; answers will vary depending on the dictionary used.

p. 53 | Exercise 2: Context Clues

11. G conduct
12. C scheme
13. A quarantine
14. H ignite
15. J ceremony
16. B interrupt
17. I consent
18. D fragrant
19. E plead
20. F management

p. 54 | Exercise 3: Like Meanings and Opposite Meanings

21. A
22. B
23. D
24. D
25. B
26. A
27. D
28. A
29. B
30. A

Lesson 14

p. 55 | Exercise 1: Wordbusting

> **NOTES**
> - For each Vocabulary Word, students should fill in at least one of the **context, structure,** and **sound** boxes.
> - Check that students vary the boxes they use throughout the exercise.
> - Make sure students look up each word in the dictionary and fill in the dictionary box; answers will vary depending on the dictionary used.

p. 57 | Exercise 2: Context Clues

11. D architect
12. G desperate
13. I glimpse
14. E sacrifice
15. B betray
16. C eternal
17. H victim
18. A realm
19. F district
20. J victorious

p. 58 | Exercise 3: Like Meanings and Opposite Meanings

21. B
22. A
23. D
24. B
25. A
26. A
27. B
28. A
29. C
30. A

Lesson 15

p. 59 | Exercise 1: Wordbusting

> **NOTES**
> - For each Vocabulary Word, students should fill in at least one of the **context, structure,** and **sound** boxes.
> - Check that students vary the boxes they use throughout the exercise.
> - Make sure students look up each word in the dictionary and fill in the dictionary box; answers will vary depending on the dictionary used.

p. 61 | Exercise 2: Context Clues

11. D descriptive
12. C flourish
13. F terrain
14. B abundant
15. A establish
16. J survey
17. H possess
18. G barrier
19. I prehistoric
20. E desirable

p. 62 | Exercise 3: Like Meanings and Opposite Meanings

21. D
22. B
23. A
24. C
25. D
26. C
27. A
28. B
29. D
30. A

Workshop Answer Key *(continued)*

Lesson 16

p. 63 | Exercise 1: Wordbusting

NOTES
- For each Vocabulary Word, students should fill in at least one of the **context, structure,** and **sound** boxes.
- Check that students vary the boxes they use throughout the exercise.
- Make sure students look up each word in the dictionary and fill in the dictionary box; answers will vary depending on the dictionary used.

p. 65 | Exercise 2: Context Clues

11. B	dramatic	17. E	feat
12. C	marvel	18. D	vicinity
13. G	irregular	19. I	extraordinary
14. F	satisfy		
15. H	leisure	20. A	inaccurate
16. J	numerous		

p. 66 | Exercise 3: Like Meanings and Opposite Meanings

21. C	26. A
22. A	27. C
23. B	28. B
24. C	29. A
25. D	30. C

Lesson 17

p. 67 | Exercise 1: Wordbusting

NOTES
- For each Vocabulary Word, students should fill in at least one of the **context, structure,** and **sound** boxes.
- Check that students vary the boxes they use throughout the exercise.
- Make sure students look up each word in the dictionary and fill in the dictionary box; answers will vary depending on the dictionary used.

p. 69 | Exercise 2: Context Clues

11. C	heir	16. H	exclaim
12. D	envy	17. F	oath
13. E	portrait	18. G	yacht
14. I	wardrobe	19. A	reign
15. B	ambitious	20. J	honorable

p. 70 | Exercise 3: Like Meanings and Opposite Meanings

21. D	26. A
22. A	27. C
23. B	28. A
24. C	29. D
25. D	30. C

Lesson 18

p. 71 | Exercise 1: Wordbusting

NOTES
- For each Vocabulary Word, students should fill in at least one of the **context, structure,** and **sound** boxes.
- Check that students vary the boxes they use throughout the exercise.
- Make sure students look up each word in the dictionary and fill in the dictionary box; answers will vary depending on the dictionary used.

p. 73 | Exercise 2: Context Clues

11. H	counterfeit	16. F	investment
12. E	request	17. I	luxurious
13. A	knapsack	18. J	transparent
14. D	ornamental	19. B	relate
15. C	solitary	20. G	arid

p. 74 | Exercise 3: Like Meanings and Opposite Meanings

21. B	26. B
22. A	27. A
23. C	28. C
24. D	29. C
25. C	30. D

Lesson 19

p.75 | Exercise 1: Wordbusting

> **NOTES**
> - For each Vocabulary Word, students should fill in at least one of the **context, structure,** and **sound** boxes.
> - Check that students vary the boxes they use throughout the exercise.
> - Make sure students look up each word in the dictionary and fill in the dictionary box; answers will vary depending on the dictionary used.

p.77 | Exercise 2: Context Clues

11. C appropriate	16. A ordinary
12. H hearty	17. E quantity
13. I occasion	18. B cultivate
14. J assume	19. G inviting
15. F gorgeous	20. D contribute

p.78 | Exercise 3: Like Meanings and Opposite Meanings

21. B	26. C
22. C	27. B
23. A	28. A
24. D	29. C
25. B	30. B

Lesson 20

p.79 | Exercise 1: Wordbusting

> **NOTES**
> - For each Vocabulary Word, students should fill in at least one of the **context, structure,** and **sound** boxes.
> - Check that students vary the boxes they use throughout the exercise.
> - Make sure students look up each word in the dictionary and fill in the dictionary box; answers will vary depending on the dictionary used.

p.81 | Exercise 2: Context Clues

11. H boast	16. B precipitation
12. A contrast	17. I export
13. E import	18. G exert
14. C tradition	19. F eliminate
15. J disadvantage	20. D luscious

p.82 | Exercise 3: Like Meanings and Opposite Meanings

21. C	26. C
22. B	27. B
23. B	28. A
24. B	29. A
25. A	30. A

Lesson 21

p.83 | Exercise 1: Wordbusting

> **NOTES**
> - For each Vocabulary Word, students should fill in at least one of the **context, structure,** and **sound** boxes.
> - Check that students vary the boxes they use throughout the exercise.
> - Make sure students look up each word in the dictionary and fill in the dictionary box; answers will vary depending on the dictionary used.

p.85 | Exercise 2: Context Clues

11. J visual	16. A genuine
12. G theme	17. E entertain
13. D inform	18. I text
14. F inspiration	19. C appreciate
15. B mammoth	20. H braille

p.86 | Exercise 3: Like Meanings and Opposite Meanings

21. D	26. B
22. B	27. A
23. C	28. D
24. A	29. C
25. A	30. A

Workshop Answer Key *(continued)*

Lesson 22

p. 87 | Exercise 1: Wordbusting

> **NOTES**
> - For each Vocabulary Word, students should fill in at least one of the **context, structure,** and **sound** boxes.
> - Check that students vary the boxes they use throughout the exercise.
> - Make sure students look up each word in the dictionary and fill in the dictionary box; answers will vary depending on the dictionary used.

p. 89 | Exercise 2: Context Clues

11. H juvenile	**16.** C furious
12. G doubtless	**17.** I campaign
13. E reduction	**18.** B characteristic
14. A plot	**19.** F urge
15. D widespread	**20.** J conscience

p. 90 | Exercise 3: Like Meanings and Opposite Meanings

21. B	**26.** B
22. C	**27.** B
23. D	**28.** A
24. C	**29.** A
25. A	**30.** C

Lesson 23

p. 91 | Exercise 1: Wordbusting

> **NOTES**
> - For each Vocabulary Word, students should fill in at least one of the **context, structure,** and **sound** boxes.
> - Check that students vary the boxes they use throughout the exercise.
> - Make sure students look up each word in the dictionary and fill in the dictionary box; answers will vary depending on the dictionary used.

p. 93 | Exercise 2: Context Clues

11. B inexpensive	**16.** G guidance
12. A issue	**17.** I villain
13. E persuade	**18.** F revolution
14. C protest	**19.** D remedy
15. J applaud	**20.** H temporary

p. 94 | Exercise 3: Like Meanings and Opposite Meanings

21. A	**26.** B
22. B	**27.** C
23. C	**28.** A
24. D	**29.** D
25. C	**30.** A

Lesson 24

p. 95 | Exercise 1: Wordbusting

> **NOTES**
> - For each Vocabulary Word, students should fill in at least one of the **context, structure,** and **sound** boxes.
> - Check that students vary the boxes they use throughout the exercise.
> - Make sure students look up each word in the dictionary and fill in the dictionary box; answers will vary depending on the dictionary used.

p. 97 | Exercise 2: Context Clues

11. F hazard	**17.** E merchandise
12. A dissolve	
13. I ballot	**18.** D corporation
14. G adjust	**19.** C employer
15. B foul	**20.** H disgust
16. J candidate	

p. 98 | Exercise 3: Like Meanings and Opposite Meanings

21. B	**26.** A
22. C	**27.** C
23. C	**28.** D
24. D	**29.** A
25. A	**30.** A

Introductory Course | *Vocabulary Workshop*

Lesson 25

p. 99 | Exercise 1: Wordbusting

NOTES
- For each Vocabulary Word, students should fill in at least one of the **context, structure,** and **sound** boxes.
- Check that students vary the boxes they use throughout the exercise.
- Make sure students look up each word in the dictionary and fill in the dictionary box; answers will vary depending on the dictionary used.

p. 101 | Exercise 2: Context Clues

11. I complaint
12. B mourning
13. E absorb
14. F tension
15. J regret
16. H debt
17. D omit
18. A security
19. G cooperate
20. C offense

p. 102 | Exercise 3: Like Meanings and Opposite Meanings

21. C
22. D
23. A
24. D
25. B
26. D
27. B
28. C
29. D
30. A

Lesson 26

p. 103 | Exercise 1: Wordbusting

NOTES
- For each Vocabulary Word, students should fill in at least one of the **context, structure,** and **sound** boxes.
- Check that students vary the boxes they use throughout the exercise.
- Make sure students look up each word in the dictionary and fill in the dictionary box; answers will vary depending on the dictionary used.

p. 105 | Exercise 2: Context Clues

11. G rebel
12. B duplicate
13. I simplify
14. J resident
15. D amateur
16. H intrusion
17. E privacy
18. F sympathy
19. A self-respect
20. C keen

p. 106 | Exercise 3: Like Meanings and Opposite Meanings

21. A
22. B
23. A
24. C
25. A
26. A
27. D
28. A
29. D
30. C

Lesson 27

p. 107 | Exercise 1: Wordbusting

NOTES
- For each Vocabulary Word, students should fill in at least one of the **context, structure,** and **sound** boxes.
- Check that students vary the boxes they use throughout the exercise.
- Make sure students look up each word in the dictionary and fill in the dictionary box; answers will vary depending on the dictionary used.

p. 109 | Exercise 2: Context Clues

11. J eavesdrop
12. H captivity
13. B survival
14. A prey
15. E decrease
16. G threat
17. F prohibit
18. I tragedy
19. C provoke
20. D migrate

p. 110 | Exercise 3: Like Meanings and Opposite Meanings

21. C
22. A
23. D
24. D
25. B
26. B
27. C
28. B
29. A
30. D

Lesson 28

p. 111 | Exercise 1: Wordbusting

NOTES

- For each Vocabulary Word, students should fill in at least one of the **context, structure,** and **sound** boxes.

- Check that students vary the boxes they use throughout the exercise.

- Make sure students look up each word in the dictionary and fill in the dictionary box; answers will vary depending on the dictionary used.

p. 113 | Exercise 2: Context Clues

11. G suburb
12. F obvious
13. J vocal
14. E unfortunate
15. H benefit
16. B reckless
17. A responsibility
18. C unite
19. D resemble
20. I severe

p. 114 | Exercise 3: Like Meanings and Opposite Meanings

21. A
22. D
23. B
24. C
25. D
26. C
27. A
28. B
29. B
30. D

Lesson 29

p. 115 | Exercise 1: Wordbusting

NOTES

- For each Vocabulary Word, students should fill in at least one of the **context, structure,** and **sound** boxes.

- Check that students vary the boxes they use throughout the exercise.

- Make sure students look up each word in the dictionary and fill in the dictionary box; answers will vary depending on the dictionary used.

p. 117 | Exercise 2: Context Clues

11. B anthem
12. H compliment
13. A rehearsal
14. J nominate
15. E engage
16. I promotion
17. F courteous
18. C justify
19. D specify
20. G qualify

p. 118 | Exercise 3: Like Meanings and Opposite Meanings

21. C
22. C
23. B
24. C
25. D
26. A
27. D
28. A
29. B
30. C

Lesson 30

p. 119 | Exercise 1: Wordbusting

NOTES

- For each Vocabulary Word, students should fill in at least one of the **context, structure,** and **sound** boxes.

- Check that students vary the boxes they use throughout the exercise.

- Make sure students look up each word in the dictionary and fill in the dictionary box; answers will vary depending on the dictionary used.

p. 121 | Exercise 2: Context Clues

11. D associate
12. F toxic
13. B apologize
14. H frantic
15. C reservoir
16. J pollute
17. E hesitate
18. I superior
19. G application
20. A impatience

p. 122 | Exercise 3: Like Meanings and Opposite Meanings

21. D
22. A
23. B
24. D
25. A
26. B
27. D
28. B
29. D
30. C

Workshop Answer Key *(continued)*

Understanding New Words and Their Uses

Lesson 1

p. 125 | Exercise 1: Multimeaning

1. C   2. B

p. 125 | Exercise 2: Word Analysis

3. A   7. astonish
4. C   8. deny
5. D   9. innumerable
6. C   10. twilight

Lesson 2

p. 127 | Exercise 1: Multimeaning

1. C   2. A

p. 127 | Exercise 2: Word Analysis

3. C   7. nuisance
4. A   8. aviation
5. B   9. collide
6. C   10. instinct

Lesson 3

p. 129 | Exercise 1: Multimeaning

1. B   2. C

p. 129 | Exercise 2: Word Analysis

3. D   7. foe
4. C   8. paralysis
5. C   9. error
6. A   10. congratulate

Lesson 4

p. 131 | Exercise 1: Multimeaning

1. D   2. C

p. 131 | Exercise 2: Word Analysis

3. C   7. imposter
4. A   8. gasp
5. A   9. portion
6. A   10. dainty

Lesson 5

p. 133 | Exercise 1: Multimeaning

1. A   2. B

p. 133 | Exercise 2: Word Analysis

3. C   7. gossip
4. C   8. ransom
5. D   9. receipt
6. A   10. bombard

Lesson 6

p. 135 | Exercise 1: Multimeaning

1. D   2. A

p. 135 | Exercise 2: Word Analysis

3. C   7. notion
4. D   8. publicity
5. A   9. analyze
6. C   10. offspring

Lesson 7

p. 137 | Exercise 1: Multimeaning

1. C   2. C

p. 137 | Exercise 2: Word Analysis

3. D   7. architect
4. C   8. realm
5. B   9. district
6. C   10. quarantine

Lesson 8

p. 139 | **Exercise 1: Multimeaning**
1. B
2. D

p. 139 | **Exercise 2: Word Analysis**
3. B
4. D
5. D
6. C
7. feat
8. barrier
9. marvel
10. vicinity

Lesson 9

p. 141 | **Exercise 1: Multimeaning**
1. C
2. A

p. 141 | **Exercise 2: Word Analysis**
3. B
4. B
5. B
6. A
7. yacht
8. arid
9. oath
10. knapsack

Lesson 10

p. 143 | **Exercise 1: Multimeaning**
1. C
2. D

p. 143 | **Exercise 2: Word Analysis**
3. B
4. A
5. D
6. C
7. quantity
8. import
9. gorgeous
10. occasion

Lesson 11

p. 145 | **Exercise 1: Multimeaning**
1. D
2. B

p. 145 | **Exercise 2: Word Analysis**
3. A
4. C
5. A
6. A
7. juvenile
8. widespread
9. theme
10. conscience

Lesson 12

p. 147 | **Exercise 1: Multimeaning**
1. A
2. C

p. 147 | **Exercise 2: Word Analysis**
3. B
4. A
5. B
6. D
7. villain
8. applaud
9. disgust
10. persuade

Lesson 13

p. 149 | **Exercise 1: Multimeaning**
1. C
2. B

p. 149 | **Exercise 2: Word Analysis**
3. C
4. D
5. B
6. D
7. tension
8. privacy
9. complaint
10. keen

Lesson 14

p. 151 | **Exercise 1: Multimeaning**
1. B
2. C

p. 151 | **Exercise 2: Word Analysis**
3. A
4. C
5. C
6. C
7. suburb
8. tragedy
9. provoke
10. severe

Lesson 15

p. 153 | **Exercise 1: Multimeaning**
1. B
2. D

p. 153 | **Exercise 2: Word Analysis**
3. C
4. D
5. B
6. A
7. engage
8. anthem
9. qualify
10. reservoir

Connecting New Words and Patterns

Lesson 1

p. 158 | Analogies

1. (B); Synonym. *Conference* and *meeting* have similar meanings, as do *people* and *persons*.
   (A) PW   (D) PO
   (C) A   (E) L

2. (E); Antonym. A *descendant* comes after an individual, while an *ancestor* comes before. The two words are opposite in meaning, as are *inside* and *outside*.
   (A) CQ or S   (C) PO
   (B) D   (D) PW

3. (C); Synonym. *Doubtful* and *unsure* both mean uncertain. *Hurt* and *harmed* are also synonyms.
   (A) PA   (D) CQ
   (B) A   (E) L

4. (B); Antonym. *Innumerable,* countless, means the opposite of *few. Safe,* which means free of danger, is the opposite of *dangerous.*
   (A) S   (D) C
   (C) D   (E) CQ

5. (A); Function. The function of *journalism* is to *inform,* just as the function of *comedy* is to *amuse.*
   (B) S   (D) CE
   (C) PO   (E) C

6. (C); Synonym. *Legend* and *myth* have similar meanings, just as the *rhythm* of a song is nearly the same thing as its *beat.*
   (A) PW   (D) A
   (B) CE   (E) PA

7. (C); Antonym. *Majority* is the opposite of *minority,* just as *odd* is the opposite of *even.*
   (A) AO   (D) PO
   (B) PW   (E) CQ

8. (A); Performer and Action. You expect a *navigator* to *steer* a ship, just as you expect a *chauffeur* to *drive* a car.
   (B) F or AO   (D) S
   (C) PW   (E) CQ

9. (D); Classification. A *flag* may be classified as a *symbol,* just as a *senator* may be classified as a *politician.*
   (A) PW   (C) PO
   (B) CE   (E) A

10. (B); Synonym. *Vivid* and *lively* have similar meanings, as do *necessary* and *needed.*
    (A) A   (D) F
    (C) L   (E) D

Lesson 2

p. 159 | Analogies

1. (C); Classification. *Aviation* may be classified as a *science,* just as *typing* may be classified as a *skill.*
   (A) S   (D) PW
   (B) L   (E) CQ

2. (A); Synonym. *Collide* and *crash* have similar meanings, as do *toss* and *hurl.*
   (B) PW   (D) PO
   (C) CE   (E) A

3. (C); Synonym. *Complex,* which means complicated, is similar in meaning to *involved,* just as *glance* is similar to *peek.*
   (A) CQ   (D) C
   (B) A   (E) CE

4. (C); Antonym. *Departure* is opposite in meaning to *arrival,* just as *left* is the opposite of *right.*
   (A) PO   (D) CE
   (B) AO   (E) L

5. (A); Synonym. *Disturb* and *bother* have similar meanings, as do to *show* and to *display.*
   (B) A   (D) L
   (C) F   (E) C

6. (C); Degree. A *fatal* accident is worse than an accident that is merely *harmful*. Similarly, a *brilliant* person is smarter than a *bright* person.
(A) C   (D) PO
(B) L   (E) PW

7. (D); Part and Whole. A *foundation* is part of a *structure* just as an *introduction* is part of an *essay*.
(A) PA   (C) L
(B) F   (E) CQ

8. (B); Synonym. *Incident* is similar in meaning to *event*, while *car* is another word for *automobile*.
(A) PA   (D) PW or L
(C) C   (E) PO

9. (D); Characteristic Quality. A *nuisance* is characteristically *annoying*, just as a *riddle* is characteristically *puzzling*.
(A) L   (C) PW
(B) PO   (E) C

10. (C); Antonym. *Rash*, which can mean reckless, is the opposite of *careful*, just as *messy* is the opposite of *neat*.
(A) CE   (D) AO
(B) S   (E) C

Lesson 3

p. 160 | Analogies

1. (A); Part and Whole. The *abdomen* is part of the *body*, just as a *trunk* is part of an *elephant*.
(B) CQ   (D) A
(C) S   (E) PA

2. (C); Antonym. *Caution* is the opposite of *carelessness*, just as *sound* is the opposite of *silence*.
(A) S   (D) CQ
(B) D   (E) PW

3. (C); Synonym. A *commotion* is similar to a *disturbance*, just as something's *value* is similar to its *worth*.
(A) PW   (D) CE
(B) A   (E) F

4. (B); Characteristic Quality. *Rubber* is characteristically *flexible*, just as *perfume* is characteristically *fragrant*.
(A) S   (D) CE
(C) A   (E) PO

5. (C); Antonym. A *foe*, or enemy, is the opposite of a *friend*, just as a *beginning* is the opposite of a *conclusion*.
(A) PA   (D) C
(B) PW   (E) D

6. (C); Cause and Effect. *Gratitude* can be the result of a *favor*. *Anger* can be the result of an *insult*.
(A) F   (D) PW
(B) L   (E) PA

7. (E); Characteristic Quality. A *rescuer* is characteristically *heroic*, just as a *prince* is characteristically *royal*.
(A) S   (C) PA
(B) PO   (D) F

8. (B); Function. The function of a *crane* is to *hoist*, or lift, heavy objects. In the same way, the function of a *truck* is to *transport*, or carry, goods.
(A) C   (D) S
(C) CQ   (E) A

9. (A); Synonym. *Maximum* is similar in meaning to *greatest*, just as *least* is similar in meaning to *smallest*.
(B) D   (D) CQ
(C) AO or F   (E) A

10. (E); Antonym. *Previous* means the opposite of *next*, just as *boring* means the opposite of *entertaining*.
(A) PO   (C) CE
(B) D   (D) S

Lesson 4

p. 161 | Analogies

1. (E); Synonym. *Acquire* and *get* have similar meanings, as do *wish* and *desire*.
(A) C   (C) PW
(B) CE   (D) A

2. (E); Characteristic Quality. *Lace* is characteristically *dainty*, just as *diamonds* are characteristically *sparkling*.
   - (A) A
   - (B) S
   - (C) F or C
   - (D) L

3. (A); Antonym. To *disguise* something is roughly the opposite of to *expose* it, while to *bore* someone is the opposite of to *entertain* that person.
   - (B) S
   - (C) PO
   - (D) CE
   - (E) PA

4. (E); Antonym. *Earnest*, which means serious, is opposite in meaning to *joking*, just as *noisy* is opposite in meaning to *quiet*.
   - (A) C
   - (B) CE
   - (C) S
   - (D) D

5. (D); Cause and Effect. A *gasp* can result from *surprise*, just as *tears* can result from *sorrow*.
   - (A) A
   - (B) D
   - (C) C
   - (E) S

6. (E); Performer and Action. You expect a *bear* to *hibernate*, just as you expect a *tourist* to *travel*.
   - (A) F
   - (B) S
   - (C) CE
   - (D) A

7. (D); Action and Object. You *inhale air*, just as you *rake leaves*.
   - (A) PO
   - (B) C
   - (C) D
   - (E) CQ

8. (B); Synonym. *Linger* and *wait* have similar meanings, as do *talk* and *chat*.
   - (A) CE
   - (C) A
   - (D) PA
   - (E) CQ

9. (A); Synonym. *Requirement* and *necessity* have similar meanings, as do the nouns *help* and *assistance*.
   - (B) L
   - (C) A
   - (D) PO
   - (E) CQ

10. (C); Characteristic Quality. A *vacuum* is characteristically *empty*, just as *lightning* is characteristically *bright*.
    - (A) S
    - (B) C
    - (D) PW
    - (E) F

Lesson 5

p. 162 | Analogies

1. (B); Synonym. *Bureau*, when it refers to a government office, means the same as *agency*. In the same way, *piece* and *section* have similar meanings.
   - (A) A
   - (C) L
   - (D) PW
   - (E) C

2. (E); Characteristic Quality. *Gasoline* is characteristically *flammable*, just as *cotton* is characteristically *absorbent*.
   - (A) A
   - (B) C
   - (C) S
   - (D) D

3. (B); Synonym. *Jeopardy* and *risk* have similar meanings, as do *strange* and *unfamiliar*.
   - (A) CE
   - (C) PW
   - (D) PO
   - (E) C

4. (C); Synonym. *Lunar* is similar in meaning to *moonlike*, just as *sunny* is similar in meaning to *bright*.
   - (A) PO
   - (B) A
   - (D) D
   - (E) F

5. (C); Location. *Medicines* can be found in a *pharmacy*, just as *spices* can be found in the *kitchen*.
   - (A) CQ
   - (B) PO
   - (D) PW
   - (E) A

6. (C); Cause and Effect. When you *pierce* something, you create a *hole*. In the same way, *dew* can cause *dampness*.
   - (A) A
   - (B) AO
   - (D) PA
   - (E) F

7. (A); Function. The function of a *crowbar* is to *pry*, just as the function of a *razor* is to *shave*.
   - (B) CQ
   - (C) S
   - (D) AO
   - (E) C

8. (C); Antonym. To *resign* from a job means the opposite of to *apply* for a job. Similarly, to *divide* a task is the opposite of *combining* several tasks.
   - (A) CE
   - (B) D
   - (D) CQ
   - (E) L

Workshop Answer Key *(continued)*

9. (C); Characteristic Quality. A *statue* is characteristically *static*, or unmoving, just as the *ocean* is characteristically *salty*.
(A) PW   (D) C
(B) A   (E) F

10. (A); Antonym. *Suspicion* means the opposite of *trust*, just as *boredom* means the opposite of *interest*.
(B) PA   (D) CQ
(C) S   (E) L or PW

Lesson 6

p. 163 | Analogies

1. (D); Classification. A *biography* may be classified as *nonfiction*, just as *biology* may be classified as *science*.
(A) A   (C) CQ
(B) D   (E) S

2. (A); Synonym. *Debate* is similar in meaning to *argue*, just as *select* is similar in meaning to *choose*.
(B) C   (D) PW or L
(C) A   (E) PO

3. (E); Classification. A *birth certificate* may be classified as a *document*, just as a *dictionary* may be classified as a *book*.
(A) AO   (C) D
(B) CQ   (D) S

4. (C); Antonym. *Essential* and *unnecessary* have opposite meanings, as do *grinning* and *frowning*.
(A) S   (D) CE
(B) PW   (E) F

5. (D); Antonym. *Generous* and *stingy* have opposite meanings, as do *rude* and *polite*.
(A) L   (C) C
(B) S   (E) PO

6. (E); Degree. Things that are *identical* are alike to a greater degree than things that are *similar*, just as something that is *boiling* is much hotter than something that is *warm*.
(A) PO   (C) S
(B) L   (D) A

7. (E); Classification. *Teaching* may be classified as a *profession*, just as *silk* may be classified as a *fabric*.
(A) PA   (C) D
(B) S   (D) CE

8. (C); Antonym. *Routine* is the opposite of *unusual*, just as *planned* is the opposite of *unexpected*.
(A) S   (D) CE
(B) C   (E) PO

9. (E); Performer and Action. You expect a *scholar* to *read*, just as you expect a *pilot* to *fly*.
(A) PW   (C) L
(B) PO   (D) S

10. (D); Synonym. *Thorough* and *complete* have nearly the same meaning, as do *broad* and *wide*.
(A) CE   (C) AO
(B) CQ   (E) A

Lesson 7

p. 164 | Analogies

1. (C); Performer and Object. An *architect* works with a *blueprint*, while a *composer* creates a *symphony*.
(A) A   (D) F
(B) C   (E) S

2. (B); Synonym. To *betray* and to *deceive* have nearly the same meaning, as do to *work* and to *labor*.
(A) A   (D) L
(C) C   (E) PO

3. (D); Classification. A *wedding* may be classified as a *ceremony*, just as *Utah* may be classified as a *state*.
(A) D   (C) A
(B) S   (E) CQ

4. (A); Synonym. *District* is similar in meaning to *section*, just as *boring* is similar in meaning to *dull*.
(B) C   (D) PO
(C) CE   (E) L

Introductory Course | *Vocabulary Workshop*

Workshop Answer Key *(continued)*

5. (B); Antonym. Something *eternal* is the opposite of something *temporary*. Similarly, *raw* is the opposite of *cooked*.
(A) S   (D) C
(C) PW   (E) CQ

6. (B); Characteristic Quality. A *rose* is characteristically *fragrant*, or sweet-smelling, just as *china* is characteristically *fragile*.
(A) PA   (D) PW
(C) L   (E) PO

7. (A); Antonym. To *ignite* a fire is the opposite of to *put out* a fire, just as *rest* is the opposite of *activity*.
(B) F   (D) CE
(C) D   (E) AO

8. (C); Synonym. *Quarantine* and *isolation* have similar meanings, as do *command* and *order*.
(A) AO   (D) CQ
(B) A   (E) CE

9. (D); Synonym. *Scheme* and *plot* have nearly the same meaning, as do *order* and *arrange*.
(A) F   (C) L
(B) A   (E) AO

10. (D); Performer and Action. A *victim* is someone who *suffers*, just as a *victor* is someone who *wins*.
(A) C   (C) A
(B) CQ   (E) L

Lesson 8

p. 165 | Analogies

1. (B); Synonym. *Abundant* and *plentiful* have nearly the same meaning, as do *rich* and *wealthy*.
(A) CQ   (D) C
(C) A   (E) PO

2. (B); Synonym. *Descriptive* and *detailed* have nearly the same meaning, as do *still* and *motionless*.
(A) A   (D) PW
(C) CQ   (E) PO

3. (A); Antonym. *Desirable* means the opposite of *disgusting*, just as *bright* means the opposite of *faded*.
(B) S   (D) AO
(C) PW   (E) D

4. (A); Antonym. *Dramatic*, or showy, means the opposite of *dull*. *Comical* means the opposite of *gloomy*.
(B) S   (D) L
(C) CQ   (E) PW

5. (C); Degree. Something *extraordinary* is much rarer than something *unusual*. In the same way, something *awful* is much worse than something that is merely *bad*.
(A) CQ   (D) A
(B) F   (E) L

6. (D); Synonym. *Flourish* and *display* are similar in meaning, just as *unselfish* is similar in meaning to *generous*.
(A) C   (C) A
(B) PA   (E) PW

7. (A); Synonym. *Possess* and *have* have nearly the same meaning, as do *lift* and *raise*.
(B) PA   (D) AO
(C) A   (E) L

8. (E); Synonym. *Prehistoric* is similar in meaning to *ancient*, just as *yell* is similar in meaning to *shout*.
(A) AO   (C) CE
(B) PA   (D) PW

9. (D); Antonym. To *satisfy* someone is the opposite of to *disappoint* someone, just as to *approve* means the opposite of to *reject*.
(A) PA   (C) CE
(B) PW   (E) S

10. (C); Synonym. *Terrain* and *ground* have nearly the same meaning, as do *ask* and *request*.
(A) L   (D) CQ
(B) A   (E) F or AO

Workshop Answer Key (continued)

Lesson 9

p. 166 | Analogies

1. (C); Antonym. *Ambitious*, or eager for advancement, means the opposite of *content*, or happy with what one already has, just as *large* means the opposite of *small*.
   (A) S   (D) F
   (B) C   (E) CQ

2. (E); Antonym. *Arid*, or dry, means the opposite of *wet*, just as *asleep* means the opposite of *awake*.
   (A) F   (C) CE
   (B) CQ   (D) PA

3. (E); Synonym. *Counterfeit* has a similar meaning to *fake*, just as *difficult* has a similar meaning to *hard*.
   (A) A   (C) F
   (B) CE   (D) CQ

4. (C); Synonym. *Envy* has nearly the same meaning as *jealousy*, just as *desire* has nearly the same meaning as *want*.
   (A) L   (D) PO
   (B) PW   (E) A

5. (B); Degree. To *exclaim* is to *say* something with a great degree of excitement. To *inspect* is to examine more carefully than merely to *glance*.
   (A) AO   (D) A
   (C) CQ   (E) CE

6. (D); Characteristic Quality. A *shrub* is characteristically *ornamental*, just as a *tool* is characteristically *useful*.
   (A) C   (C) L
   (B) F   (E) A

7. (D); Performer and Action. You expect a *king* to *reign* over his subjects, just as you expect a *waiter* to *serve* food to customers.
   (A) C   (C) L
   (B) PW   (E) D

8. (E); Characteristic Quality. A *loner* is characteristically *solitary*, just as a *ballerina* is characteristically *graceful*.
   (A) C   (C) S
   (B) A   (D) PW

9. (A); Characteristic Quality. *Glass* is characteristically *transparent*, or see-through. A *window* is characteristically *breakable*.
   (B) A   (D) PW
   (C) AO   (E) CE

10. (C); Part and Whole. An *outfit* is part of your *wardrobe*, just as a *wrench* is part of a *tool set*.
    (A) PO   (D) CQ
    (B) F   (E) A

Lesson 10

p. 167 | Analogies

1. (C); Antonym. *Appropriate* means the opposite of *unsuitable*, just as *fresh* means the opposite of *stale*.
   (A) CE   (D) S
   (B) CQ   (E) PW

2. (A); Synonym. *Boast* and *brag* have nearly the same meaning , as do *try* and *attempt*.
   (B) A   (D) CQ
   (C) CE   (E) AO

3. (D); Action and Object. You *cultivate* a *garden*, just as you *harvest* a *crop*.
   (A) CE   (C) L
   (B) A   (E) PA

4. (A); Antonym. *Eliminate*, which means to get rid of, means the opposite of *include*, just as *start* means the opposite of *finish*.
   (B) C   (D) AO
   (C) S   (E) L

5. (D); Action and Object. You can *export* *goods*, just as you can *write* a *letter*.
   (A) S   (C) L
   (B) D   (E) PO

6. (E); Synonym. *Inviting* and *attractive* have similar meanings, as do *incorrect* and *wrong*.
   (A) A   (C) PO
   (B) CQ   (D) CE

Workshop Answer Key *(continued)*

7. (E); Classification. A *birthday* may be classified as an *occasion*, just as a *dictionary* may be classified as a *book*.
(A) S   (C) L
(B) PO   (D) PA

8. (B); Synonym. *Ordinarily* and *usually* have nearly the same meaning, as do *quickly* and *fast*.
(A) F   (D) CE
(C) PW   (E) L

9. (C); Classification. *Snow* may be classified as *precipitation*, just as *golf* may be classified as a *sport*.
(A) L   (D) A
(B) S   (E) AO

10. (B); Synonym. *Tradition* and *custom* have similar meanings, as do *filth* and *dirt*.
(A) PW   (D) F or AO
(C) CQ   (E) L

Lesson 11

p. 168 | Analogies

1. (B); Antonym. To *appreciate*, or think highly of, is the opposite of *despise*, just as to *interest* is the opposite of to *bore*.
(A) PA   (D) S
(C) CE or A (E) C

2. (E); Action and Object. A person *reads* braille, just as a person *writes* an *essay*.
(A) A   (C) C
(B) S or D (D) PA

3. (D); Performer and Action. You expect a *politician* to *campaign*, just as you expect an *athlete* to *compete*.
(A) CQ   (C) A
(B) PW   (E) S

4. (A); Function. The function of *conscience* is to *guide* one's actions, just as the function of a *brain* is to *think*.
(B) CE   (D) PO
(C) PW   (E) CQ

5. (C); Performer and Action. You expect a *performer* to *entertain* an audience, just as you expect an *author* to *write* books.
(A) A   (D) PW
(B) F   (E) S

6. (B); Degree. Someone who is *furious* is angrier than someone who is *annoyed*. Someone who is *delighted* is more pleased than someone who is merely *glad*.
(A) PW   (D) AO
(C) A   (E) L

7. (D); Synonym. *Genuine* and *real* have nearly the same meaning, as do *solo* and *alone*.
(A) A   (C) AO
(B) PA   (E) L

8. (A); Antonym. *Juvenile*, as an adjective meaning immature, is opposite in meaning to *mature*, just as *combined* is opposite in meaning to *separate*.
(B) D   (D) L
(C) S   (E) AO or F

9. (C); Synonym. *Theme* is similar in meaning to *subject*, just as *habit* is similar in meaning to *custom*.
(A) A   (D) AO
(B) PW   (E) C

10. (C); Degree. *Urge* suggests a stronger degree of persuasion than *suggest*. In the same way, to *crash* suggests a stronger degree of impact than to *bump*.
(A) F or AO (D) AO
(B) CE   (E) A

Lesson 12

p. 169 | Analogies

1. (D); Performer and Object. A *voter* uses a *ballot* to vote, in the same way that a *customer* uses an *order form* to place an order.
(A) PW   (C) AO
(B) L   (E) S

2. (B); Synonym. *Dissolve* and *melt* are similar in meaning, as are *wash* and *cleanse*.

(A) PA	(D) PO
(C) C	(E) CQ

3. (A); Synonym. *Guidance* and *advice* are similar in meaning, as are *penalty* and *punishment*.

(B) PO	(D) PW
(C) A	(E) AO

4. (A); Synonym. *Hazard* and *danger* are similar in meaning, as are *chance* and *opportunity*.

(B) C	(D) CE
(C) AO	(E) A

5. (C); Antonym. *Inexpensive* and *costly* have opposite meanings, as do *dressy* and *casual*.

(A) C or CQ	(D) CQ
(B) S	(E) AO

6. (D); Location. *Merchandise* can be found in a *mall*, just as *groceries* can be found in a *supermarket*.

(A) PO	(C) PW
(B) CQ	(E) C

7. (A); Antonym. *Protest* roughly means the opposite of *agree*, just as *raise* means the opposite of *lower*.

(B) C	(D) CQ
(C) AO	(E) CE

8. (B); Synonym. *Remedy* and *cure* are similar in meaning, as are *memory* and *recollection*.

(A) A	(D) PW
(C) CQ	(E) C

9. (D); Synonym. *Revolution* and *revolt* have similar meanings, as do *street* and *avenue*.

(A) PA	(C) F
(B) PO	(E) AO

10. (A); Antonym. *Temporary*, or short-term, means the opposite of *permanent*, just as *calm* means the opposite of *upset*.

(B) C	(D) D
(C) CQ	(E) S

Lesson 13

p.170 | Analogies

1. (E); Antonym. *Amateur* is the opposite of *professional*, just as *neat* is the opposite of *disorderly*.

(A) S	(C) C
(B) PO	(D) CQ

2. (C); Cause and Effect. A *problem* can cause someone to make a *complaint*, just as *success* can cause people to give *praise*.

(A) CQ	(D) AO
(B) F	(E) C

3. (E); Action and Object. You *pay* off a *debt*, just as you *obey* a *law*.

(A) PO	(C) S
(B) L	(D) C

4. (C); Synonym. A *duplicate* of something is the same thing as a *copy* of it, just as someone's *position* is the same thing as his or her *location*.

(A) F	(D) PW
(B) PO	(E) CQ

5. (A); Cause and Effect. *Death* can cause people to go into *mourning*, just as *victory* can cause people to have a *celebration*.

(B) L	(D) C
(C) AO	(E) PA

6. (E); Antonym. To *omit* is the opposite of to *include*, just as to *pay* is the opposite of to *borrow*.

(A) PA	(C) PW
(B) S	(D) AO

7. (B); Antonym. To *rebel* is the opposite of to *obey*, just as to *bore* is roughly the opposite of to *entertain*.

(A) S	(D) PW
(C) PA	(E) C

8. (C); Classification. *Regret* can be classified as a *feeling*, just as *pleasantness* can be classified as an *attitude*.

(A) L	(D) PA
(B) AO	(E) CQ

Workshop Answer Key *(continued)*

9. (B); Synonym. *Self-respect* and *self-esteem* have nearly the same meaning, as do *faith* and *belief*.
(A) C   (D) A
(C) PW (E) AO

10. (D); Synonym. *Sympathy* is similar in meaning to *pity*, as *robbery* is similar in meaning to *theft*.
(A) A   (C) AO
(B) CQ (E) C or AO

Lesson 14

p. 171 | Analogies

1. (D); Antonym. *Obvious*, which means clearly seen, is opposite in meaning to *hidden*, just as *completed* and *unfinished* have opposite meanings.
(A) S   (C) F or AO
(B) D   (E) AO

2. (E); Characteristic Quality. *Prey*, a hunted animal, is characteristically *hunted*, just as an *artist* is characteristically *inspired*, or impelled to create.
(A) F   (C) CE
(B) AO (D) C

3. (D); Antonym. *Prohibit* means the opposite of *allow*, just as *defend* means roughly the opposite of *attack*.
(A) PO (C) S
(B) CQ or C (E) PA

4. (A); Antonym. *Reckless* means the opposite of *careful*, just as *clumsy* means the opposite of *graceful*.
(B) C   (D) S
(C) L   (E) D

5. (D); Degree. Things that *match* are more alike in appearance than things that *resemble* one another. In the same way, to *demand* something is to request it much more strongly than to *suggest* it.
(A) L   (C) CQ
(B) PW (E) AO

6. (C); Synonym. *Responsibility* is similar in meaning to *duty*, just as *job* is similar in meaning to *occupation*.
(A) C   (D) A
(B) PO (E) CQ

7. (B); Synonym. The *suburbs* of a city are nearly the same as its *outskirts*, just as the word *areas* can be used to refer to the *sections* of a town.
(A) CE (D) L
(C) C   (E) F

8. (D); Cause and Effect. A *tragedy* can cause *suffering*, just as a *delay* can cause *tardiness*.
(A) PW (C) C
(B) D   (E) AO

9. (A); Antonym. To *unite* is the opposite of to *divide*, just as to *work* is the opposite of to *loaf*.
(B) C   (D) L
(C) PO (E) AO

10. (C); Characteristic Quality. A *parrot* is characteristically *vocal*, or talkative, just as a *library* is characteristically *quiet*.
(A) F   (D) C
(B) S   (E) L

Lesson 15

p. 172 | Analogies

1. (E); Antonym. To *compliment* means the opposite of to *insult*, just as to *disappoint* means the opposite of to *please*.
(A) PO (C) C
(B) PA (D) S

2. (C); Antonym. *Courteous* is opposite in meaning to *impolite*, just as *expensive* is nearly opposite in meaning to *cheap*.
(A) PA (D) S
(B) CQ (E) C

3. (A); Degree. Someone who is *frantic* is more unsettled than someone who is *upset*. In the same way, something that is *wild* is more active than something that is *lively*.
(B) L   (D) A
(C) C   (E) PA

21

4. (A); Synonym. To *hesitate* and to *pause* are similar in meaning, just as to *walk* and to *stroll* are similar in meaning.
   (B) PW   (D) C
   (C) L   (E) A

5. (C); Cause and Effect. *Delays* can cause *impatience*, just as *dryness* can cause *thirst*.
   (A) D   (D) S
   (B) PA   (E) PW

6. (E); Action and Object. One can *pollute* a *mind*, just as one can *paint* a *picture*.
   (A) A   (C) PW
   (B) D   (D) CE

7. (B); Synonym. A *rehearsal*, or practice, is similar to a *drill*, just as a *tune* is similar to a *melody*.
   (A) A   (D) F
   (C) AO   (E) PW

8. (E); Function. The function of a *reservoir* is to *store* water, just as the function of a *paper clip* is to *join* pieces of paper.
   (A) S   (C) PA
   (B) A   (D) D

9. (E); Degree. *Superior* suggests greater quality than does *average*, just as *love* suggests stronger affection than does *like*.
   (A) AO   (C) CQ
   (B) PA   (D) C or AO

10. (D); Antonym. *Toxic* is the opposite of *pure*, just as *difficult* is the opposite of *easy*.
    (A) PW   (C) CQ
    (B) S   (E) PO

Reading New Words in Context

Lesson 1

p. 176 | Exercise: Reading Strategically

1. B		11. A
2. D		12. D
3. A		13. B
4. D		14. C
5. C		15. A
6. B		16. C
7. B		17. C
8. B		18. B
9. D		19. D
10. C		20. A

Lesson 2

p. 180 | Exercise: Reading Strategically

1. D		11. C
2. D		12. A
3. A		13. B
4. B		14. C
5. C		15. D
6. C		16. B
7. B		17. C
8. C		18. B
9. A		19. D
10. B		20. A

Lesson 3

p. 184 | Exercise: Reading Strategically

1. B		11. C
2. C		12. B
3. A		13. B
4. A		14. A
5. D		15. C
6. B		16. B
7. C		17. A
8. B		18. D
9. D		19. C
10. C		20. A

Lesson 4

p. 188 | Exercise: Reading Strategically

1. B	11. A		
2. D	12. B		
3. C	13. D		
4. A	14. D		
5. A	15. C		
6. D	16. A		
7. C	17. A		
8. D	18. C		
9. D	19. C		
10. B	20. D		

Lesson 5

p. 192 | Exercise: Reading Strategically

1. D	11. D
2. A	12. B
3. D	13. A
4. A	14. A
5. C	15. B
6. A	16. C
7. C	17. B
8. B	18. B
9. A	19. D
10. D	20. D

Lesson 6

p. 196 | Exercise: Reading Strategically

1. B	11. D
2. C	12. A
3. A	13. B
4. D	14. D
5. C	15. C
6. C	16. A
7. B	17. A
8. A	18. C
9. A	19. D
10. C	20. D

Lesson 7

p. 200 | Exercise: Reading Strategically

1. B	11. C
2. A	12. B
3. D	13. A
4. D	14. B
5. A	15. C
6. A	16. D
7. B	17. A
8. A	18. A
9. B	19. C
10. D	20. C

Lesson 8

p. 204 | Exercise: Reading Strategically

1. A	11. D
2. D	12. A
3. B	13. B
4. C	14. C
5. C	15. C
6. A	16. D
7. C	17. B
8. B	18. D
9. D	19. C
10. B	20. A

Lesson 9

p. 208 | Exercise: Reading Strategically

1. C	11. B
2. A	12. B
3. D	13. A
4. A	14. B
5. D	15. A
6. C	16. B
7. C	17. D
8. D	18. C
9. A	19. C
10. B	20. B

Workshop Answer Key (continued)

Lesson 10

p. 212 | Exercise: Reading Strategically

1. D	11. D
2. A	12. C
3. B	13. A
4. C	14. D
5. C	15. B
6. D	16. C
7. D	17. C
8. A	18. A
9. C	19. B
10. D	20. C

Lesson 11

p. 216 | Exercise: Reading Strategically

1. B	11. B
2. C	12. C
3. C	13. D
4. B	14. A
5. D	15. B
6. A	16. C
7. C	17. D
8. C	18. B
9. D	19. C
10. A	20. A

Lesson 12

p. 220 | Exercise: Reading Strategically

1. C	11. B
2. A	12. A
3. A	13. C
4. B	14. B
5. D	15. C
6. A	16. D
7. D	17. D
8. D	18. B
9. A	19. C
10. C	20. A

Lesson 13

p. 224 | Exercise: Reading Strategically

1. C	11. A
2. B	12. C
3. B	13. D
4. C	14. C
5. A	15. B
6. D	16. B
7. B	17. D
8. D	18. C
9. A	19. B
10. A	20. A

Lesson 14

p. 228 | Exercise: Reading Strategically

1. C	11. D
2. D	12. A
3. B	13. B
4. C	14. B
5. A	15. B
6. B	16. A
7. B	17. D
8. D	18. B
9. C	19. C
10. A	20. C

Lesson 15

p. 232 | Exercise: Reading Strategically

1. A	11. A
2. D	12. C
3. A	13. D
4. B	14. A
5. B	15. B
6. D	16. C
7. C	17. B
8. B	18. C
9. B	19. A
10. C	20. D

Tests Answer Key

Formative Assessment

p.3 | Test 1

1. D	6. B
2. A	7. A
3. C	8. B
4. A	9. D
5. D	10. C

p.4 | Test 2

1. C	6. A
2. D	7. A
3. D	8. C
4. C	9. A
5. C	10. B

p.5 | Test 3

1. D	6. D
2. D	7. D
3. C	8. D
4. A	9. B
5. A	10. B

p.6 | Test 4

1. C	6. D
2. B	7. C
3. A	8. B
4. B	9. C
5. C	10. C

p.7 | Test 5

1. D	6. B
2. A	7. C
3. B	8. D
4. A	9. A
5. A	10. B

p.8 | Test 6

1. B	6. A
2. A	7. A
3. B	8. C
4. C	9. A
5. D	10. D

p.9 | Test 7

1. D	6. D
2. B	7. B
3. B	8. B
4. A	9. C
5. A	10. D

p.10 | Test 8

1. C	6. B
2. A	7. D
3. D	8. A
4. B	9. C
5. A	10. B

p.11 | Test 9

1. C	6. C
2. D	7. D
3. A	8. B
4. D	9. D
5. C	10. C

p.12 | Test 10

1. B	6. B
2. A	7. B
3. B	8. C
4. A	9. D
5. C	10. C

p.13 | Test 11

1. A	6. A
2. C	7. A
3. A	8. A
4. D	9. B
5. B	10. D

p.14 | Test 12

1. A	6. C
2. C	7. A
3. B	8. B
4. D	9. C
5. B	10. B

ANSWER KEY

25

Tests Answer Key *(continued)*

p. 15 | Test 13

1. C		6. B	
2. B		7. B	
3. B		8. C	
4. A		9. D	
5. B		10. B	

p. 16 | Test 14

1. B		6. B	
2. D		7. D	
3. A		8. D	
4. B		9. C	
5. D		10. A	

p. 17 | Test 15

1. B		6. C	
2. A		7. D	
3. C		8. C	
4. D		9. B	
5. A		10. C	

p. 18 | Test 16

1. B		6. D	
2. A		7. B	
3. B		8. C	
4. B		9. A	
5. B		10. B	

p. 19 | Test 17

1. B		6. A	
2. A		7. A	
3. D		8. C	
4. C		9. A	
5. D		10. D	

p. 20 | Test 18

1. C		6. D	
2. D		7. D	
3. C		8. C	
4. A		9. B	
5. D		10. A	

p. 21 | Test 19

1. B		6. A	
2. D		7. D	
3. C		8. C	
4. B		9. B	
5. D		10. D	

p. 22 | Test 20

1. B		6. B	
2. C		7. A	
3. D		8. C	
4. A		9. D	
5. B		10. C	

p. 23 | Test 21

1. A		6. D	
2. C		7. C	
3. B		8. B	
4. A		9. A	
5. B		10. B	

p. 24 | Test 22

1. A		6. A	
2. A		7. D	
3. B		8. B	
4. A		9. B	
5. C		10. B	

p. 25 | Test 23

1. C		6. C	
2. C		7. D	
3. B		8. A	
4. A		9. C	
5. B		10. D	

p. 26 | Test 24

1. A		6. D	
2. B		7. D	
3. A		8. C	
4. B		9. B	
5. B		10. D	

p. 27 | Test 25

1. B	6. D
2. B	7. C
3. A	8. C
4. A	9. A
5. C	10. B

p. 28 | Test 26

1. B	6. C
2. D	7. B
3. A	8. C
4. B	9. D
5. B	10. A

p. 29 | Test 27

1. B	6. A
2. A	7. A
3. B	8. A
4. B	9. A
5. D	10. B

p. 30 | Test 28

1. B	6. A
2. B	7. B
3. A	8. C
4. D	9. B
5. C	10. C

p. 31 | Test 29

1. D	6. A
2. A	7. C
3. A	8. C
4. B	9. A
5. B	10. C

p. 32 | Test 30

1. D	6. D
2. C	7. C
3. B	8. A
4. B	9. B
5. B	10. D

Summative Assessment

p. 35 | Test 1 Part A

1. majority	11. exception
2. detect	12. departure
3. collapse	13. symbols
4. astonish	14. twilight
5. session	15. unexpectedly
6. disturb	16. error
7. generation	17. vivid
8. disastrous	18. reliable
9. definite	19. legend
10. incident	20. descendants

21. B	36. B
22. C	37. C
23. C	38. C
24. B	39. C
25. C	40. D
26. D	41. B
27. D	42. A
28. C	43. C
29. A	44. D
30. C	45. C
31. C	46. B
32. D	47. B
33. D	48. C
34. B	49. B
35. A	50. C

p. 41 | Test 1 Part B

51. reference	61. gasp
52. hoist	62. discomfort
53. requirement	63. pharmacy
54. linger	64. acquire
55. disguise	65. pry
56. competition	66. portion
57. imitate	67. hibernate
58. conceal	68. flexible
59. paralysis	69. lunar
60. pierce	70. license

71. C
72. A
73. C
74. B
75. B
76. A
77. D
78. B
79. B
80. B
81. C
82. B
83. A
84. D
85. C

86. D
87. C
88. A
89. D
90. A
91. B
92. B
93. D
94. C
95. D
96. C
97. B
98. D
99. D
100. C

p. 47 | Test 2 Part A

1. career
2. publicity
3. terrain
4. possess
5. descriptive
6. scholar
7. establish
8. offspring
9. determination
10. quarantine

11. barrier
12. destination
13. sacrifice
14. routine
15. desperate
16. ceremony
17. flourish
18. realm
19. architect
20. fragrant

21. B
22. D
23. A
24. B
25. A
26. D
27. C
28. C
29. C
30. B
31. D
32. D
33. A
34. B
35. A

36. D
37. C
38. D
39. A
40. B
41. B
42. A
43. A
44. D
45. C
46. C
47. B
48. A
49. C
50. C

p. 53 | Test 2 Part B

51. vicinity
52. ordinarily
53. heir
54. tradition
55. portraits
56. boast
57. assume
58. occasion
59. precipitation
60. inviting

61. knapsack
62. exert
63. disadvantage
64. feat
65. investment
66. quantity
67. import
68. cultivate
69. arid
70. contribute

71. D
72. B
73. B
74. A
75. B
76. A
77. C
78. D
79. B
80. D
81. A
82. C
83. B
84. B
85. C

86. B
87. D
88. C
89. A
90. D
91. B
92. A
93. C
94. B
95. D
96. D
97. B
98. B
99. D
100. C

p. 59 | Test 3 Part A

1. inspiration
2. doubtless
3. absorb
4. appreciate
5. villains
6. hazard
7. mammoth
8. reduction
9. juvenile
10. cooperate

11. protest
12. inform
13. inexpensive
14. candidate
15. temporary
16. persuade
17. remedy
18. merchandise
19. widespread
20. revolution

21. A	**36.** A	**71.** D	**86.** C
22. C	**37.** B	**72.** A	**87.** C
23. D	**38.** D	**73.** B	**88.** C
24. D	**39.** C	**74.** A	**89.** B
25. B	**40.** A	**75.** A	**90.** B
26. D	**41.** C	**76.** D	**91.** D
27. B	**42.** B	**77.** B	**92.** B
28. B	**43.** A	**78.** C	**93.** A
29. B	**44.** D	**79.** B	**94.** D
30. B	**45.** C	**80.** A	**95.** C
31. C	**46.** C	**81.** C	**96.** C
32. D	**47.** B	**82.** B	**97.** B
33. C	**48.** B	**83.** B	**98.** A
34. D	**49.** D	**84.** D	**99.** C
35. B	**50.** C	**85.** A	**100.** D

p. 65 | **Test 3 Part B**

51. amateur	**61.** tragedy
52. simplify	**62.** responsibility
53. survival	**63.** decrease
54. duplicate	**64.** prey
55. Reckless	**65.** rebel
56. application	**66.** severe
57. obvious	**67.** threat
58. resident	**68.** justify
59. impatience	**69.** prohibit
60. benefit	**70.** rehearsal

Workshop Answer Key

Making New Words Your Own

Lesson 1

p. 3 | Exercise 1: Wordbusting

> **NOTES**
> - For each Vocabulary Word, students should fill in at least one of the **context, structure,** and **sound** boxes.
> - Check that students vary the boxes they use throughout the exercise.
> - Make sure students look up each word in the dictionary and fill in the dictionary box; answers will vary depending on the dictionary used.

p. 5 | Exercise 2: Context Clues

11. E	humane	**16.** A	alien
12. H	mortal	**17.** G	diplomatic
13. D	planetary	**18.** F	tranquil
14. B	satellite	**19.** I	ghastly
15. C	galaxy	**20.** J	velocity

p. 6 | Exercise 3: Like Meanings and Opposite Meanings

21. B	**26.** B
22. C	**27.** D
23. C	**28.** D
24. C	**29.** C
25. D	**30.** B

Lesson 2

p. 7 | Exercise 1: Wordbusting

> **NOTES**
> - For each Vocabulary Word, students should fill in at least one of the **context, structure,** and **sound** boxes.
> - Check that students vary the boxes they use throughout the exercise.
> - Make sure students look up each word in the dictionary and fill in the dictionary box; answers will vary depending on the dictionary used.

p. 9 | Exercise 2: Context Clues

11. G	luminous	**16.** J	invade
12. E	fascinate	**17.** A	overture
13. B	ally	**18.** I	avert
14. H	fugitive	**19.** C	gesture
15. F	destiny	**20.** D	stellar

p. 10 | Exercise 3: Like Meanings and Opposite Meanings

21. A	**26.** B
22. D	**27.** B
23. A	**28.** A
24. C	**29.** B
25. A	**30.** A

Lesson 3

p. 11 | Exercise 1: Wordbusting

> **NOTES**
> - For each Vocabulary Word, students should fill in at least one of the **context, structure,** and **sound** boxes.
> - Check that students vary the boxes they use throughout the exercise.
> - Make sure students look up each word in the dictionary and fill in the dictionary box; answers will vary depending on the dictionary used.

p. 13 | Exercise 2: Context Clues

11. J	eventual	**16.** I	defiant
12. C	grotesque	**17.** H	technique
13. D	inferior	**18.** F	absurd
14. E	controversial	**19.** A	obsolete
15. G	mere	**20.** B	abstract

p. 14 | Exercise 3: Like Meanings and Opposite Meanings

21. A	**26.** A
22. D	**27.** B
23. A	**28.** D
24. A	**29.** A
25. B	**30.** C

Workshop Answer Key (continued)

FIRST COURSE

Lesson 4

p. 15 | Exercise 1: Wordbusting

NOTES
- For each Vocabulary Word, students should fill in at least one of the **context, structure,** and **sound** boxes.
- Check that students vary the boxes they use throughout the exercise.
- Make sure students look up each word in the dictionary and fill in the dictionary box; answers will vary depending on the dictionary used.

p. 17 | Exercise 2: Context Clues

11. B deliberate
12. H originality
13. E conform
14. A impact
15. G recoil
16. D consequence
17. I distort
18. J reality
19. C excess
20. F offend

p. 18 | Exercise 3: Like Meanings and Opposite Meanings

21. C
22. A
23. D
24. A
25. A
26. A
27. C
28. C
29. B
30. D

Lesson 5

p. 19 | Exercise 1: Wordbusting

NOTES
- For each Vocabulary Word, students should fill in at least one of the **context, structure,** and **sound** boxes.
- Check that students vary the boxes they use throughout the exercise.
- Make sure students look up each word in the dictionary and fill in the dictionary box; answers will vary depending on the dictionary used.

p. 21 | Exercise 2: Context Clues

11. H haunt
12. J leash
13. C supervise
14. A congregate
15. B hover
16. E signify
17. D motive
18. I maturity
19. G loiter
20. F ignorance

p. 22 | Exercise 3: Like Meanings and Opposite Meanings

21. B
22. A
23. C
24. D
25. B
26. A
27. B
28. B
29. B
30. A

Lesson 6

p. 23 | Exercise 1: Wordbusting

NOTES
- For each Vocabulary Word, students should fill in at least one of the **context, structure,** and **sound** boxes.
- Check that students vary the boxes they use throughout the exercise.
- Make sure students look up each word in the dictionary and fill in the dictionary box; answers will vary depending on the dictionary used.

p. 25 | Exercise 2: Context Clues

11. A threshold
12. D audible
13. H subtle
14. G candid
15. F notorious
16. B conspicuous
17. E modest
18. J diaphragm
19. I lenient
20. C idle

p. 26 | Exercise 3: Like Meanings and Opposite Meanings

21. A
22. D
23. C
24. D
25. C
26. C
27. A
28. B
29. C
30. B

Workshop Answer Key (continued)

Lesson 7

p. 27 | Exercise 1: Wordbusting

> **NOTES**
> - For each Vocabulary Word, students should fill in at least one of the **context, structure,** and **sound** boxes.
> - Check that students vary the boxes they use throughout the exercise.
> - Make sure students look up each word in the dictionary and fill in the dictionary box; answers will vary depending on the dictionary used.

p. 29 | Exercise 2: Context Clues

11. J	anticipate	**16.** C	fulfill
12. H	caliber	**17.** A	porcelain
13. G	eloquent	**18.** I	placid
14. B	maintain	**19.** E	aggravate
15. F	phase	**20.** D	distract

p. 30 | Exercise 3: Like Meanings and Opposite Meanings

21. A		**26.** B	
22. D		**27.** B	
23. C		**28.** A	
24. B		**29.** D	
25. B		**30.** C	

Lesson 8

p. 31 | Exercise 1: Wordbusting

> **NOTES**
> - For each Vocabulary Word, students should fill in at least one of the **context, structure,** and **sound** boxes.
> - Check that students vary the boxes they use throughout the exercise.
> - Make sure students look up each word in the dictionary and fill in the dictionary box; answers will vary depending on the dictionary used.

p. 33 | Exercise 2: Context Clues

11. I	dashing	**16.** G	principally
12. B	tiresome	**17.** C	frail
13. H	dismal	**18.** E	optional
14. A	spontaneous	**19.** D	obligation
15. J	flaw	**20.** F	obstinate

p. 34 | Exercise 3: Like Meanings and Opposite Meanings

21. A		**26.** D	
22. B		**27.** D	
23. C		**28.** C	
24. D		**29.** B	
25. D		**30.** B	

Lesson 9

p. 35 | Exercise 1: Wordbusting

> **NOTES**
> - For each Vocabulary Word, students should fill in at least one of the **context, structure,** and **sound** boxes.
> - Check that students vary the boxes they use throughout the exercise.
> - Make sure students look up each word in the dictionary and fill in the dictionary box; answers will vary depending on the dictionary used.

p. 37 | Exercise 2: Context Clues

11. F	comparable	**16.** H	myth
12. D	formal	**17.** A	profound
13. E	authentic	**18.** I	legendary
14. J	immortal	**19.** G	interpret
15. C	contemplate	**20.** B	dual

p. 38 | Exercise 3: Like Meanings and Opposite Meanings

21. C		**26.** D	
22. C		**27.** C	
23. A		**28.** A	
24. A		**29.** A	
25. D		**30.** D	

Workshop Answer Key (continued)

Lesson 10

p. 39 | Exercise 1: Wordbusting

> **NOTES**
> - For each Vocabulary Word, students should fill in at least one of the **context, structure,** and **sound** boxes.
> - Check that students vary the boxes they use throughout the exercise.
> - Make sure students look up each word in the dictionary and fill in the dictionary box; answers will vary depending on the dictionary used.

p. 41 | Exercise 2: Context Clues

11. D crucial
12. C gratified
13. I indispensable
14. A cherish
15. F vigor
16. G consistent
17. B resolve
18. H versatile
19. E designate
20. J mythology

p. 42 | Exercise 3: Like Meanings and Opposite Meanings

21. B
22. B
23. B
24. C
25. D
26. A
27. D
28. B
29. D
30. B

Lesson 11

p. 43 | Exercise 1: Wordbusting

> **NOTES**
> - For each Vocabulary Word, students should fill in at least one of the **context, structure,** and **sound** boxes.
> - Check that students vary the boxes they use throughout the exercise.
> - Make sure students look up each word in the dictionary and fill in the dictionary box; answers will vary depending on the dictionary used.

p. 45 | Exercise 2: Context Clues

11. C merit
12. A illustrious
13. E initial
14. D legitimate
15. H moderate
16. I discrimination
17. J unison
18. B guarantee
19. G moral
20. F partial

p. 46 | Exercise 3: Like Meanings and Opposite Meanings

21. D
22. A
23. B
24. C
25. C
26. A
27. B
28. D
29. C
30. B

Lesson 12

p. 47 | Exercise 1: Wordbusting

> **NOTES**
> - For each Vocabulary Word, students should fill in at least one of the **context, structure,** and **sound** boxes.
> - Check that students vary the boxes they use throughout the exercise.
> - Make sure students look up each word in the dictionary and fill in the dictionary box; answers will vary depending on the dictionary used.

p. 49 | Exercise 2: Context Clues

11. F notable
12. G elective
13. D constitution
14. E indirect
15. A hypocrite
16. I segregation
17. J veto
18. C indefinite
19. B prudent
20. H judicial

p. 50 | Exercise 3: Like Meanings and Opposite Meanings

21. A
22. A
23. D
24. D
25. D
26. B
27. B
28. C
29. D
30. D

Workshop Answer Key *(continued)*

Lesson 13

p. 51 | Exercise 1: Wordbusting

> **NOTES**
> - For each Vocabulary Word, students should fill in at least one of the **context, structure,** and **sound** boxes.
> - Check that students vary the boxes they use throughout the exercise.
> - Make sure students look up each word in the dictionary and fill in the dictionary box; answers will vary depending on the dictionary used.

p. 53 | Exercise 2: Context Clues

11. J	credible	16. F	manuscript
12. E	revise	17. B	mastery
13. A	grammatical	18. H	participate
14. D	legible	19. G	refrain
15. I	tutor	20. C	usage

p. 54 | Exercise 3: Like Meanings and Opposite Meanings

21. A	26. C
22. C	27. D
23. C	28. B
24. D	29. A
25. D	30. A

Lesson 14

p. 55 | Exercise 1: Wordbusting

> **NOTES**
> - For each Vocabulary Word, students should fill in at least one of the **context, structure,** and **sound** boxes.
> - Check that students vary the boxes they use throughout the exercise.
> - Make sure students look up each word in the dictionary and fill in the dictionary box; answers will vary depending on the dictionary used.

p. 57 | Exercise 2: Context Clues

11. A	forum	16. G	narration
12. B	faculty	17. I	dialogue
13. F	prose	18. H	persuasion
14. E	literary	19. D	editorial
15. J	symbolic	20. C	journal

p. 58 | Exercise 3: Like Meanings and Opposite Meanings

21. A	26. C
22. C	27. A
23. B	28. D
24. D	29. C
25. A	30. B

Lesson 15

p. 59 | Exercise 1: Wordbusting

> **NOTES**
> - For each Vocabulary Word, students should fill in at least one of the **context, structure,** and **sound** boxes.
> - Check that students vary the boxes they use throughout the exercise.
> - Make sure students look up each word in the dictionary and fill in the dictionary box; answers will vary depending on the dictionary used.

p. 61 | Exercise 2: Context Clues

11. C	adhere	16. A	tactics
12. I	penetrate	17. D	minority
13. B	forbidding	18. E	participant
14. H	recommend	19. F	opponent
15. G	maneuver	20. J	yield

p. 62 | Exercise 3: Like Meanings and Opposite Meanings

21. D	26. D
22. A	27. D
23. D	28. B
24. D	29. B
25. A	30. C

Workshop Answer Key (continued)

FIRST COURSE

Lesson 16

p. 63 | Exercise 1: Wordbusting

NOTES
- For each Vocabulary Word, students should fill in at least one of the **context, structure,** and **sound** boxes.
- Check that students vary the boxes they use throughout the exercise.
- Make sure students look up each word in the dictionary and fill in the dictionary box; answers will vary depending on the dictionary used.

p. 65 | Exercise 2: Context Clues

11. B officially
12. I opposition
13. G pursue
14. E hardy
15. A scholarship
16. C expand
17. J excel
18. F fatigue
19. H obstacle
20. D intellect

p. 66 | Exercise 3: Like Meanings and Opposite Meanings

21. C
22. D
23. A
24. B
25. D
26. C
27. D
28. A
29. D
30. B

Lesson 17

p. 67 | Exercise 1: Wordbusting

NOTES
- For each Vocabulary Word, students should fill in at least one of the **context, structure,** and **sound** boxes.
- Check that students vary the boxes they use throughout the exercise.
- Make sure students look up each word in the dictionary and fill in the dictionary box; answers will vary depending on the dictionary used.

p. 69 | Exercise 2: Context Clues

11. F intolerable
12. C maternal
13. J rival
14. E crisis
15. A self-conscious
16. I adopt
17. B blemish
18. D anguish
19. H inhabit
20. G immature

p. 70 | Exercise 3: Like Meanings and Opposite Meanings

21. B
22. A
23. C
24. B
25. C
26. B
27. A
28. C
29. B
30. D

Lesson 18

p. 71 | Exercise 1: Wordbusting

NOTES
- For each Vocabulary Word, students should fill in at least one of the **context, structure,** and **sound** boxes.
- Check that students vary the boxes they use throughout the exercise.
- Make sure students look up each word in the dictionary and fill in the dictionary box; answers will vary depending on the dictionary used.

p. 73 | Exercise 2: Context Clues

11. G timid
12. J hesitation
13. B acute
14. F hysterical
15. A wretched
16. D irritable
17. E ridicule
18. C tendency
19. H turmoil
20. I vague

p. 74 | Exercise 3: Like Meanings and Opposite Meanings

21. A
22. D
23. B
24. B
25. B
26. A
27. C
28. D
29. C
30. A

ANSWER KEY

35

Workshop Answer Key (continued)

Lesson 19

p. 75 | Exercise 1: Wordbusting

NOTES
- For each Vocabulary Word, students should fill in at least one of the **context, structure,** and **sound** boxes.
- Check that students vary the boxes they use throughout the exercise.
- Make sure students look up each word in the dictionary and fill in the dictionary box; answers will vary depending on the dictionary used.

p. 77 | Exercise 2: Context Clues

11. F fortress	16. A pageant
12. H era	17. C serf
13. J grandeur	18. E tyrant
14. D barbarous	19. I proclamation
15. G monarchy	20. B baron

p. 78 | Exercise 3: Like Meanings and Opposite Meanings

21. C	26. D
22. B	27. B
23. C	28. C
24. A	29. C
25. C	30. D

Lesson 20

p. 79 | Exercise 1: Wordbusting

NOTES
- For each Vocabulary Word, students should fill in at least one of the **context, structure,** and **sound** boxes.
- Check that students vary the boxes they use throughout the exercise.
- Make sure students look up each word in the dictionary and fill in the dictionary box; answers will vary depending on the dictionary used.

p. 81 | Exercise 2: Context Clues

11. I absolute	16. E status
12. D perilous	17. A illusion
13. C banish	18. J toil
14. F lure	19. G valiant
15. B cultural	20. H vengeance

p. 82 | Exercise 3: Like Meanings and Opposite Meanings

21. D	26. A
22. D	27. B
23. D	28. D
24. B	29. C
25. D	30. D

Lesson 21

p. 83 | Exercise 1: Wordbusting

NOTES
- For each Vocabulary Word, students should fill in at least one of the **context, structure,** and **sound** boxes.
- Check that students vary the boxes they use throughout the exercise.
- Make sure students look up each word in the dictionary and fill in the dictionary box; answers will vary depending on the dictionary used.

p. 85 | Exercise 2: Context Clues

11. I optical	16. F endurance
12. E antiseptic	17. D parasite
13. J organism	18. A nutrition
14. B edible	19. C immune
15. G pigment	20. H glucose

p. 86 | Exercise 3: Like Meanings and Opposite Meanings

21. B	26. C
22. A	27. C
23. C	28. C
24. C	29. B
25. D	30. D

Lesson 22

p. 87 | Exercise 1: Wordbusting

NOTES

- For each Vocabulary Word, students should fill in at least one of the **context, structure,** and **sound** boxes.
- Check that students vary the boxes they use throughout the exercise.
- Make sure students look up each word in the dictionary and fill in the dictionary box; answers will vary depending on the dictionary used.

p. 89 | Exercise 2: Context Clues

11. A camouflage	**16.** B naturalist
12. F seasonal	**17.** I zoology
13. G habitat	**18.** D nocturnal
14. H mammal	**19.** E undergrowth
15. C temperate	**20.** J preservation

p. 90 | Exercise 3: Like Meanings and Opposite Meanings

21. A	**26.** B
22. A	**27.** D
23. C	**28.** C
24. B	**29.** A
25. D	**30.** B

Lesson 23

p. 91 | Exercise 1: Wordbusting

NOTES

- For each Vocabulary Word, students should fill in at least one of the **context, structure,** and **sound** boxes.
- Check that students vary the boxes they use throughout the exercise.
- Make sure students look up each word in the dictionary and fill in the dictionary box; answers will vary depending on the dictionary used.

p. 93 | Exercise 2: Context Clues

11. B compute	**16.** G futile
12. I exceed	**17.** J percentage
13. H relinquish	**18.** F substantial
14. D efficiency	**19.** E prestige
15. C fundamental	**20.** A competent

p. 94 | Exercise 3: Like Meanings and Opposite Meanings

21. C	**26.** A
22. B	**27.** B
23. B	**28.** B
24. D	**29.** D
25. D	**30.** B

Lesson 24

p. 95 | Exercise 1: Wordbusting

NOTES

- For each Vocabulary Word, students should fill in at least one of the **context, structure,** and **sound** boxes.
- Check that students vary the boxes they use throughout the exercise.
- Make sure students look up each word in the dictionary and fill in the dictionary box; answers will vary depending on the dictionary used.

p. 97 | Exercise 2: Context Clues

11. C economical	**17.** E compensate
12. H utility	**18.** I memorandum
13. J stationery	
14. B recognition	**19.** G logical
15. A metropolitan	**20.** D financial
16. F cancel	

p. 98 | Exercise 3: Like Meanings and Opposite Meanings

21. A	**26.** B
22. D	**27.** B
23. D	**28.** B
24. B	**29.** C
25. C	**30.** C

Lesson 25

p. 99 | **Exercise 1: Wordbusting**

> **NOTES**
> - For each Vocabulary Word, students should fill in at least one of the **context, structure,** and **sound** boxes.
> - Check that students vary the boxes they use throughout the exercise.
> - Make sure students look up each word in the dictionary and fill in the dictionary box; answers will vary depending on the dictionary used.

p. 101 | **Exercise 2: Context Clues**

11. A accord	16. G manual
12. J debris	17. E coincide
13. D approximate	18. F mechanism
14. C chaos	19. H kernel
15. B elaborate	20. I surplus

p. 102 | **Exercise 3: Like Meanings and Opposite Meanings**

21. A	26. B
22. B	27. D
23. C	28. A
24. D	29. C
25. A	30. B

Lesson 26

p. 103 | **Exercise 1: Wordbusting**

> **NOTES**
> - For each Vocabulary Word, students should fill in at least one of the **context, structure,** and **sound** boxes.
> - Check that students vary the boxes they use throughout the exercise.
> - Make sure students look up each word in the dictionary and fill in the dictionary box; answers will vary depending on the dictionary used.

p. 105 | **Exercise 2: Context Clues**

11. J confirm	16. I commit
12. B abrupt	17. F random
13. A probability	18. E radiate
14. D repel	19. G infinite
15. H magnitude	20. C inert

p. 106 | **Exercise 3: Like Meanings and Opposite Meanings**

21. A	26. B
22. A	27. A
23. D	28. D
24. D	29. D
25. C	30. A

Lesson 27

p. 107 | **Exercise 1: Wordbusting**

> **NOTES**
> - For each Vocabulary Word, students should fill in at least one of the **context, structure,** and **sound** boxes.
> - Check that students vary the boxes they use throughout the exercise.
> - Make sure students look up each word in the dictionary and fill in the dictionary box; answers will vary depending on the dictionary used.

p. 109 | **Exercise 2: Context Clues**

11. C exotic	16. G diversity
12. D geological	17. A navigable
13. E glacial	18. H aerial
14. I ecosystem	19. J via
15. F barren	20. B tributary

p. 110 | **Exercise 3: Like Meanings and Opposite Meanings**

21. C	26. C
22. D	27. B
23. B	28. C
24. C	29. D
25. D	30. C

Workshop Answer Key *(continued)*

Lesson 28

p. 111 | Exercise 1: Wordbusting

NOTES
- For each Vocabulary Word, students should fill in at least one of the **context, structure,** and **sound** boxes.
- Check that students vary the boxes they use throughout the exercise.
- Make sure students look up each word in the dictionary and fill in the dictionary box; answers will vary depending on the dictionary used.

p. 113 | Exercise 2: Context Clues

11. I encounter	**16.** H inquisitive
12. G challenge	**17.** C universal
13. J unpredictable	**18.** D propel
14. F poach	**19.** A alternate
15. E vital	**20.** B effect

p. 114 | Exercise 3: Like Meanings and Opposite Meanings

21. C	**26.** A
22. A	**27.** B
23. D	**28.** C
24. D	**29.** B
25. B	**30.** C

Lesson 29

p. 115 | Exercise 1: Wordbusting

NOTES
- For each Vocabulary Word, students should fill in at least one of the **context, structure,** and **sound** boxes.
- Check that students vary the boxes they use throughout the exercise.
- Make sure students look up each word in the dictionary and fill in the dictionary box; answers will vary depending on the dictionary used.

p. 117 | Exercise 2: Context Clues

11. H capacity	**16.** J stability
12. G intricate	**17.** D reception
13. E perpetual	**18.** C digital
14. B prompt	**19.** I minimum
15. A speculate	**20.** F intermediate

p. 118 | Exercise 3: Like Meanings and Opposite Meanings

21. C	**26.** C
22. C	**27.** B
23. A	**28.** B
24. D	**29.** C
25. C	**30.** B

Lesson 30

p. 119 | Exercise 1: Wordbusting

NOTES
- For each Vocabulary Word, students should fill in at least one of the **context, structure,** and **sound** boxes.
- Check that students vary the boxes they use throughout the exercise.
- Make sure students look up each word in the dictionary and fill in the dictionary box; answers will vary depending on the dictionary used.

p. 121 | Exercise 2: Context Clues

11. G stationary	**16.** H involuntary
12. D germinate	**17.** I precaution
13. B submerged	**18.** E proportion
14. J conifer	**19.** A precise
15. F photosynthesis	**20.** C preliminary

p.122 | Exercise 3: Like Meanings and Opposite Meanings

21. B	**26.** C
22. D	**27.** B
23. A	**28.** A
24. C	**29.** C
25. B	**30.** D

Workshop Answer Key *(continued)*

Understanding New Words and Their Uses

Lesson 1

p. 125 | Exercise 1: Multimeaning

1. B
2. C

p. 125 | Exercise 2: Word Analysis

3. C
4. D
5. C
6. A
7. ghastly
8. velocity
9. invade
10. fascinate

Lesson 2

p. 127 | Exercise 1: Multimeaning

1. B
2. C

p. 127 | Exercise 2: Word Analysis

3. D
4. A
5. B
6. A
7. eventual
8. mere
9. technique
10. obsolete

Lesson 3

p. 129 | Exercise 1: Multimeaning

1. D
2. D

p. 129 | Exercise 2: Word Analysis

3. B
4. D
5. A
6. B
7. motive
8. notorious
9. haunt
10. supervise

Lesson 4

p. 131 | Exercise 1: Multimeaning

1. A
2. C

p. 131 | Exercise 2: Word Analysis

3. D
4. B
5. B
6. D
7. frail
8. obligation
9. porcelain
10. flaw

Lesson 5

p. 133 | Exercise 1: Multimeaning

1. C
2. B

p. 133 | Exercise 2: Word Analysis

3. A
4. C
5. C
6. B
7. cherish
8. gratify
9. resolve
10. designate

Lesson 6

p. 135 | Exercise 1: Multimeaning

1. B
2. D

p. 135 | Exercise 2: Word Analysis

3. C
4. B
5. B
6. C
7. moral
8. elective
9. illustrious
10. partial

Lesson 7

p. 137 | Exercise 1: Multimeaning

1. C
2. B

p. 137 | Exercise 2: Word Analysis

3. A
4. B
5. B
6. A
7. participate
8. refrain
9. journal
10. prose

Lesson 8

p. 139 | Exercise 1: Multimeaning

1. D
2. C

p. 139 | Exercise 2: Word Analysis

3. D
4. B
5. C
6. B
7. yield
8. intellect
9. opposition
10. expand

Workshop Answer Key *(continued)*

Lesson 9

p. 141 | **Exercise 1: Multimeaning**

   1. C   **2.** B

p. 141 | **Exercise 2: Word Analysis**

   3. B   **7.** inhabit
   4. D   **8.** maternal
   5. A   **9.** ridicule
   6. C   **10.** adopt

Lesson 10

p. 143 | **Exercise 1: Multimeaning**

   1. D   **2.** C

p. 143 | **Exercise 2: Word Analysis**

   3. B   **7.** vengeance
   4. C   **8.** fortress
   5. B   **9.** monarchy
   6. B   **10.** banish

Lesson 11

p. 145 | **Exercise 1: Multimeaning**

   1. B   **2.** C

p. 145 | **Exercise 2: Word Analysis**

   3. A   **7.** pigment
   4. C   **8.** optical
   5. A   **9.** nutrition
   6. A   **10.** edible

Lesson 12

p. 147 | **Exercise 1: Multimeaning**

   1. B   **2.** C

p. 147 | **Exercise 2: Word Analysis**

   3. A   **7.** financial
   4. C   **8.** logical
   5. D   **9.** substantial
   6. A   **10.** percentage

Lesson 13

p. 149 | **Exercise 1: Multimeaning**

   1. C   **2.** D

p. 149 | **Exercise 2: Word Analysis**

   3. B   **7.** kernel
   4. A   **8.** debris
   5. A   **9.** manual
   6. C   **10.** probability

Lesson 14

p. 151 | **Exercise 1: Multimeaning**

   1. C   **2.** C

p. 151 | **Exercise 2: Word Analysis**

   3. B   **7.** encounter
   4. B   **8.** via
   5. B   **9.** vital
   6. B   **10.** glacial

Lesson 15

p. 153 | **Exercise 1: Multimeaning**

   1. C   **2.** C

p. 153 | **Exercise 2: Word Analysis**

   3. A   **7.** reception
   4. D   **8.** stationary
   5. C   **9.** precise
   6. A   **10.** minimum

Workshop Answer Key *(continued)*

Connecting New Words and Patterns

Lesson 1

p. 158 | Analogies

1. (D); Synonym. *Alien* is similar in meaning to *foreign*, just as *normal* is similar in meaning to *usual*.
(A) F	(C) C
(B) CQ	(E) A

2. (A); Synonym. *Diplomatic* is similar in meaning to *tactful*, just as *polite* is similar in meaning to *well-mannered*.
(B) CQ	(D) A
(C) PW	(E) PO

3. (B); Part and Whole. A *star* is part of a *galaxy*, or a system of stars, in the same way that a *bulb* is part of a *lamp*.
(A) C	(D) A
(C) AO	(E) S

4. (C); Characteristic Quality. A *gesture* is characteristically *expressive*, just as a *letter* is characteristically a *written* document.
(A) C	(D) L
(B) PW	(E) D

5. (B); Degree. *Ghastly* suggests a greater degree of dreadfulness than *unpleasant* does, just as *overpowering* suggests a greater degree of strength than *strong* does.
(A) PO	(D) L
(C) AO	(E) A

6. (A); Characteristic Quality. A *star* is characteristically *luminous*, meaning shining or reflecting light, in the same way that a *winner* is characteristically *proud*.
(B) CE	(D) PW
(C) D	(E) F

7. (E); Part and Whole. An *overture* is the first part of an *opera*, just as an *introduction* is the first part of an *essay*.
(A) C	(C) L
(B) A	(D) F or S

8. (A); Synonym. *Planetary*, or terrestrial (representing the earth), is similar in meaning to *global*. In the same way, *strange* is similar in meaning to *unfamiliar*.
(B) CQ	(D) PW
(C) CE	(E) L

9. (E); Classification. A *moon* can be classified as a *satellite*, just as a *sun* can be classified as a *star*.
(A) AO or F	(C) A
(B) F	(D) PO

10. (D); Synonym. To be *stellar* is to be *superior*, and the two are thus similar in meaning. To be *regular* is considered to be *ordinary*, and the two are similar in meaning.
(A) PW	(C) CE
(B) CQ	(E) A

Lesson 2

p. 159 | Analogies

1. (B); Synonym. *Consequence* and *result* have nearly the same meaning, as do *solution* and *answer*.
(A) A	(D) C
(C) D	(E) PO

2. (C); Characteristic Quality. *Politics* is characteristically *controversial*, just as a *maze* is characteristically *complicated*.
(A) AO or A	(D) D
(B) S or D	(E) CE

3. (B); Antonym. A *defiant* person is the opposite of a *cooperative* person, as a *hurtful* action is the opposite of a *helpful* action.
(A) PO	(D) AO
(C) S or D	(E) CQ

4. (D); Synonym. *Deliberate* and *purposeful* have nearly the same meaning, as do *fortunate* and *lucky*.
(A) F	(C) D
(B) C	(E) A

5. (D); Synonym. *Distort* and *twist* have nearly the same meaning, as do *throw* and *toss*.

(A) A
(C) L
(B) C
(E) PO

6. (E); Degree. *Grotesque* suggests a greater degree of strangeness than *odd* does, just as *deadly* suggests a greater degree of destructiveness than *harmful* does.

(A) A or CE
(C) AO
(B) PW
(D) S

7. (A); Antonym. *Inferior* and *superior* are opposite in meaning, as are *boring* and *interesting*.

(B) S
(D) PO
(C) D
(E) C

8. (B); Synonym. *Originality* and *freshness* have nearly the same meaning, as do *enthusiasm* and *eagerness*.

(A) AO
(D) A
(C) PW
(E) CQ

9. (A); Antonym. *Reality* is the opposite of *fantasy*, just as *fact* is the opposite of *fiction*.

(B) PA
(D) CE
(C) L
(E) C

10. (A); Synonym. *Recoil* and *retreat* have nearly the same meaning, as do *begin* and *start*.

(B) CQ
(D) AO or F
(C) D
(E) L

Lesson 3

p. 160 | Analogies

1. (E); Synonym. *Candid* and *frank* have nearly the same meaning, as do *honest* and *truthful*.

(A) CQ
(C) PW
(B) C
(D) PO

2. (D); Classification. The *diaphragm* can be classified as a *muscle*, just as a *peach* can be classified as a *fruit*.

(A) PW
(C) PA
(B) F
(E) D

3. (C); Performer and Action. You expect a *ghost* to *haunt*, just as you expect a *leprechaun* to *trick* people.

(A) S or D
(D) C
(B) PO
(E) PW

4. (C); Performer and Action. You expect a *hummingbird* to *hover*, just as you expect a *squirrel* to *scamper*.

(A) D
(D) S or CE
(B) AO
(E) L

5. (E); Antonym. *Idle*, or inactive, means the opposite of *busy*, just as *serious* means the opposite of *joking*.

(A) PO
(C) F
(B) CQ
(D) C

6. (D); Antonym. *Ignorance* and *knowledge* are opposite in meaning, as are *health* and *sickness*.

(A) D
(C) PA
(B) AO
(E) F

7. (C); Performer and Object. A dog *trainer* uses a *leash*, just as a *gymnast* uses a *balance beam*.

(A) AO
(D) CQ
(B) L
(E) PA

8. (D); Antonym. A *lenient* parent is the opposite of a *strict* parent, just as a *harsh* climate is the opposite of a *mild* climate.

(A) CQ
(C) C
(B) CE
(E) AO

9. (B); Antonym. *Modest* and *vain* are opposite in meaning, as are *fearless* and *afraid*.

(A) S
(D) CQ
(C) F
(E) C

10. (A); Antonym. *Subtle* and *obvious* have opposite meanings, as do *clear* and *confused*.

(B) L
(D) CE
(C) C
(E) D

Workshop Answer Key *(continued)*

Lesson 4

p. 161 | Analogies

1. (C); Antonym. To *aggravate*, or worsen, is the opposite of to *improve*, just as to *damage* is the opposite of to *repair*.
(A) S   (D) PW
(B) F   (E) PO

2. (D); Synonym. *Dashing* and *stylish* have nearly the same meaning, as do *lively* and *exciting*.
(A) A   (C) PA
(B) PW   (E) F

3. (A); Antonym. *Dismal* and *cheerful* have opposite meanings, as do *disappointed* and *delighted*.
(B) AO   (D) PO
(C) CE   (E) F

4. (C); Synonym. A *flaw* is similar to a *defect*, just as an *error* is almost the same thing as a *mistake*.
(A) D   (D) PW
(B) F   (E) C

5. (C); Antonym. *Frail*, or weak, means the opposite of *sturdy*, just as *wet* means the opposite of *dry*.
(A) S   (D) C
(B) CE   (E) L

6. (B); Antonym. To *maintain* something is the opposite of to *neglect* it, just as to *create* something is the opposite of to *destroy* it.
(A) C   (D) PW
(C) D   (E) PO

7. (B); Synonym. *Obligation* and *duty* have nearly the same meaning, as do *task* and *job*.
(A) PA   (D) F
(C) PW   (E) D

8. (A); Synonym. *Phase* is similar in meaning to *stage*, just as *zone* is similar in meaning to *area*.
(B) F   (D) CQ
(C) PW   (E) C

9. (D); Characteristic Quality. *Laughter* is characteristically *spontaneous*, or unplanned, just as a *celebration* is characteristically *joyous*.
(A) D   (C) C
(B) A   (E) L

10. (E); Synonym. *Tiresome* and *boring* have nearly the same meaning, as do *irritable* and *touchy*.
(A) CE   (C) PW
(B) AO   (D) A

Lesson 5

p. 162 | Analogies

1. (B); Synonym. *Consistent* is similar in meaning to *regular*, just as *usual* is similar in meaning to *ordinary*.
(A) AO   (D) C
(C) PW   (E) PO

2. (A); Synonym. *Contemplate* and *consider* have nearly the same meaning, as do *admit* and *confess*.
(B) C   (D) CQ
(C) D   (E) CE

3. (E); Antonym. *Crucial* and *unimportant* are opposite in meaning, as are *loud* and *silent*.
(A) S   (C) C
(B) L   (D) CE

4. (C); Characteristic Quality. A *tuxedo* is characteristically *formal*, or dressy, just as *satin* is characteristically *smooth*.
(A) PA   (D) L
(B) A   (E) PW

5. (D); Synonym. *Indispensable* and *essential* both mean necessary or required, just as *nice* and *pleasant* both mean agreeable.
(A) AO   (C) A
(B) C   (E) PA

6. (D); Action and Object. You *interpret*, or *determine*, the meaning of symbols, just as you *deliver* a *speech*.
(A) S   (C) D
(B) L   (E) PA

Workshop Answer Key *(continued)*

7. (A); Degree. *Legendary* suggests even greater renown than *well known* does, just as *demand* suggests greater urgency and force than *request* does.
(B) AO   (D) PO
(C) A   (E) L

8. (D); Characteristic Quality. A *myth* is characteristically *traditional,* or passed down through generations, just as a *feather* is *light.*
(A) PO   (C) F
(B) A   (E) D

9. (B); Part and Whole. A *legend* is part of a culture's *mythology,* just as a *tail* is part of a *cat.*
(A) A   (D) CQ
(C) L   (E) F

10. (A); Synonym. *Vigor* and *strength* have nearly the same meaning, as do *delicateness* and *fragility.*
(B) C   (D) L
(C) F   (E) CE

Lesson 6

p. 163 | Analogies

1. (A); Synonym. A *guarantee* is similar to a *promise,* just as a *sign* is similar to an *indication.*
(B) AO   (D) D
(C) L   (E) CQ

2. (C); Characteristic Quality. A *hypocrite,* one whose actions are inconsistent with his or her words, is characteristically *insincere,* just as a *thief* is characteristically *dishonest.*
(A) D   (D) S
(B) PW   (E) PO

3. (E); Synonym. *Illustrious* and *famous* have nearly the same meaning, as do *silly* and *foolish.*
(A) C   (C) D
(B) PA   (D) L

4. (B); Antonym. *Indefinite* and *certain* are opposite in meaning, as are *confusing* and *clear.*
(A) PA   (D) F
(C) PW   (E) S

5. (A); Part and Whole. An *initial* is one part of a *name,* just as a *title* is one part of a *book.*
(B) S   (D) AO
(C) D or CE   (E) CQ

6. (C); Synonym. *Merit* is similar in meaning to *worth,* just as *ability* is similar in meaning to *skill.*
(A) PW   (D) D
(B) F   (E) PO

7. (C); Synonym. *Moderate* and *mild* have nearly the same meaning, as do *easy* and *simple.*
(A) D   (D) CE
(B) PW   (E) C

8. (E); Antonym. *Momentary* and *permanent* are opposite in meaning, as are *brief* and *endless.*
(A) PO   (C) S
(B) CQ   (D) L

9. (A); Synonym. When *partial* is used to describe someone who favors one person over another, *partial* and *unfair* have nearly the same meaning. *Raw* and *uncooked* are also similar in meaning.
(B) A   (D) C
(C) CQ   (E) L

10. (C); Action and Object. You can *veto,* or refuse to approve, a *proposal,* just as you can *accept* an *invitation.*
(A) CE   (D) S
(B) C   (E) PO

Lesson 7

p. 164 | Analogies

1. (D); Synonym. *Credible* and *believable* have nearly the same meaning, as do *loyal* and *faithful.*
(A) C   (C) D
(B) L   (E) F

2. (E); Part and Whole. A *teacher* is part of the *faculty*, just as a *singer* is part of the *choir*.
   (A) L   (C) S or AO or D
   (B) C   (D) PA

3. (C); Characteristic Quality. A *forum*, or assembly, is characteristically *public*, just as *garbage* is characteristically *smelly*.
   (A) AO   (D) PW
   (B) C   (E) A

4. (C); Synonym. A *journal* is the same as a *diary*, just as a *tale* is the same as a *story*.
   (A) C   (D) CQ
   (B) PW   (E) CE

5. (A); Synonym. *Legible* and *readable* have similar meanings, as do *gentle* and *tender*.
   (B) F   (D) CQ
   (C) PW   (E) CE

6. (E); Characteristic Quality. An *author* is characteristically *literary*, just as a *chemist* is characteristically *scientific*.
   (A) F   (C) L
   (B) C   (D) PW

7. (B); Performer and Object. A *writer* prepares a *manuscript*, just as a *chef* prepares a *recipe*.
   (A) CE   (D) PA
   (C) PW   (E) A

8. (B); Cause and Effect. *Practice* can cause *mastery* of a skill, just as *repetition* can cause *memorization* of information.
   (A) C   (D) AO
   (C) D   (E) A

9. (D); Synonym. A *persuasion*, or strong belief, is similar to an *opinion*, just as a *thought* is similar to an *idea*.
   (A) AO   (C) CQ
   (B) D   (E) L

10. (B); Performer and Action. You expect a *tutor* to *teach*, just as you expect a *chef* to *cook*.
    (A) A   (D) D
    (C) PA   (E) PO

Lesson 8

p. 165 | Analogies

1. (A); Synonym. To *adhere* and to *stick* have similar meanings, as do to *hint* and to *suggest*.
   (B) F   (D) PO
   (C) CQ   (E) L

2. (C); Antonym. To *expand* and to *contract* are opposite in meaning, as are to *grow* and to *wither*.
   (A) S   (D) D
   (B) CQ   (E) L

3. (D); Synonym. *Fatigue* means almost the same thing as *exhaustion*, just as *energy* and *power* have similar meanings.
   (A) F   (C) PW
   (B) L   (E) CE

4. (E); Antonym. *Forbidding* is opposite in meaning to *inviting* in the same way that *opposite* and *identical* are opposite in meaning.
   (A) PW   (C) CE
   (B) AO or F   (D) D

5. (C); Performer and Action. A *student* can *excel*, meaning to do extremely well, just as a *carpenter* can *build* something.
   (A) F   (D) PW
   (B) S   (E) C

6. (E); Antonym. *Hardy* and *weak* are opposite in meaning, as are *dry* and *moist*.
   (A) S   (C) D
   (B) C   (D) PW

7. (E); Antonym. An *opponent* is the opposite of a *teammate*, just as an *enemy* is the opposite of a *friend*.
   (A) S   (C) CQ
   (B) AO   (D) C

8. (B); Synonym. *Pursue* is similar in meaning to *chase*, just as *start* is similar in meaning to *begin*.
   (A) PO   (D) CQ
   (C) AO   (E) C

9. (D); Synonym.   *Recommend* is similar in meaning to *advise*, just as *order* is similar in meaning to *command*.
   (A) PW   (C) C
   (B) CQ   (E) A

10. (C); Performer and Object.   A *student* receives a *scholarship*, just as an *employee* receives a *paycheck*.
   (A) A   (D) F
   (B) PW   (E) L

Lesson 9

p. 166 | Analogies

1. (C); Synonym.   When *acute* and *sharp* describe hearing or pain, for example, they have nearly the same meaning, just as *plain* and *simple* have nearly the same meaning.
   (A) D   (D) A
   (B) L   (E) CQ

2. (C); Action and Object.   You *adopt* a *plan*, just as you *borrow* a *book*.
   (A) PA   (D) PO
   (B) CQ   (E) PW

3. (D); Synonym.   *Anguish* has nearly the same meaning as *agony*, just as *happiness* has nearly the same meaning as *joy*.
   (A) PA   (C) PW
   (B) C   (E) CE

4. (E); Cause and Effect.   *Hesitation* can be caused by *uncertainty*, just as *damage* can be caused by a *storm*.
   (A) PW   (C) S
   (B) C   (D) A

5. (B); Synonym.   *Hysterical* and *wild* have nearly the same meaning, as do *tame* and *gentle*.
   (A) CE   (D) PW
   (C) A   (E) PO

6. (C); Antonym.   *Irritable* and *calm* are opposite in meaning, as are *evil* and *good*.
   (A) CQ   (D) L
   (B) C   (E) S

7. (D); Cause and Effect.   *Ridicule* can cause *embarrassment*, just as *praise* can cause *confidence*.
   (A) S   (C) PA
   (B) A   (E) AO

8. (D); Antonym.   *Timid* means the opposite of *confident*, just as *attached* means the opposite of *separated*.
   (A) PW   (C) C
   (B) CQ   (E) S

9. (A); Antonym.   *Vague* means the opposite of *definite*, just as *overcast* weather is the opposite of *clear* weather.
   (B) D   (D) CE
   (C) S   (E) PA

10. (D); Degree.   *Wretched* suggests a greater degree of sadness than *unhappy* does, just as *excellent* suggests a greater degree of quality than *adequate* does.
   (A) S   (C) L or PW
   (B) CE   (E) CQ

Lesson 10

p. 167 | Analogies

1. (A); Synonym.   *Barbarous* and *cruel* have similar meanings, as do *polite* and *well-mannered*.
   (B) CQ   (D) PW
   (C) A   (E) C

2. (D); Classification.   A *baron* may be classified as a *nobleman*, just as a *truck* may be classified as a *vehicle*.
   (A) S   (C) PW
   (B) PA   (E) CQ

3. (A); Synonym.   *Cultural* and *educational* are similar in meaning as are *story* and *tale*.
   (B) F   (D) L
   (C) A   (E) PW

4. (C); Function.   The function of a *fortress* is to *protect*, just as the function of a *weapon* is to *harm*.
   (A) L   (D) S
   (B) A   (E) PW

5. (E); Synonym. *Grandeur* is similar in meaning to *magnificence*, just as *courage* is similar in meaning to *bravery*.
(A) CQ (C) F
(B) C (D) CE

6. (C); Classification. A *monarchy* can be classified as a *government* ruled by a king or queen, just as *French* can be classified as a *language*.
(A) CE or PW (D) AO
(B) CQ (E) PO

7. (A); Antonym. *Perilous*, which means full of danger, is opposite in meaning to *safe*. *Uneasy* and *calm* also have opposite meanings.
(B) S (D) PA
(C) D (E) C

8. (E); Cause and Effect. *Toil*, or work, can cause *exhaustion*, just as *success* can cause *pride*.
(A) S (C) C
(B) A (D) PW

9. (B); Characteristic Quality. A *tyrant* is characteristically *unjust* in the same way that *velvet* is characteristically *soft*.
(A) C (D) PA
(C) F (E) L

10. (D); Antonym. *Vengeance* and *forgiveness* are opposite in meaning, as are *roughness* and *smoothness*.
(A) L (C) C
(B) PO or PA (E) AO

Lesson 11

p. 168 | Analogies

1. (C); Antonym. *Edible*, which means eatable, is opposite in meaning to *poisonous*, just as *fresh* is opposite in meaning to *stale*.
(A) D or S (D) CQ
(B) PO (E) PA

2. (C); Synonym. *Endurance* and *patience* have similar meanings, as do *truthfulness* and *honesty*.
(A) PO (D) L
(B) PW (E) CQ

3. (B); Classification. *Glucose* is a type of *sugar*, just as *spaghetti* is a type of *food*.
(A) CQ (D) F
(C) S (E) CE

4. (A); Characteristic Quality. A *habitat* is characteristically a *natural* environment, just as the *ocean* is characteristically *deep*.
(B) S or D (D) A
(C) CE or D (E) F or AO

5. (B); Classification. A *whale* is classified as a *mammal*, just as a *termite* is classified as an *insect*.
(A) CE (D) AO
(C) PO or L (E) D

6. (E); Performer and Object. *Naturalists* study *trees*, just as *beauticians* work with *hair*.
(A) CQ (C) AO
(B) PW (D) PA

7. (D); Function. The function of *nutrition* is to *nourish*, just as the function of *exercise* is to *strengthen*.
(A) CQ (C) D
(B) PW (E) AO

8. (C); Synonym. *Organism* means nearly the same thing as *living thing*, just as *trousers* means nearly the same thing as *pants*.
(A) PO (D) CQ
(B) CE (E) L

9. (B); Synonym. A *temperate* climate is the same as a *mild* climate. *Excited* and *thrilled* also have the same meaning.
(A) L (D) PW
(C) C (E) AO

10. (B); Classification. *Zoology* is classified as a *science*, just as *German* is a *language*.
(A) A (D) S
(C) PO (E) E

Lesson 12

p. 169 | Analogies

1. (C); Action and Object. You can *cancel* an *appointment*, just as you can *plan* a *party*.
(A) C
(D) L
(B) F
(E) PW

2. (C); Degree. *Competent* suggests a lesser level of performance than *excellent* does, just as *naughty* suggests a lesser degree of wickedness than *evil* does.
(A) CQ
(D) PW
(B) AO
(E) C

3. (D); Antonym. *Efficiency* is the opposite of *wastefulness*, just as *tender* is the opposite of *rough*.
(A) C
(C) S or D
(B) PO
(E) CE

4. (B); Synonym. *Fundamental* and *basic* have nearly the same meaning, as do *difficult* and *hard*.
(A) PA
(D) A
(C) F
(E) L

5. (B); Antonym. A *futile* action is the opposite of an *effective* action, just as a *valuable* thing is the opposite of a *worthless* thing.
(A) PA
(D) AO
(C) C
(E) PW

6. (E); Synonym. *Logical* and *reasonable* have nearly the same meaning, as do *keen* and *sharp*.
(A) CE
(C) PA
(B) PO
(D) PW

7. (D); Function. The function of a *memorandum* is to *remind*, just as the function of a *story* is to *entertain*.
(A) PW
(C) CQ
(B) PA
(E) AO

8. (B); Cause and Effect. *Recognition*, or approval, can cause someone to feel *pride*. *Approval* can cause a person to feel *pleasure*.
(A) CQ
(D) PO
(C) C
(E) L

9. (B); Location. *Stationery* can be found in a *desk*, just as *folders* can be found in a *file cabinet*.
(A) F
(D) CQ
(C) D
(E) S

10. (C); Classification. *Electricity* is classified as a *utility*, just as a *piano* is classified as an *instrument*.
(A) L
(D) D
(B) AO
(E) F

Lesson 13

p. 170 | Analogies

1. (C); Characteristic Quality. A *cliff* is characteristically *abrupt*, or steep, just as a *peak* is characteristically *high*.
(A) PW
(D) D
(B) F
(E) PA

2. (B); Cause and Effect. *Debris* can be caused by *destruction*, just as *ashes* can be caused by *fire*.
(A) S
(D) PA
(C) AO
(E) PW

3. (E); Synonym. *Diversity* is similar in meaning to *variety*. In the same way, *regular* is similar in meaning to *everyday*.
(A) A
(C) PA
(B) CQ
(D) AO

4. (D); Synonym. *Elaborate* is similar in meaning to *complicated*, just as *ornamented* is similar in meaning to *decorated*.
(A) C
(C) CQ
(B) CE
(E) L

5. (D); Antonym. *Infinite* and *limited* have opposite meanings, as do *lengthy* and *brief*.
(A) PO
(C) S
(B) F
(E) D

6. (B); Characteristic Quality. A *kernel*, the center of something, is characteristically *central*, just as a *plate* is characteristically *circular*.
(A) AO
(D) S
(C) C
(E) A

7. (C); Function. The function of a *manual* is to *instruct*, just as the function of a *wheelchair* is to *transport*.
(A) D   (D) S
(B) C   (E) L

8. (D); Part and Whole. A *mechanism* is part of a *clock*, just as a *skeleton* is part of a *body*.
(A) C   (C) CQ
(B) F   (E) D

9. (A); Antonym. *Repel* and *attract* have opposite meanings, as do *push* and *pull*.
(B) PA or F   (D) D
(C) CQ   (E) F

10. (C); Synonym. *Surplus* and *extra* have nearly the same meaning, as do *crooked* and *bent*.
(A) PA   (D) L
(B) C   (E) PO

Lesson 14

p. 171 | Analogies

1. (D); Antonym. A *barren* field is the opposite of a *fertile* field, just as being *poor* is the opposite of being *rich*.
(A) AO   (C) PO
(B) F   (E) CQ

2. (D); Characteristic Quality. An *encounter* is characteristically *unexpected*, just as a *party* is characteristically *entertaining*.
(A) PA   (C) C
(B) D   (E) PO

3. (C); Synonym. *Exotic* and *foreign* have similar meanings, as do *regular* and *ordinary*.
(A) PW   (D) CQ
(B) D   (E) PA

4. (D); Characteristic Quality. A *chimpanzee* is characteristically *inquisitive*, or curious, just as an *eel* is characteristically *slippery*.
(A) C   (C) D
(B) AO or F   (E) L

5. (B); Characteristic Quality. An *ocean* is characteristically *navigable*, allowing the passage of ships, just as a *whistle* is characteristically *shrill*.
(A) AO   (D) C
(C) D   (E) PW

6. (D); Performer and Action. A *hunter* could *poach*, or hunt illegally, just as a *doctor* can *heal*.
(A) C   (C) D
(B) S or CE   (E) CQ

7. (C); Function. The function of a *propeller* is to *propel*, or move something forward, just as the function of a *rudder* is to *steer*.
(A) PO   (D) D
(B) PW   (E) CQ

8. (D); Classification. A *tributary* is a river or stream that flows into a larger *river*, just as a *road* is a smaller and less developed route than a *highway*.
(A) PA   (C) AO
(B) L   (E) CE

9. (A); Characteristic Quality. A *surprise* is characteristically *unpredictable*, just as a *fire* is characteristically *hot*.
(B) C   (D) F or PO
(C) L   (E) S

10. (C); Synonym. *Vital* and *essential* have nearly the same meaning, as do *wanted* and *desired*.
(A) CE   (D) L
(B) F   (E) PW

Lesson 15

p. 172 | Analogies

1. (B); Antonym. *Discrimination*, which can mean making unfair judgments about people, is opposite in meaning to *fairness*. In the same way, *finish* and *begin* are opposite in meaning.
(A) PO   (D) C
(C) CQ   (E) CE

2. (C); Antonym. *Intricate*, or complex, means the opposite of *simple*, just as *fancy* means the opposite of *plain*.
(A) PA
(D) CQ
(B) L
(E) PW

3. (E); Characteristic Quality. A *hiccup* is characteristically *involuntary*, just as *enlistment* in the armed services in the United States is characteristically *voluntary*.
(A) L
(C) AO
(B) S
(D) PO

4. (E); Synonym. *Perpetual* is similar in meaning to *eternal*, just as *attached* is similar in meaning to *joined*.
(A) D
(C) CE
(B) PW
(D) CQ

5. (D); Cause and Effect. *Safety* is the effect of using *precaution*, just as *tiredness* is the effect of *sleeplessness*.
(A) C or PW
(C) L
(B) PO
(E) PW

6. (D); Synonym. *Prompt* and *quick* have nearly the same meaning, as do *safe* and *secure*.
(A) PW
(C) CE
(B) D
(E) C

7. (E); Synonym. *Relinquish* and *surrender* are similar in meaning, just as *clue* and *hint* are similar in meaning.
(A) AO
(C) F
(B) PA
(D) A

8. (A); Synonym. *Speculate* and *think* have nearly the same meaning, as do *ask* and *request*.
(B) PW
(D) C
(C) F
(E) AO

9. (C); Antonym. *Stationary*, or still, means the opposite of *movable*, just as *broken* means the opposite of *fixed*.
(A) AO
(D) CE
(B) CQ
(E) F

10. (D); Characteristic Quality. A *sunken ship* is characteristically *submerged*, or underwater, just as a pirate's *treasure* is characteristically *buried*.
(A) PO
(C) C
(B) CE
(E) L

Reading New Words in Context

Lesson 1

p. 176 | Exercise: Reading Strategically

1. A		**11.** D	
2. D		**12.** B	
3. C		**13.** B	
4. A		**14.** A	
5. B		**15.** A	
6. B		**16.** B	
7. D		**17.** C	
8. C		**18.** D	
9. C		**19.** B	
10. C		**20.** C	

Lesson 2

p. 180 | Exercise: Reading Strategically

1. C		**11.** D	
2. A		**12.** D	
3. A		**13.** A	
4. C		**14.** B	
5. D		**15.** C	
6. C		**16.** B	
7. D		**17.** B	
8. A		**18.** A	
9. B		**19.** A	
10. C		**20.** C	

Workshop Answer Key *(continued)*

Lesson 3

p. 185 | Exercise: Reading Strategically

1. D	**11.** C
2. C	**12.** B
3. A	**13.** B
4. B	**14.** D
5. C	**15.** A
6. D	**16.** B
7. D	**17.** B
8. C	**18.** B
9. A	**19.** C
10. B	**20.** D

Lesson 4

p. 188 | Exercise: Reading Strategically

1. A	**11.** D
2. A	**12.** D
3. D	**13.** C
4. A	**14.** B
5. C	**15.** B
6. B	**16.** A
7. B	**17.** D
8. D	**18.** C
9. D	**19.** D
10. D	**20.** A

Lesson 5

p. 192 | Exercise: Reading Strategically

1. A	**11.** D
2. B	**12.** A
3. C	**13.** C
4. D	**14.** C
5. B	**15.** C
6. C	**16.** D
7. D	**17.** C
8. A	**18.** A
9. C	**19.** D
10. B	**20.** B

Lesson 6

p. 196 | Exercise: Reading Strategically

1. D	**11.** D
2. C	**12.** D
3. D	**13.** D
4. B	**14.** A
5. A	**15.** D
6. C	**16.** C
7. D	**17.** A
8. D	**18.** D
9. C	**19.** D
10. A	**20.** C

Lesson 7

p. 200 | Exercise: Reading Strategically

1. A	**11.** C
2. D	**12.** D
3. B	**13.** B
4. B	**14.** A
5. D	**15.** A
6. C	**16.** B
7. D	**17.** C
8. C	**18.** D
9. B	**19.** C
10. A	**20.** C

Lesson 8

p. 205 | Exercise: Reading Strategically

1. C	**11.** C
2. C	**12.** D
3. B	**13.** A
4. C	**14.** D
5. A	**15.** C
6. B	**16.** D
7. B	**17.** A
8. C	**18.** B
9. B	**19.** D
10. A	**20.** C

First Course | *Vocabulary Workshop*

Workshop Answer Key *(continued)*

FIRST COURSE

Lesson 9

p. 208 | Exercise: Reading Strategically

1.	B	11.	A
2.	D	12.	B
3.	A	13.	B
4.	C	14.	A
5.	B	15.	C
6.	B	16.	D
7.	D	17.	B
8.	C	18.	A
9.	D	19.	C
10.	C	20.	C

Lesson 10

p. 212 | Exercise: Reading Strategically

1.	A	11.	C
2.	B	12.	A
3.	C	13.	A
4.	C	14.	D
5.	C	15.	D
6.	D	16.	C
7.	D	17.	D
8.	A	18.	B
9.	C	19.	B
10.	C	20.	B

Lesson 11

p. 216 | Exercise: Reading Strategically

1.	B	11.	C
2.	D	12.	C
3.	C	13.	D
4.	A	14.	B
5.	C	15.	A
6.	B	16.	D
7.	B	17.	D
8.	D	18.	D
9.	A	19.	C
10.	A	20.	C

Lesson 12

p. 221 | Exercise: Reading Strategically

1.	C	11.	B
2.	B	12.	B
3.	B	13.	B
4.	C	14.	C
5.	D	15.	A
6.	A	16.	D
7.	B	17.	B
8.	A	18.	C
9.	C	19.	A
10.	D	20.	D

Lesson 13

p. 224 | Exercise: Reading Strategically

1.	A	11.	D
2.	D	12.	D
3.	C	13.	A
4.	B	14.	C
5.	A	15.	A
6.	B	16.	D
7.	C	17.	A
8.	D	18.	B
9.	C	19.	A
10.	C	20.	D

Lesson 14

p. 228 | Exercise: Reading Strategically

1.	C	11.	C
2.	C	12.	C
3.	A	13.	D
4.	A	14.	C
5.	D	15.	A
6.	C	16.	D
7.	C	17.	D
8.	D	18.	D
9.	B	19.	B
10.	B	20.	C

Workshop Answer Key *(continued)*

Lesson 15

p. 232 | Exercise: Reading Strategically

1. B	**11.** B
2. C	**12.** D
3. C	**13.** A
4. C	**14.** A
5. C	**15.** C
6. B	**16.** B
7. C	**17.** C
8. D	**18.** B
9. C	**19.** B
10. B	**20.** B

Tests Answer Key

Formative Assessment

p. 3 | Test 1

1. B	6. A
2. D	7. B
3. B	8. B
4. A	9. D
5. D	10. A

p. 4 | Test 2

1. C	6. B
2. C	7. A
3. C	8. A
4. A	9. D
5. C	10. D

p. 5 | Test 3

1. D	6. B
2. D	7. B
3. C	8. C
4. D	9. A
5. C	10. D

p. 6 | Test 4

1. C	6. A
2. C	7. B
3. A	8. B
4. C	9. B
5. B	10. D

p. 7 | Test 5

1. A	6. D
2. B	7. B
3. A	8. A
4. B	9. C
5. C	10. C

p. 8 | Test 6

1. A	6. C
2. C	7. D
3. C	8. C
4. B	9. D
5. A	10. A

p. 9 | Test 7

1. D	6. A
2. B	7. D
3. C	8. B
4. B	9. B
5. B	10. D

p. 10 | Test 8

1. A	6. C
2. A	7. C
3. A	8. B
4. B	9. D
5. A	10. D

p. 11 | Test 9

1. C	6. B
2. C	7. A
3. A	8. A
4. D	9. A
5. C	10. C

p. 12 | Test 10

1. C	6. D
2. A	7. D
3. A	8. A
4. B	9. B
5. C	10. C

p. 13 | Test 11

1. B	6. B
2. B	7. D
3. A	8. B
4. C	9. D
5. A	10. C

p. 14 | Test 12

1. C	6. B
2. C	7. A
3. C	8. C
4. B	9. A
5. D	10. D

p. 15 | Test 13

1. C	6. B
2. D	7. B
3. C	8. C
4. B	9. A
5. A	10. D

p. 16 | Test 14

1. A	6. D
2. C	7. D
3. B	8. A
4. B	9. B
5. C	10. A

p. 17 | Test 15

1. A	6. B
2. B	7. D
3. A	8. B
4. B	9. B
5. C	10. D

p. 18 | Test 16

1. C	6. C
2. C	7. A
3. A	8. B
4. A	9. D
5. D	10. B

p. 19 | Test 17

1. B	6. C
2. A	7. D
3. B	8. B
4. D	9. A
5. A	10. C

p. 20 | Test 18

1. C	6. B
2. A	7. D
3. D	8. A
4. C	9. C
5. B	10. A

p. 21 | Test 19

1. C	6. D
2. A	7. A
3. C	8. C
4. D	9. D
5. B	10. C

p. 22 | Test 20

1. B	6. D
2. B	7. A
3. A	8. A
4. C	9. D
5. A	10. B

p. 23 | Test 21

1. C	6. D
2. C	7. A
3. C	8. A
4. A	9. B
5. D	10. B

p. 24 | Test 22

1. A	6. A
2. C	7. D
3. C	8. D
4. B	9. B
5. B	10. C

p. 25 | Test 23

1. B	6. D
2. B	7. A
3. B	8. C
4. A	9. B
5. C	10. D

p. 26 | Test 24

1. C	6. D
2. A	7. A
3. B	8. A
4. C	9. B
5. D	10. B

p. 27 | Test 25

1. B	6. D
2. B	7. A
3. B	8. C
4. B	9. C
5. D	10. C

p. 28 | Test 26

1. A	6. C
2. B	7. A
3. A	8. A
4. B	9. C
5. C	10. B

p. 29 | Test 27

1. C	6. B
2. D	7. D
3. C	8. C
4. D	9. C
5. B	10. A

p. 30 | Test 28

1. D	6. B
2. A	7. B
3. C	8. A
4. D	9. D
5. B	10. B

p. 31 | Test 29

1. A	6. C
2. D	7. D
3. C	8. C
4. A	9. B
5. B	10. A

p. 32 | Test 30

1. C	6. C
2. B	7. A
3. B	8. B
4. D	9. C
5. A	10. D

Summative Assessment

p. 35 | Test 1 Part A

1. consequence	11. threshold
2. inferior	12. maturity
3. caliber	13. fulfill
4. distract	14. versatile
5. contemplate	15. fascinate
6. comparable	16. anticipate
7. defiant	17. legendary
8. motive	18. resolve
9. consistent	19. obsolete
10. dashing	20. conspicuous

21. B	36. C
22. A	37. D
23. A	38. C
24. A	39. D
25. C	40. A
26. B	41. C
27. C	42. B
28. B	43. D
29. D	44. C
30. A	45. B
31. D	46. D
32. D	47. D
33. A	48. B
34. A	49. A
35. A	50. C

p. 41 | Test 1 Part B

51. abstract	61. profound
52. controversial	62. grotesque
53. conform	63. distort
54. absurd	64. aggravate
55. designate	65. obligation
56. porcelain	66. offend
57. deliberate	67. originality
58. spontaneous	68. gratify
59. crucial	69. vigor
60. technique	70. impact

71. B
72. A
73. D
74. C
75. B
76. A
77. A
78. D
79. C
80. C
81. D
82. A
83. C
84. A
85. D

86. C
87. C
88. B
89. B
90. A
91. C
92. A
93. C
94. B
95. D
96. C
97. C
98. D
99. C
100. B

p. 47 | Test 2 Part A

1. elective
2. judicial
3. participate
4. status
5. timid
6. legitimate
7. revise
8. adhere
9. intellect
10. constitution

11. minority
12. segregate
13. moral
14. pursue
15. hesitation
16. tactics
17. initial
18. obstacles
19. partial
20. tendency

21. A
22. C
23. C
24. D
25. C
26. B
27. A
28. B
29. A
30. B
31. C
32. C
33. B
34. A
35. C

36. C
37. B
38. C
39. C
40. D
41. B
42. B
43. B
44. C
45. A
46. D
47. B
48. C
49. D
50. C

p. 53 | Test 2 Part B

51. era
52. turmoil
53. forum
54. notable
55. officially
56. credible
57. valiant
58. unison
59. veto
60. adopt

61. opponent
62. refrain
63. persuasion
64. illusion
65. discrimination
66. crisis
67. intolerable
68. fatigue
69. guarantee
70. recommend

71. B
72. D
73. B
74. B
75. C
76. A
77. B
78. A
79. D
80. C
81. A
82. D
83. B
84. A
85. D

86. B
87. B
88. B
89. D
90. A
91. C
92. A
93. D
94. A
95. D
96. C
97. A
98. B
99. C
100. B

p. 59 | Test 3 Part A

1. zoology
2. magnitude
3. naturalist
4. mammal
5. habitat
6. preservation
7. barren
8. glacial
9. seasonal
10. undergrowth

11. tributary
12. diversity
13. camouflage
14. challenge
15. navigable
16. effect
17. ecosystem
18. organism
19. vital
20. precautions

21. B
22. D
23. A
24. C
25. D
26. C
27. A
28. A
29. C
30. A
31. A
32. C
33. A
34. A
35. C

36. A
37. C
38. B
39. D
40. B
41. A
42. D
43. C
44. B
45. A
46. B
47. D
48. C
49. D
50. C

71. B
72. C
73. B
74. C
75. A
76. A
77. C
78. A
79. C
80. A
81. B
82. A
83. B
84. B
85. A

86. D
87. C
88. B
89. C
90. D
91. D
92. B
93. B
94. D
95. B
96. D
97. C
98. A
99. A
100. C

p. 65 | Test 3 Part B

51. speculate
52. accord
53. relinquish
54. futile
55. competent
56. capacity
57. exceed
58. probability
59. preliminary
60. fundamental

61. manual
62. logical
63. precise
64. efficiency
65. economical
66. utility
67. elaborate
68. minimum
69. radiate
70. proportion

Workshop Answer Key

Making New Words Your Own

Lesson 1

p. 3 | **Exercise 1: Wordbusting**

> **NOTES**
> - For each Vocabulary Word, students should fill in at least one of the **context, structure,** and **sound** boxes.
> - Check that students vary the boxes they use throughout the exercise.
> - Make sure students look up each word in the dictionary and fill in the dictionary box; answers will vary depending on the dictionary used.

p. 5 | **Exercise 2: Context Clues**

11. D probable	16. B romantic
12. G ruthless	17. I eminent
13. A epidemic	18. J picturesque
14. C myriad	19. H intentional
15. E appalling	20. F contagious

p. 6 | **Exercise 3: Like Meanings and Opposite Meanings**

21. A	26. D
22. A	27. C
23. C	28. B
24. B	29. C
25. B	30. D

Lesson 2

p. 7 | **Exercise 1: Wordbusting**

> **NOTES**
> - For each Vocabulary Word, students should fill in at least one of the **context, structure,** and **sound** boxes.
> - Check that students vary the boxes they use throughout the exercise.
> - Make sure students look up each word in the dictionary and fill in the dictionary box; answers will vary depending on the dictionary used.

p. 9 | **Exercise 2: Context Clues**

11. H knoll	16. C barbarism
12. B calamity	17. G abuse
13. E deceive	18. D novelty
14. I sincerity	19. J bewilder
15. F baffle	20. A folklore

p. 10 | **Exercise 3: Like Meanings and Opposite Meanings**

21. D	26. C
22. B	27. A
23. C	28. C
24. A	29. C
25. B	30. A

Lesson 3

p. 11 | **Exercise 1: Wordbusting**

> **NOTES**
> - For each Vocabulary Word, students should fill in at least one of the **context, structure,** and **sound** boxes.
> - Check that students vary the boxes they use throughout the exercise.
> - Make sure students look up each word in the dictionary and fill in the dictionary box; answers will vary depending on the dictionary used.

p. 13 | **Exercise 2: Context Clues**

11. B strategy	16. E ferocious
12. D inevitable	17. J valid
13. H catastrophe	18. A ecology
14. F aggressive	19. C sanctuary
15. G motivate	20. I intelligible

p. 14 | **Exercise 3: Like Meanings and Opposite Meanings**

21. C	26. A
22. A	27. C
23. D	28. C
24. C	29. B
25. C	30. A

Workshop Answer Key (continued)

Lesson 4

p. 15 | Exercise 1: Wordbusting

> **NOTES**
> - For each Vocabulary Word, students should fill in at least one of the **context, structure,** and **sound** boxes.
> - Check that students vary the boxes they use throughout the exercise.
> - Make sure students look up each word in the dictionary and fill in the dictionary box; answers will vary depending on the dictionary used.

p. 17 | Exercise 2: Context Clues

11. I	defy	**16.** D	anthology
12. A	misdeed	**17.** G	pacify
13. E	mystical	**18.** B	nourish
14. C	integrity	**19.** H	advent
15. J	alliance	**20.** F	sustain

p. 18 | Exercise 3: Like Meanings and Opposite Meanings

21. C	**26.** A
22. C	**27.** D
23. B	**28.** A
24. B	**29.** C
25. D	**30.** D

Lesson 5

p. 19 | Exercise 1: Wordbusting

> **NOTES**
> - For each Vocabulary Word, students should fill in at least one of the **context, structure,** and **sound** boxes.
> - Check that students vary the boxes they use throughout the exercise.
> - Make sure students look up each word in the dictionary and fill in the dictionary box; answers will vary depending on the dictionary used.

p. 21 | Exercise 2: Context Clues

11. B	calculation	**17.** C	accessory
12. J	gallery	**18.** I	valor
13. F	customary	**19.** G	complement
14. E	badger		
15. A	vitality	**20.** D	convert
16. H	intervene		

p. 22 | Exercise 3: Like Meanings and Opposite Meanings

21. A	**26.** C
22. A	**27.** A
23. C	**28.** D
24. A	**29.** C
25. C	**30.** A

Lesson 6

p. 23 | Exercise 1: Wordbusting

> **NOTES**
> - For each Vocabulary Word, students should fill in at least one of the **context, structure,** and **sound** boxes.
> - Check that students vary the boxes they use throughout the exercise.
> - Make sure students look up each word in the dictionary and fill in the dictionary box; answers will vary depending on the dictionary used.

p. 25 | Exercise 2: Context Clues

11. C	fragile	**17.** J	adjacent
12. G	harmonious	**18.** H	artisan
13. B	pulverize	**19.** F	deceased
14. I	glorify	**20.** A	multicolored
15. D	attain		
16. E	incomparable		

p. 26 | Exercise 3: Like Meanings and Opposite Meanings

21. C	**26.** B
22. C	**27.** A
23. A	**28.** D
24. C	**29.** B
25. C	**30.** C

Workshop Answer Key *(continued)*

Lesson 7

p. 27 | Exercise 1: Wordbusting

NOTES

- For each Vocabulary Word, students should fill in at least one of the **context**, **structure**, and **sound** boxes.

- Check that students vary the boxes they use throughout the exercise.

- Make sure students look up each word in the dictionary and fill in the dictionary box; answers will vary depending on the dictionary used.

p. 29 | Exercise 2: Context Clues

11. D	menagerie	17. J	phenom-enon
12. B	isolation		
13. I	revelation	18. C	delegate
14. F	discord	19. G	feline
15. E	posterity	20. A	confedera-tion
16. H	foresight		

p. 30 | Exercise 3: Like Meanings and Opposite Meanings

21. B	26. B
22. A	27. D
23. A	28. D
24. D	29. C
25. B	30. C

Lesson 8

p. 31 | Exercise 1: Wordbusting

NOTES

- For each Vocabulary Word, students should fill in at least one of the **context**, **structure**, and **sound** boxes.

- Check that students vary the boxes they use throughout the exercise.

- Make sure students look up each word in the dictionary and fill in the dictionary box; answers will vary depending on the dictionary used.

p. 33 | Exercise 2: Context Clues

11. G	descend	17. B	inherit
12. E	menace	18. C	gnarled
13. H	adequate	19. A	advanta-geous
14. I	enhance		
15. F	inflexible	20. D	incite
16. J	mutual		

p. 34 | Exercise 3: Like Meanings and Opposite Meanings

21. C	26. B
22. B	27. B
23. D	28. D
24. C	29. B
25. A	30. C

Lesson 9

p. 35 | Exercise 1: Wordbusting

NOTES

- For each Vocabulary Word, students should fill in at least one of the **context**, **structure**, and **sound** boxes.

- Check that students vary the boxes they use throughout the exercise.

- Make sure students look up each word in the dictionary and fill in the dictionary box; answers will vary depending on the dictionary used.

p. 37 | Exercise 2: Context Clues

11. J	impel	16. H	adapt
12. D	potential	17. E	basis
13. I	restore	18. A	petition
14. C	assumption	19. G	omission
15. B	controversy	20. F	primitive

p. 38 | Exercise 3: Like Meanings and Opposite Meanings

21. A	26. C
22. C	27. A
23. C	28. C
24. B	29. D
25. D	30. A

Workshop Answer Key (continued)

Lesson 10

p. 39 | Exercise 1: Wordbusting

NOTES
- For each Vocabulary Word, students should fill in at least one of the **context, structure,** and **sound** boxes.
- Check that students vary the boxes they use throughout the exercise.
- Make sure students look up each word in the dictionary and fill in the dictionary box; answers will vary depending on the dictionary used.

p. 41 | Exercise 2: Context Clues

11. C immense
12. A creative
13. F insoluble
14. D consecutive
15. B feasible
16. G diction
17. J durable
18. I ingenious
19. H hilarious
20. E ordeal

p. 42 | Exercise 3: Like Meanings and Opposite Meanings

21. A
22. D
23. B
24. A
25. C
26. B
27. D
28. C
29. C
30. C

Lesson 11

p. 43 | Exercise 1: Wordbusting

NOTES
- For each Vocabulary Word, students should fill in at least one of the **context, structure,** and **sound** boxes.
- Check that students vary the boxes they use throughout the exercise.
- Make sure students look up each word in the dictionary and fill in the dictionary box; answers will vary depending on the dictionary used.

p. 45 | Exercise 2: Context Clues

11. E emigrate
12. J malnutrition
13. A aristocrat
14. G refuge
15. H censorship
16. F optimism
17. I morale
18. C deport
19. B famine
20. D decade

p. 46 | Exercise 3: Like Meanings and Opposite Meanings

21. A
22. D
23. A
24. B
25. D
26. D
27. B
28. A
29. C
30. B

Lesson 12

p. 47 | Exercise 1: Wordbusting

NOTES
- For each Vocabulary Word, students should fill in at least one of the **context, structure,** and **sound** boxes.
- Check that students vary the boxes they use throughout the exercise.
- Make sure students look up each word in the dictionary and fill in the dictionary box; answers will vary depending on the dictionary used.

p. 49 | Exercise 2: Context Clues

11. C anxiety
12. A urban
13. I boycott
14. E multitude
15. B nationality
16. G naturalization
17. F predicament
18. H propaganda
19. D resolute
20. J burly

p. 50 | Exercise 3: Like Meanings and Opposite Meanings

21. A
22. B
23. A
24. C
25. D
26. C
27. D
28. B
29. A
30. C

Workshop Answer Key (continued)

Lesson 13

p. 51 | Exercise 1: Wordbusting

NOTES

- For each Vocabulary Word, students should fill in at least one of the **context, structure,** and **sound** boxes.
- Check that students vary the boxes they use throughout the exercise.
- Make sure students look up each word in the dictionary and fill in the dictionary box; answers will vary depending on the dictionary used.

p. 53 | Exercise 2: Context Clues

11. F boisterous	16. E accessible
12. J hospitable	17. I dilapidated
13. C bankrupt	18. A premiere
14. H fraudulent	19. G riotous
15. B impulsive	20. D transit

p. 54 | Exercise 3: Like Meanings and Opposite Meanings

21. A	26. C
22. A	27. A
23. C	28. A
24. D	29. B
25. C	30. B

Lesson 14

p. 55 | Exercise 1: Wordbusting

NOTES

- For each Vocabulary Word, students should fill in at least one of the **context, structure,** and **sound** boxes.
- Check that students vary the boxes they use throughout the exercise.
- Make sure students look up each word in the dictionary and fill in the dictionary box; answers will vary depending on the dictionary used.

p. 57 | Exercise 2: Context Clues

11. H acceptance	16. I jubilation
12. D grieve	17. B thrive
13. C immigrate	18. J prosecute
14. A intensity	19. G privilege
15. E exaggeration	20. F circulate

p. 58 | Exercise 3: Like Meanings and Opposite Meanings

21. D	26. C
22. C	27. B
23. D	28. A
24. C	29. D
25. D	30. C

Lesson 15

p. 59 | Exercise 1: Wordbusting

NOTES

- For each Vocabulary Word, students should fill in at least one of the **context, structure,** and **sound** boxes.
- Check that students vary the boxes they use throughout the exercise.
- Make sure students look up each word in the dictionary and fill in the dictionary box; answers will vary depending on the dictionary used.

p. 61 | Exercise 2: Context Clues

11. A humidity	16. J dissect
12. G dedicate	17. B tumult
13. E memento	18. H dispense
14. D depose	19. C haven
15. F restrain	20. I exertion

p. 62 | Exercise 3: Like Meanings and Opposite Meanings

21. A	26. B
22. C	27. C
23. D	28. A
24. D	29. B
25. B	30. D

Lesson 16

p. 63 | Exercise 1: Wordbusting

> **NOTES**
> - For each Vocabulary Word, students should fill in at least one of the **context**, **structure**, and **sound** boxes.
> - Check that students vary the boxes they use throughout the exercise.
> - Make sure students look up each word in the dictionary and fill in the dictionary box; answers will vary depending on the dictionary used.

p. 65 | Exercise 2: Context Clues

11. I hamper	**16.** F recuperate
12. B imperative	**17.** E presume
13. D inconsiderate	**18.** C negligent
14. J intercept	**19.** H liable
15. A spacious	**20.** G impose

p. 66 | Exercise 3: Like Meanings and Opposite Meanings

21. D	**26.** C
22. B	**27.** D
23. B	**28.** A
24. B	**29.** B
25. D	**30.** D

Lesson 17

p. 67 | Exercise 1: Wordbusting

> **NOTES**
> - For each Vocabulary Word, students should fill in at least one of the **context**, **structure**, and **sound** boxes.
> - Check that students vary the boxes they use throughout the exercise.
> - Make sure students look up each word in the dictionary and fill in the dictionary box; answers will vary depending on the dictionary used.

p. 69 | Exercise 2: Context Clues

11. A capital	**16.** B elegant
12. G haughty	**17.** F occupant
13. C gracious	**18.** J aroma
14. H manageable	**19.** I probation
15. E monopoly	**20.** D frequency

p. 70 | Exercise 3: Like Meanings and Opposite Meanings

21. C	**26.** B
22. B	**27.** C
23. D	**28.** A
24. A	**29.** B
25. D	**30.** B

Lesson 18

p. 71 | Exercise 1: Wordbusting

> **NOTES**
> - For each Vocabulary Word, students should fill in at least one of the **context**, **structure**, and **sound** boxes.
> - Check that students vary the boxes they use throughout the exercise.
> - Make sure students look up each word in the dictionary and fill in the dictionary box; answers will vary depending on the dictionary used.

p. 73 | Exercise 2: Context Clues

11. B prearrange	**16.** G saturate
12. E dismantle	**17.** I sedate
13. D remote	**18.** F embarrass
14. J populate	**19.** C baste
15. H rigid	**20.** A diminish

p. 74 | Exercise 3: Like Meanings and Opposite Meanings

21. A	**26.** A
22. C	**27.** B
23. C	**28.** C
24. C	**29.** D
25. D	**30.** B

Workshop Answer Key *(continued)*

Lesson 19

p. 75 | Exercise 1: Wordbusting

> **NOTES**
> - For each Vocabulary Word, students should fill in at least one of the **context, structure,** and **sound** boxes.
> - Check that students vary the boxes they use throughout the exercise.
> - Make sure students look up each word in the dictionary and fill in the dictionary box; answers will vary depending on the dictionary used.

p. 77 | Exercise 2: Context Clues

11. D liberate
12. F notify
13. E access
14. J pleasantry
15. A provision
16. I circumnavigate
17. C regime
18. B accommodations
19. H remorse
20. G evacuate

p. 78 | Exercise 3: Like Meanings and Opposite Meanings

21. C
22. B
23. D
24. A
25. B
26. B
27. A
28. C
29. D
30. B

Lesson 20

p. 79 | Exercise 1: Wordbusting

> **NOTES**
> - For each Vocabulary Word, students should fill in at least one of the **context, structure,** and **sound** boxes.
> - Check that students vary the boxes they use throughout the exercise.
> - Make sure students look up each word in the dictionary and fill in the dictionary box; answers will vary depending on the dictionary used.

p. 81 | Exercise 2: Context Clues

11. C disagreeable
12. E thrifty
13. G humiliate
14. I verify
15. J jeopardize
16. A adept
17. D dingy
18. F persistent
19. B titanic
20. H maroon

p. 82 | Exercise 3: Like Meanings and Opposite Meanings

21. D
22. D
23. A
24. A
25. A
26. C
27. A
28. B
29. D
30. A

Lesson 21

p. 83 | Exercise 1: Wordbusting

> **NOTES**
> - For each Vocabulary Word, students should fill in at least one of the **context, structure,** and **sound** boxes.
> - Check that students vary the boxes they use throughout the exercise.
> - Make sure students look up each word in the dictionary and fill in the dictionary box; answers will vary depending on the dictionary used.

p. 85 | Exercise 2: Context Clues

11. H tariff
12. J satire
13. E salutation
14. I sable
15. D pun
16. G premier
17. C obituary
18. F foreword
19. A diplomat
20. B aspiration

p. 86 | Exercise 3: Like Meanings and Opposite Meanings

21. C
22. A
23. D
24. B
25. A
26. B
27. C
28. D
29. A
30. D

Lesson 22

p. 87 | Exercise 1: Wordbusting

> **NOTES**
> - For each Vocabulary Word, students should fill in at least one of the **context**, **structure**, and **sound** boxes.
> - Check that students vary the boxes they use throughout the exercise.
> - Make sure students look up each word in the dictionary and fill in the dictionary box; answers will vary depending on the dictionary used.

p. 89 | Exercise 2: Context Clues

11. E quaint
12. H quench
13. G urgent
14. J blockade
15. C neutral
16. I confiscate
17. B generate
18. A indelible
19. D obscure
20. F pewter

p. 90 | Exercise 3: Like Meanings and Opposite Meanings

21. D
22. B
23. A
24. C
25. C
26. A
27. B
28. C
29. A
30. D

Lesson 23

p. 91 | Exercise 1: Wordbusting

> **NOTES**
> - For each Vocabulary Word, students should fill in at least one of the **context**, **structure**, and **sound** boxes.
> - Check that students vary the boxes they use throughout the exercise.
> - Make sure students look up each word in the dictionary and fill in the dictionary box; answers will vary depending on the dictionary used.

p. 93 | Exercise 2: Context Clues

11. J intolerance
12. C activate
13. F petty
14. A charitable
15. E pious
16. D colossal
17. G tarnish
18. B invariable
19. I eccentric
20. H confide

p. 94 | Exercise 3: Like Meanings and Opposite Meanings

21. B
22. C
23. A
24. A
25. C
26. B
27. C
28. C
29. D
30. A

Lesson 24

p. 95 | Exercise 1: Wordbusting

> **NOTES**
> - For each Vocabulary Word, students should fill in at least one of the **context**, **structure**, and **sound** boxes.
> - Check that students vary the boxes they use throughout the exercise.
> - Make sure students look up each word in the dictionary and fill in the dictionary box; answers will vary depending on the dictionary used.

p. 97 | Exercise 2: Context Clues

11. E clarify
12. H irk
13. A essay
14. J proposal
15. B sarcasm
16. I successor
17. C apt
18. G summit
19. D temperament
20. F deduction

p. 98 | Exercise 3: Like Meanings and Opposite Meanings

21. C
22. C
23. A
24. D
25. B
26. D
27. A
28. C
29. B
30. C

Workshop Answer Key *(continued)*

Lesson 25

p. 99 | Exercise 1: Wordbusting

> **NOTES**
> - For each Vocabulary Word, students should fill in at least one of the **context, structure,** and **sound** boxes.
> - Check that students vary the boxes they use throughout the exercise.
> - Make sure students look up each word in the dictionary and fill in the dictionary box; answers will vary depending on the dictionary used.

p. 101 | Exercise 2: Context Clues

11. A	contemporary	16. J	occurrence
12. I	climax	17. D	therapy
13. E	casual	18. F	famished
14. B	anonymous	19. H	fragment
15. G	literal	20. C	fictitious

p. 102 | Exercise 3: Like Meanings and Opposite Meanings

21. B	26. C
22. A	27. B
23. C	28. D
24. D	29. B
25. C	30. B

Lesson 26

p. 103 | Exercise 1: Wordbusting

> **NOTES**
> - For each Vocabulary Word, students should fill in at least one of the **context, structure,** and **sound** boxes.
> - Check that students vary the boxes they use throughout the exercise.
> - Make sure students look up each word in the dictionary and fill in the dictionary box; answers will vary depending on the dictionary used.

p. 105 | Exercise 2: Context Clues

11. H	endorse	16. A	dispatch
12. B	condemn	17. F	intrigue
13. E	falter	18. G	modify
14. C	dictate	19. D	emphasize
15. J	improvise	20. I	dilute

p. 106 | Exercise 3: Like Meanings and Opposite Meanings

21. A	26. C
22. C	27. A
23. C	28. A
24. B	29. B
25. B	30. B

Lesson 27

p. 107 | Exercise 1: Wordbusting

> **NOTES**
> - For each Vocabulary Word, students should fill in at least one of the **context, structure,** and **sound** boxes.
> - Check that students vary the boxes they use throughout the exercise.
> - Make sure students look up each word in the dictionary and fill in the dictionary box; answers will vary depending on the dictionary used.

p. 109 | Exercise 2: Context Clues

11. I	category	16. G	demolish
12. C	illuminate	17. B	distraction
13. F	testify	18. H	denial
14. J	detach	19. A	articulate
15. D	inclination	20. E	upbraid

p. 110 | Exercise 3: Like Meanings and Opposite Meanings

21. D	26. B
22. A	27. D
23. D	28. A
24. C	29. B
25. C	30. C

Workshop Answer Key *(continued)*

Lesson 28

p. 111 | Exercise 1: Wordbusting

NOTES
- For each Vocabulary Word, students should fill in at least one of the **context, structure,** and **sound** boxes.
- Check that students vary the boxes they use throughout the exercise.
- Make sure students look up each word in the dictionary and fill in the dictionary box; answers will vary depending on the dictionary used.

p. 113 | Exercise 2: Context Clues

11. G secluded
12. H superficial
13. F tangible
14. E braggart
15. I unique
16. D derive
17. A eligible
18. C extensive
19. B imply
20. J miscellaneous

p. 114 | Exercise 3: Like Meanings and Opposite Meanings

21. A
22. B
23. C
24. D
25. A
26. B
27. D
28. B
29. D
30. B

Lesson 29

p. 115 | Exercise 1: Wordbusting

NOTES
- For each Vocabulary Word, students should fill in at least one of the **context, structure,** and **sound** boxes.
- Check that students vary the boxes they use throughout the exercise.
- Make sure students look up each word in the dictionary and fill in the dictionary box; answers will vary depending on the dictionary used.

p. 117 | Exercise 2: Context Clues

11. G malfunction
12. F technology
13. B hypothesis
14. H warranty
15. D rebate
16. C synthetic
17. E arrogant
18. J commute
19. I congest
20. A considerate

p. 118 | Exercise 3: Like Meanings and Opposite Meanings

21. A
22. D
23. B
24. B
25. B
26. D
27. C
28. B
29. C
30. D

Lesson 30

p. 119 | Exercise 1: Wordbusting

NOTES
- For each Vocabulary Word, students should fill in at least one of the **context, structure,** and **sound** boxes.
- Check that students vary the boxes they use throughout the exercise.
- Make sure students look up each word in the dictionary and fill in the dictionary box; answers will vary depending on the dictionary used.

p. 121 | Exercise 2: Context Clues

11. J agenda
12. D parasitic
13. H aeronautics
14. I planetarium
15. E hydraulic
16. G photogenic
17. C antibiotics
18. A erosion
19. F automaton
20. B respiration

p. 122 | Exercise 3: Like Meanings and Opposite Meanings

21. A
22. D
23. B
24. C
25. B
26. D
27. B
28. B
29. B
30. B

Workshop Answer Key (continued)

Understanding New Words and Their Uses

Lesson 1

p. 125 | Exercise 1: Multimeaning

1. D
2. A

p. 125 | Exercise 2: Word Analysis

3. A
4. A
5. B
6. A
7. appalling
8. barbarism
9. knoll
10. novelty

Lesson 2

p. 127 | Exercise 1: Multimeaning

1. B
2. B

p. 127 | Exercise 2: Word Analysis

3. C
4. A
5. C
6. C
7. sustain
8. catastrophe
9. ferocious
10. intelligible

Lesson 3

p. 129 | Exercise 1: Multimeaning

1. A
2. C

p. 129 | Exercise 2: Word Analysis

3. C
4. B
5. A
6. C
7. convert
8. glorify
9. fragile
10. deceased

Lesson 4

p. 131 | Exercise 1: Multimeaning

1. D
2. D

p. 131 | Exercise 2: Word Analysis

3. B
4. D
5. D
6. B
7. posterity
8. gnarled
9. inflexible
10. phenomenon

Lesson 5

p. 133 | Exercise 1: Multimeaning

1. B
2. C

p. 133 | Exercise 2: Word Analysis

3. D
4. A
5. C
6. B
7. primitive
8. adapt
9. feasible
10. omission

Lesson 6

p. 135 | Exercise 1: Multimeaning

1. D
2. C

p. 135 | Exercise 2: Word Analysis

3. C
4. D
5. D
6. B
7. burly
8. urban
9. nationality
10. boycott

Lesson 7

p. 137 | Exercise 1: Multimeaning

1. A
2. D

p. 137 | Exercise 2: Word Analysis

3. C
4. A
5. D
6. A
7. riotous
8. boisterous
9. jubilation
10. immigrate

Lesson 8

p. 139 | Exercise 1: Multimeaning

1. C
2. A

p. 139 | Exercise 2: Word Analysis

3. A
4. A
5. C
6. C
7. haven
8. humidity
9. recuperate
10. dispense

Lesson 9

p. 141 | Exercise 1: Multimeaning

1. B   2. D

p. 141 | Exercise 2: Word Analysis

3. D	7. diminish
4. A	8. saturate
5. A	9. monopoly
6. B	10. populate

Lesson 10

p. 143 | Exercise 1: Multimeaning

1. D   2. B

p. 143 | Exercise 2: Word Analysis

3. B	7. liberate
4. C	8. pleasantry
5. A	9. humiliate
6. C	10. evacuate

Lesson 11

p. 145 | Exercise 1: Multimeaning

1. A   2. D

p. 145 | Exercise 2: Word Analysis

3. D	7. obituary
4. C	8. pun
5. C	9. indelible
6. B	10. tariff

Lesson 12

p. 147 | Exercise 1: Multimeaning

1. B   2. C

p. 147 | Exercise 2: Word Analysis

3. C	7. pious
4. A	8. petty
5. A	9. summit
6. B	10. successor

Lesson 13

p. 149 | Exercise 1: Multimeaning

1. C   2. C

p. 149 | Exercise 2: Word Analysis

3. D	7. modify
4. C	8. climax
5. A	9. falter
6. B	10. dictate

Lesson 14

p. 151 | Exercise 1: Multimeaning

1. B   2. C

p. 151 | Exercise 2: Word Analysis

3. A	7. demolish
4. C	8. unique
5. B	9. imply
6. D	10. secluded

Lesson 15

p. 153 | Exercise 1: Multimeaning

1. C   2. D

p. 153 | Exercise 2: Word Analysis

3. D	7. hypothesis
4. B	8. erosion
5. A	9. hydraulic
6. A	10. parasitic

Connecting New Words and Patterns

Lesson 1

p. 158 | Analogies

1. (E); Characteristic Quality. *Abuse* is characteristically *cruel*, just as a *celebration* is characteristically *joyful*.
(A) D   (C) AO
(B) F   (D) PW

Workshop Answer Key *(continued)*

2. (B); Degree. *Appalling* means very *upsetting,* just as *fascinating* means very *interesting.*
- (A) PO
- (C) C
- (D) CE
- (E) L

3. (D); Synonym. *Baffle* is similar in meaning to *confuse,* just as *attempt* is similar in meaning to *try.*
- (A) CE
- (B) C
- (C) CQ
- (E) PW

4. (C); Cause and Effect. A *calamity,* or disaster, can cause *distress,* just as *winning* can cause *happiness.*
- (A) PO
- (B) CQ
- (D) PA
- (E) AO

5. (D); Performer and Action. You expect a *liar* to *deceive* you, just as you expect a *hero* to *rescue* you.
- (A) CQ
- (B) A
- (C) C
- (E) S or AO

6. (A); Cause and Effect. An *epidemic,* or mass illness, can cause *fear,* just as a *puzzle* can cause *confusion.*
- (B) PO
- (C) D or S
- (D) C
- (E) S

7. (C); Degree. A *knoll* is a smaller hill than a *mountain.* A *ditch* is a shallower trough than a *canyon.*
- (A) L
- (B) PW
- (D) CQ
- (E) AO

8. (A); Performer and Object. A *novelty* is the creation of an *inventor,* just as a *symphony* is the creation of a *composer.*
- (B) L
- (C) PA
- (D) PW
- (E) CE

9. (E); Antonym. *Probable* and *unlikely* have opposite meanings, as do *sad* and *happy.*
- (A) L
- (B) PO
- (C) F
- (D) C

10. (B); Synonym. *Ruthless* is similar in meaning to *merciless,* just as *famous* is similar in meaning to *well-known.*
- (A) PA
- (C) CQ
- (D) A
- (E) CE

Lesson 2

p. 159 | Analogies

1. (D); Synonym. *Advent* is similar in meaning to *arrival,* just as *faithfulness* is similar in meaning to *loyalty.*
- (A) D
- (B) F
- (C) C
- (E) CQ

2. (D); Characteristic Quality. A *bully* is characteristically *aggressive,* or quick to attack, just as an *expert* is characteristically *confident.*
- (A) S
- (B) CE
- (C) D
- (E) PW

3. (B); Cause and Effect. *Confusion* can result from *catastrophe,* just as *sorrow* can result from grieving a *death.*
- (A) PO
- (C) A
- (D) PW
- (E) C

4. (E); Classification. *Ecology* may be classified as a *science,* just as *algebra* may be classified as a branch of *mathematics.*
- (A) L
- (B) F
- (C) CQ
- (D) PO

5. (A); Antonym. *Ferocious* and *gentle* are opposite in meaning, as are *pleased* and *dissatisfied.*
- (B) PO
- (C) AO
- (D) D
- (E) L

6. (E); Antonym. *Motivate* and *discourage* have opposite meanings, just as do *tarnished* and *polished.*
- (A) F
- (B) CQ
- (C) PO
- (D) S

7. (D); Function. The function of *food* is to *nourish,* just as the function of a *raincoat* is to *protect.*
- (A) AO
- (B) D
- (C) C
- (E) PW

8. (E); Antonym. *Pacify* and *provoke* have opposite meanings, as do *refuse* and *accept.*
- (A) C
- (B) PO
- (C) L
- (D) D

9. (C); Part and Whole. A *sanctuary* is part of a *church*, just as an *axle* is part of a *truck*. Or, (A); Synonym. A *sanctuary*, any church or temple, and *church* have similar meanings, as do *past* and *previous*.
(A) S   (D) PA
(B) F   (E) CQ

10. (B); Synonym. *Strategy* is similar in meaning to *method*, just as *intention* is similar in meaning to *purpose*.
(A) CE   (D) C
(C) PA   (E) PW

Lesson 3

p. 160 | Analogies

1. (D); Classification. A *belt* may be classified as an *accessory*, just as a *bracelet* may be classified as a type of *jewelry*.
(A) AO   (C) PA
(B) S   (E) CE

2. (E); Performer and Object. An *artisan* can make or paint *pottery* in the same way an *architect* makes or works with a *blueprint*.
(A) C   (C) CE
(B) A   (D) AO

3. (D); Classification. A *badger* is a type of *animal*, just as *granite* is a type of *rock*.
(A) L   (C) PA
(B) CQ   (E) PO

4. (B); Performer and Object. A *math whiz* makes *calculations*, while a *chemist* works with *formulas*.
(A) S   (D) D
(C) PW   (E) CE

5. (B); Antonym. *Customary* behavior is the opposite of *unusual* behavior, as a *thoughtful* action is the opposite of an *inconsiderate* action.
(A) PW   (D) PO
(C) F   (E) C

6. (E); Characteristic Quality. An *egg* is characteristically *fragile*, or breakable, just as the *desert* is characteristically *dry*.
(A) CE   (C) S
(B) A   (D) PO

7. (D); Location. A *painting* can be found in a *gallery*, just as an *easel* can be found in a *studio*.
(A) PW   (C) D
(B) CE   (E) CQ

8. (C); Antonym. *Glorify* and *degrade* have opposite meanings, as do *succeed* and *fail*.
(A) CQ   (D) C
(B) L   (E) F

9. (D); Characteristic Quality. A *rainbow* is characteristically *multicolored*, just as a *pillow* is characteristically *soft*.
(A) A   (C) F
(B) L   (E) PA

10. (E); Synonym. *Vitality* and *energy* have nearly the same meaning, as do *sadness* and *sorrow*.
(A) CQ   (C) AO
(B) PA   (D) PW

Lesson 4

p. 161 | Analogies

1. (E); Degree. *Adequate* is a lesser quality of performance than *excellent*, just as *tired* is a lesser degree of exhaustion than *frazzled*.
(A) S   (C) PW
(B) PA   (D) C

2. (C); Performer and Action. You expect a *delegate* to *represent* others, just as you expect an *actor* to *perform*.
(A) C   (D) F
(B) CQ   (E) S

3. (D); Antonym. *Descend* and *rise* have opposite meanings, as do *shove* and *pull*.
(A) PO   (C) D
(B) CQ   (E) PW

4. (C); Antonym. *Discord* and *harmony* have opposite meanings, as do *war* and *peace*.
(A) CQ   (D) C
(B) F   (E) PW

5. (C). Function. The function of a *decoration* is to *enhance*, just as the function of *fertilizer* is to *enrich*.
(A) C   (D) D
(B) AO   (E) CE

6. (C); Part and Whole. *Whiskers* are part of a *feline*, or cat, just as a *paw* is part of a *kitten*.
(A) PO   (D) AO
(B) S   (E) C

7. (B); Performer and Action. You expect an *heiress* to *inherit*, just as you expect a *thief* to *steal*.
(A) S   (D) PW
(C) L   (E) CQ

8. (B); Cause and Effect. *Isolation* can cause *loneliness*, as *experience* can increase *confidence*.
(A) PA   (D) L
(C) PW   (E) PO

9. (B); Characteristic Quality. A *menace*, or threat, is characteristically *frightening* in the same way that *crime* is characteristically *offensive*.
(A) S   (D) F
(C) A   (E) PO

10. (B); Characteristic Quality. A *menagerie* of animals is characteristically *caged*, just as a *crime* is characteristically *illegal*.
(A) S   (D) C
(C) PW   (E) AO

Lesson 5

p. 162 | Analogies

1. (A); Synonym. *Adapt*, which can mean to change something to make it fit a new use, is similar in meaning to *modify*. In the same way, *thoughtful* and *considerate* are similar in meaning.
(B) CQ   (D) PO
(C) AO   (E) CE

2. (E); Synonym. *Basis* is similar in meaning to *foundation*, as *sign* is similar in meaning to *indication*.
(A) CQ   (C) PW
(B) F   (D) D

3. (E); Antonym. *Consecutive* and *interrupted* are opposite in meaning, as are *fresh* and *stale*.
(A) D   (C) PW
(B) S   (D) L

4. (D); Synonym. *Controversy* is similar in meaning to *dispute*, as *promise* is similar in meaning to *pledge*.
(A) PA   (C) AO
(B) CQ   (E) C

5. (D); Characteristic Quality. An *artist* is characteristically *creative*, just as a *chemist* is characteristically *scientific*.
(A) PO   (C) S
(B) CE   (E) L

6. (E); Characteristic Quality. *Leather* is characteristically *durable*, or long-lasting, just as *sand* is characteristically *gritty*.
(A) PW   (C) AO
(B) F   (D) L

7. (D); Degree. *Hilarious* means very *funny*, just as *nasty* means very *unpleasant*.
(A) PA   (C) PW
(B) A   (E) CE

8. (C); Degree. *Immense* means very *large*, just as *frantic* means very *nervous*.
(A) PO   (D) S
(B) L   (E) C

9. (D); Characteristic Quality. An *inventor* is characteristically *ingenious*, or inventive, just as a *monkey* is characteristically *curious*.
(A) PW   (C) F
(B) PA   (E) PO

10. (D); Synonym. *Primitive* and *crude* are similar in meaning, as are *complex* and *complicated*.
(A) PW   (C) PA
(B) L   (E) C

Lesson 6

p. 163 | Analogies

1. (D); Classification. A *princess* is a type of *aristocrat*, just as a *sailboat* is a type of *vessel*.
(A) AO   (C) PA
(B) A   (E) PW

2. (A); Characteristic Quality. A *football player* is characteristically *burly*, just as a *ballet dancer* is characteristically *graceful*.
   - (B) S
   - (C) C
   - (D) PA
   - (E) F

3. (A); Part and Whole. A *year* is part of a *decade* in the same way that a *roof* is part of a *house*.
   - (B) A or D
   - (C) CE
   - (D) C
   - (E) PA

4. (D); Cause and Effect. A *famine* can result from a *war*, just as *destruction* is the likely result of a *hurricane*.
   - (A) A
   - (B) CQ
   - (C) L
   - (E) D

5. (D); Cause and Effect. *Malnutrition* can cause *death*, just as a *fever* can cause *sweating*.
   - (A) AO
   - (B) L
   - (C) PA
   - (E) A

6. (C); Synonym. *Multitude* and *crowd* are similar in meaning, just as *ceremony* and *service* are similar in meaning.
   - (A) AO
   - (B) PO
   - (D) C
   - (E) CQ

7. (E); Function. The function of *propaganda* is to *persuade*, just as the function of a *newspaper* is to *inform*.
   - (A) C
   - (B) CE
   - (C) PW
   - (D) L

8. (A); Characteristic Quality. A *refuge* is characteristically *safe*, just as an *anchor* is characteristically *heavy*.
   - (B) S
   - (C) F
   - (D) L
   - (E) D

9. (D); Synonym. *Resolute* and *determined* have similar meanings, as do *steady* and *regular*.
   - (A) A
   - (B) C
   - (C) PO
   - (E) AO

10. (C); Antonym. *Urban* and *rural* have opposite meanings, as do *firm* and *unsteady*.
    - (A) L
    - (B) PO
    - (D) C
    - (E) F

Lesson 7

p. 164 | Analogies

1. (C); Antonym. *Accessible*, which can mean obtainable, is opposite in meaning to *unobtainable*, just as *shout* and *whisper* are opposite in meaning.
   - (A) PA
   - (B) PW
   - (D) PO
   - (E) C

2. (A); Antonym. *Bankrupt* means the opposite of *rich*, just as *torn* means the opposite of *mended*.
   - (B) D
   - (C) C
   - (D) L
   - (E) CQ

3. (A); Antonym. *Boisterous* and *calm* have opposite meanings, as do *violent* and *peaceful*.
   - (B) PA
   - (C) AO
   - (D) PW
   - (E) PO

4. (E); Characteristic Quality. *Old ruins* are characteristically *dilapidated*, or in poor condition, just as *parachuting* is characteristically *dangerous*.
   - (A) L
   - (B) A
   - (C) C
   - (D) F

5. (B); Characteristic Quality. An *embezzler* is characteristically *fraudulent* in the same way that a *miser* is characteristically *stingy*.
   - (A) L
   - (C) PA
   - (D) A
   - (E) C

6. (A); Synonym. *Grieve* and *mourn* have similar meanings, as do *haul* and *carry*.
   - (B) CE
   - (C) F
   - (D) AO
   - (E) CQ

7. (A); Degree. A *hospitable* person is much friendlier than a merely *civil* person. And to *search* means to look more thoroughly than to *peek*.
   - (B) CQ
   - (C) C
   - (D) CE
   - (E) AO

8. (D); Cause and Effect. *Victory* can cause *jubilation*, or celebration, just as *loss* can cause *sadness*.
   - (A) PO
   - (B) S
   - (C) PA
   - (E) F

9. (C); Degree. *Riotous* means very *lively*, while *shudder* means to *quiver* violently.
   (A) PO   (D) PA
   (B) CE   (E) A

10. (C); Synonym. *Transit* and *passage* are similar in meaning, just as are *ripe* and *mature*.
    (A) PA   (D) D
    (B) A   (E) CQ

Lesson 8

p. 165 | Analogies

1. (A); Performer and Action. You expect a *biologist* to *dissect* something, just as you expect a *professor* to *teach*.
   (B) F   (D) AO
   (C) S   (E) CE

2. (E); Characteristic Quality. A *haven* is characteristically *safe*, just as *treasure* is characteristically *valuable*.
   (A) PW   (C) D
   (B) A   (D) PO

3. (D); Antonym. *Hamper* and *help* have opposite meanings, as do *criticize* and *praise*.
   (A) C   (C) S
   (B) L   (E) PA

4. (C); Characteristic Quality. *Humidity* is characteristically *damp*, just as *sleet* is characteristically *cold*.
   (A) D   (D) L
   (B) AO   (E) PW

5. (B); Synonym. *Inconsiderate* is similar in meaning to *selfish*, just as *evil* is similar in meaning to *wicked*.
   (A) CE   (D) PW
   (C) C   (E) CQ

6. (D); Function. The function of a *memento* is to *remind*, just as the function of an *exploration* is to *discover*.
   (A) PO   (C) D
   (B) PW   (E) CQ

7. (B); Performer and Action. You expect a *patient* to *recuperate*, just as you expect a *physician* to *examine* someone.
   (A) C   (D) PW
   (C) D or S   (E) CE

8. (D); Function. The function of a *seat belt* is to *restrain* someone, just as the function of a *reservoir* is to *hold* water.
   (A) D or S   (C) PW
   (B) A   (E) CQ

9. (B); Characteristic Quality. A *mansion* is characteristically *spacious*, or roomy, just as the *sea* is characteristically *salty*.
   (A) AO   (D) S
   (C) PW   (E) PA

10. (E); Synonym. *Tumult* and *uproar* have similar meanings, as do *confusion* and *disorder*.
    (A) L   (C) CQ
    (B) D   (D) F or L

Lesson 9

p. 166 | Analogies

1. (C); Cause and Effect. An *aroma*, or smell, is the effect of *baking*, just as an *accident* can be the result of *speeding*.
   (A) AO   (D) PO
   (B) F   (E) C

2. (B); Action and Object. You *baste* a *turkey*, just as you *trim* a *tree*.
   (A) PA   (D) L
   (C) CE   (E) CQ

3. (C); Performer and Object. An *investor* works with *capital*, just as a *realtor* works with *land*.
   (A) C   (D) L
   (B) CE   (E) PW

4. (E); Antonym. *Elegant* and *crude* have opposite meanings, as do *serious* and *amusing*.
   (A) S   (C) L
   (B) C   (D) PW

5. (D); Antonym. *Haughty,* or standoffish, means the opposite of *friendly,* just as *wealthy* means the opposite of *poor.*
(A) D (C) AO
(B) F (E) CQ

6. (E); Synonym. *Occupant* and *resident* have the same meaning, as do *shrub* and *bush.*
(A) PW (C) C
(B) F (D) D

7. (A); Synonym. *Remote* is similar in meaning to *distant,* as *hard* is similar in meaning to *difficult.*
(B) C (D) PO
(C) D (E) L

8. (B); Antonym. *Rigid,* or stiff, means the opposite of *flexible,* just as *damaged* means the opposite of *repaired.*
(A) PO (D) PA
(C) AO (E) PW

9. (A); Antonym. *Sedate,* or calm, and *rowdy* have opposite meanings, as do *protect* and *endanger.*
(B) PW (D) C
(C) CE (E) D

10. (C); Degree. When you *moisten* something, you don't wet it as thoroughly as when you *saturate* it, just as when you *sprinkle* something you don't dispense as much water as when you *pour* water onto it.
(A) CQ (D) C
(B) L (E) S

Lesson 10

p. 167 | Analogies

1. (D); Synonym. *Dingy* and *shabby* have similar meanings, as do *private* and *personal.*
(A) C (C) F
(B) A (E) PW

2. (C); Degree. Something that is *disagreeable* is not as bad as something that is *horrible,* while a *difficult* task is not as hard as an *impossible* task.
(A) PA (D) CQ
(B) A (E) PW

3. (C); Action and Object. You *evacuate* a *building,* and you *entertain* a *crowd.*
(A) S (D) L
(B) A (E) CQ

4. (B); Antonym. *Humiliate* and *flatter* have opposite meanings, as do *criticize* and *compliment.*
(A) L (D) PO
(C) PW (E) S

5. (A); Antonym. *Liberate,* or free, and *capture* have opposite meanings, as do *feed* and *starve.*
(B) CE or D (D) AO
(C) S (E) PW

6. (D); Classification. *Maroon* may be classified as a *color,* just as a *diamond* may be classified as a *gem.*
(A) AO (C) L
(B) F (E) PW

7. (E); Synonym. *Notify* and *inform* have similar meanings, as do *fasten* and *attach.*
(A) PW (C) PO
(B) D (D) CE

8. (C); Cause and Effect. *Remorse* can result from *wrongdoing,* just as *forgiveness* can be gained from an *apology.*
(A) F (D) PW
(B) AO (E) PA

9. (D); Degree. Someone who is *miserly* holds on to his or her money even more tightly than someone who is *thrifty.* Similarly, the acts of a *wicked* person are more harmful than the acts of a *mischievous* person.
(A) F (C) CE
(B) CQ (E) C

10. (A); Performer and Action. A *witness* can *verify* information, just as an *athlete* can *play* a sport.
(B) CQ (D) PW
(C) C (E) L

Workshop Answer Key *(continued)*

Lesson 11

p. 168 | Analogies

1. (B); Synonym. *Aspiration* and *ambition* have nearly the same meaning, as do *wish* and *desire*.
(A) F   (D) AO
(C) CQ   (E) C

2. (A); Action and Object. The police *confiscate*, or take away, someone's *weapon*, as a robber *robs* a *bank*.
(B) PW   (D) CQ
(C) PA   (E) L

3. (B); Performer and Action. You expect a *diplomat* to *represent* a nation, just as you expect a *captain* to *lead* a team.
(A) S   (D) C
(C) PW   (E) D

4. (A); Function. The function of a *foreword* is to *introduce* something, while the function of a *conclusion* is to *summarize* something.
(B) A   (D) L
(C) PW   (E) AO

5. (E); Synonym. *Generate* and *produce* are similar in meaning, as are *contribute* and *give*.
(A) PW   (C) A
(B) PA   (D) CQ

6. (C); Antonym. *Obscure*, or vague, means the opposite of *clear*, just as *private* means the opposite of *public*.
(A) L   (D) S
(B) C or CE   (E) PO

7. (B); Characteristic Quality. *Pewter* is a *gray* metal, and a *lemon* is a *sour* fruit.
(A) CE   (D) A
(C) S   (E) PO

8. (A); Function. The function of a *beverage* is to *quench* thirst, just as the function of a *sponge* is to *absorb* water.
(B) C   (D) PO
(C) CQ   (E) PW

9. (D); Classification. A *sable* is a type of *mammal*, just as a *maple* is a type of *tree*.
(A) S   (C) AO
(B) CE   (E) PA

10. (A); Part and Whole. A *salutation*, or greeting, is part of a *letter*, just as the *trunk* is part of a *tree*.
(B) S   (D) CQ
(C) PO   (E) D

Lesson 12

p. 169 | Analogies

1. (A); Antonym. *Charitable*, or generous, means the opposite of *stingy*, just as *stubborn*, or unyielding, means the opposite of *flexible*.
(B) S   (D) F
(C) CQ   (E) D

2. (E); Degree. *Colossal* means bigness to a greater degree than *large*. In the same way, to *demand* is more extreme than to *suggest*.
(A) S   (C) AO
(B) C   (D) PO

3. (D); Action and Object. You *confide* a *secret*, just as you *tell* a *tale*.
(A) F   (C) CQ
(B) L   (E) PW

4. (C); Part and Whole. A *conclusion* is part of an *essay*, just as a *chapter* is part of a *textbook*.
(A) PA   (D) A
(B) C   (E) S

5. (B); Synonym. *Irk* and *irritate* are similar in meaning, as are *build* and *construct*.
(A) C   (D) A
(C) CE   (E) AO

6. (D); Antonym. *Petty* and *important* have opposite meanings, as do *innocent* and *guilty*.
(A) PO   (C) L
(B) S   (E) CQ

Workshop Answer Key *(continued)*

7. (E); Characteristic Quality. A *believer* is characteristically *pious*, just as an *artist* is characteristically *talented*.
(A) PO   (C) S
(B) L   (D) AO

8. (C); Part and Whole. A *summit* is part of a *mountain*, just as a *mouth* is part of a *river*.
(A) PA   (D) A
(B) L   (E) PO

9. (A); Synonym. *Tarnish* and *disgrace* have similar meanings, as do *need* and *require*.
(B) CE   (D) PO
(C) C   (E) PW

10. (B); Synonym. *Temperament* is similar in meaning to *manner*, as *region* is similar in meaning to *area*.
(A) PA   (D) D
(C) CQ   (E) PW

Lesson 13

p. 170 | Analogies

1. (C); Synonym. *Casual* and *informal* have nearly the same meaning, as do *regular* and *ordinary*.
(A) CQ   (D) F
(B) PO   (E) D

2. (A); Action and Object. You *condemn* a *building*, and you *sign* a *contract*.
(B) S   (D) PA
(C) C   (E) A

3. (E); Action and Object. You *dispatch*, or send off, an *ambulance*, just as you *send* a *telegram*.
(A) CE   (C) L
(B) S   (D) PW

4. (E); Synonym. To *emphasize* a point means about the same thing as to *stress* a point, just as to *realize* the difficulty of a situation means the same thing as to *understand* the difficulty of a situation.
(A) C   (C) CQ
(B) PA   (D) L

5. (D); Action and Object. You *endorse*, or sign, the back of a *check*, just as congress *raises taxes*.
(A) PW   (C) CQ
(B) PA   (E) D

6. (A); Degree. *Famished* means very *hungry*, just as *skinny* means very *slim*.
(B) CQ   (D) C
(C) L   (E) A

7. (E); Antonym. *Fictitious* and *real* have opposite meanings, as do *worried* and *unconcerned*.
(A) PW   (C) AO
(B) PA   (D) D

8. (D); Characteristic Quality. A *fragment* is characteristically *incomplete*, just as *chrome* is characteristically *shiny*.
(A) A   (C) PW
(B) AO   (E) CE

9. (B); Performer and Action. You expect an *actor* to *improvise*, just as you expect a *poet* to *recite* poetry.
(A) L   (D) C
(C) S   (E) PW

10. (D); Synonym. *Modify* and *alter* are similar in meaning, as are *copy* and *imitate*.
(A) PW   (C) AO
(B) PO   (E) D

Lesson 14

p. 171 | Analogies

1. (D); Characteristic Quality. A *braggart* characteristically *boasts*. In the same way, a *rose* is characteristically *fragrant*.
(A) C   (C) L
(B) PA   (E) D

2. (E); Degree. To *demolish* is to *damage* completely, just as to *recover* is to *improve* completely.
(A) L   (C) CE
(B) CQ   (D) PW or PA

ANSWER KEY   **79**

Workshop Answer Key *(continued)*

3. (C); Antonym. *Denial* is the opposite of *acceptance*, as *encouragement* is the opposite of *disapproval*.
   (A) F
   (B) PA
   (D) PW
   (E) L

4. (D); Synonym. *Detach* and *disconnect* have similar meanings, as do *mend* and *repair*.
   (A) D
   (B) PO
   (C) CQ
   (E) C

5. (A); Synonym. *Eligible* and *qualified* have nearly the same meaning, as do *ready* and *prepared*.
   (B) A
   (C) L
   (D) D
   (E) C

6. (B); Function. The function of a *lantern* is to *illuminate,* or provide light, just as the function of a *refrigerator* is to *chill* food.
   (A) AO
   (C) A
   (D) PW
   (E) CQ

7. (E); Antonym. *Secluded* and *public,* or open, have opposite meanings, as do *deserted* and *crowded.*
   (A) PA
   (B) L or PW
   (C) F
   (D) PO

8. (A); Characteristic Quality. A *scrape* is characteristically *superficial,* or near the surface, while a *gash* is characteristically *deep.*
   (B) L
   (C) PW
   (D) PA
   (E) F

9. (B); Synonym. *Tangible* and *touchable* have similar meanings, as do *odd* and *strange.*
   (A) PO
   (C) CE
   (D) PA
   (E) AO

10. (B); Performer and Action. You expect a *witness* to *testify* in court, just as you expect a *shopper* to *spend* money.
    (A) CQ
    (C) AO
    (D) D
    (E) C

Lesson 15

p. 172 | Analogies

1. (E); Function. The function of *antibiotics* is to *fight* disease. In the same way, the function of *vaccinations* is to *protect* against disease.
   (A) CE
   (B) PO
   (C) A
   (D) CQ

2. (A); Synonym. An *automaton* is similar to a *robot,* just as a *bureau* is similar to a *dresser.*
   (B) F
   (C) PO
   (D) C
   (E) PW

3. (B); Synonym. *Congest* and *clog* are similar in meaning, as are *employ* and *hire.*
   (A) A
   (C) D or L
   (D) CQ
   (E) PW

4. (D); Characteristic Quality. A *hypothesis,* or theory, is characteristically *unproven,* just as a *lie* is characteristically *untrue.*
   (A) PO
   (B) A
   (C) PW
   (E) PA

5. (C); Antonym. *Parasitic,* when used to describe someone who lives at the expense of others, means about the opposite of *independent,* just as *damaged* means about the opposite of *perfect.*
   (A) L
   (B) F
   (D) CQ
   (E) S

6. (D); Characteristic Quality. A *fashion model* is characteristically *photogenic,* just as *steel* is characteristically *strong.*
   (A) PO
   (B) PW
   (C) AO
   (E) C

7. (B); Classification. A *planetarium* may be classified as a *building,* just as an *orange* may be classified as a *fruit.*
   (A) D
   (C) PO
   (D) CQ
   (E) PW

8. (E); Synonym. *Respiration* and *breathing* have nearly the same meaning, as do *exchange* and *trade.*
   (A) PA
   (B) L
   (C) CQ
   (D) AO

9. (B); Antonym. *Synthetic* and *natural* are opposite in meaning, just as *ill* and *healthy* are.
(A) PA
(D) CE
(C) C
(E) PW

10. (A); Function. The function of a *warranty*, or guarantee, is to *assure* a purchaser, just as the function of an *investigation* is to *solve* a crime.
(B) S
(D) AO
(C) PA
(E) CQ

Reading New Words in Context

Lesson 1

p. 176 | Exercise: Reading Strategically

1. A	**11.** C
2. B	**12.** A
3. B	**13.** D
4. B	**14.** C
5. D	**15.** B
6. C	**16.** B
7. C	**17.** A
8. D	**18.** B
9. C	**19.** A
10. B	**20.** D

Lesson 2

p. 180 | Exercise: Reading Strategically

1. B	**11.** B
2. C	**12.** B
3. A	**13.** A
4. D	**14.** A
5. C	**15.** B
6. D	**16.** C
7. D	**17.** D
8. D	**18.** D
9. A	**19.** A
10. A	**20.** B

Lesson 3

p. 184 | Exercise: Reading Strategically

1. B	**11.** A
2. D	**12.** B
3. A	**13.** B
4. C	**14.** D
5. A	**15.** C
6. C	**16.** D
7. C	**17.** D
8. A	**18.** D
9. C	**19.** C
10. B	**20.** B

Lesson 4

p. 188 | Exercise: Reading Strategically

1. A	**11.** A
2. A	**12.** A
3. B	**13.** B
4. B	**14.** A
5. D	**15.** B
6. C	**16.** C
7. C	**17.** D
8. B	**18.** D
9. C	**19.** C
10. C	**20.** B

Lesson 5

p. 193 | Exercise: Reading Strategically

1. D	**11.** D
2. D	**12.** B
3. B	**13.** B
4. B	**14.** D
5. C	**15.** B
6. C	**16.** A
7. D	**17.** A
8. A	**18.** A
9. C	**19.** D
10. C	**20.** C

Workshop Answer Key *(continued)*

SECOND COURSE

Lesson 6

p. 196 | **Exercise: Reading Strategically**

1.	D	11.	D
2.	A	12.	B
3.	B	13.	A
4.	B	14.	B
5.	D	15.	A
6.	C	16.	C
7.	A	17.	C
8.	B	18.	D
9.	A	19.	D
10.	C	20.	B

Lesson 7

p. 200 | **Exercise: Reading Strategically**

1.	C	11.	B
2.	B	12.	A
3.	C	13.	C
4.	A	14.	C
5.	D	15.	D
6.	B	16.	B
7.	C	17.	D
8.	B	18.	B
9.	D	19.	A
10.	C	20.	D

Lesson 8

p. 205 | **Exercise: Reading Strategically**

1.	B	11.	B
2.	A	12.	B
3.	B	13.	D
4.	B	14.	A
5.	D	15.	B
6.	A	16.	C
7.	C	17.	A
8.	D	18.	A
9.	C	19.	C
10.	C	20.	A

Lesson 9

p. 208 | **Exercise: Reading Strategically**

1.	A	11.	A
2.	A	12.	B
3.	C	13.	A
4.	B	14.	A
5.	C	15.	B
6.	B	16.	C
7.	D	17.	D
8.	D	18.	D
9.	C	19.	C
10.	C	20.	B

Lesson 10

p. 213 | **Exercise: Reading Strategically**

1.	C	11.	C
2.	A	12.	B
3.	B	13.	C
4.	C	14.	B
5.	D	15.	A
6.	C	16.	A
7.	C	17.	C
8.	A	18.	D
9.	D	19.	B
10.	C	20.	B

Lesson 11

p. 216 | **Exercise: Reading Strategically**

1.	C	11.	A
2.	A	12.	B
3.	B	13.	A
4.	B	14.	A
5.	D	15.	B
6.	C	16.	C
7.	A	17.	D
8.	D	18.	B
9.	C	19.	C
10.	C	20.	B

Lesson 12

p. 220 | **Exercise: Reading Strategically**

1. B	**11.** B
2. C	**12.** A
3. C	**13.** C
4. A	**14.** D
5. C	**15.** B
6. D	**16.** A
7. A	**17.** C
8. B	**18.** A
9. D	**19.** A
10. A	**20.** B

Lesson 13

p. 224 | **Exercise: Reading Strategically**

1. B	**11.** B
2. A	**12.** C
3. B	**13.** D
4. B	**14.** A
5. D	**15.** B
6. A	**16.** C
7. A	**17.** D
8. C	**18.** C
9. C	**19.** D
10. A	**20.** B

Lesson 14

p. 228 | **Exercise: Reading Strategically**

1. A	**11.** B
2. A	**12.** B
3. B	**13.** B
4. B	**14.** A
5. D	**15.** B
6. C	**16.** C
7. C	**17.** D
8. C	**18.** D
9. A	**19.** D
10. C	**20.** B

Lesson 15

p. 232 | **Exercise: Reading Strategically**

1. D	**11.** D
2. D	**12.** B
3. B	**13.** D
4. B	**14.** B
5. A	**15.** C
6. C	**16.** A
7. C	**17.** A
8. D	**18.** C
9. C	**19.** B
10. C	**20.** C

Tests Answer Key

SECOND COURSE

Formative Assessment

p. 3 | Test 1

1. B	**6.** D
2. D	**7.** B
3. C	**8.** A
4. B	**9.** B
5. D	**10.** A

p. 4 | Test 2

1. B	**6.** C
2. A	**7.** D
3. A	**8.** C
4. B	**9.** B
5. A	**10.** D

p. 5 | Test 3

1. A	**6.** A
2. B	**7.** A
3. D	**8.** A
4. D	**9.** A
5. C	**10.** B

p. 6 | Test 4

1. C	**6.** D
2. B	**7.** C
3. A	**8.** D
4. B	**9.** C
5. A	**10.** B

p. 7 | Test 5

1. D	**6.** C
2. A	**7.** B
3. C	**8.** B
4. C	**9.** C
5. A	**10.** B

p. 8 | Test 6

1. A	**6.** D
2. D	**7.** A
3. D	**8.** A
4. B	**9.** C
5. C	**10.** D

p. 9 | Test 7

1. B	**6.** A
2. D	**7.** A
3. C	**8.** B
4. C	**9.** D
5. A	**10.** D

p. 10 | Test 8

1. C	**6.** B
2. D	**7.** D
3. A	**8.** B
4. C	**9.** B
5. C	**10.** B

p. 11 | Test 9

1. A	**6.** A
2. B	**7.** B
3. A	**8.** D
4. C	**9.** C
5. D	**10.** A

p. 12 | Test 10

1. D	**6.** C
2. C	**7.** D
3. B	**8.** B
4. C	**9.** A
5. B	**10.** C

p. 13 | Test 11

1. D	**6.** A
2. C	**7.** B
3. B	**8.** D
4. B	**9.** D
5. C	**10.** C

p. 14 | Test 12

1. A	**6.** D
2. B	**7.** B
3. D	**8.** D
4. A	**9.** B
5. C	**10.** A

Tests Answer Key *(continued)*

p. 15 | Test 13

1. A	6. C
2. C	7. A
3. A	8. D
4. A	9. B
5. B	10. C

p. 16 | Test 14

1. A	6. D
2. C	7. C
3. D	8. A
4. B	9. B
5. A	10. C

p. 17 | Test 15

1. B	6. C
2. A	7. B
3. B	8. B
4. C	9. A
5. D	10. C

p. 18 | Test 16

1. D	6. A
2. A	7. A
3. C	8. C
4. B	9. B
5. B	10. A

p. 19 | Test 17

1. B	6. C
2. C	7. D
3. D	8. A
4. A	9. A
5. A	10. B

p. 20 | Test 18

1. C	6. A
2. B	7. A
3. D	8. C
4. D	9. B
5. C	10. A

p. 21 | Test 19

1. C	6. A
2. C	7. D
3. D	8. D
4. A	9. B
5. D	10. B

p. 22 | Test 20

1. C	6. D
2. D	7. D
3. C	8. C
4. D	9. C
5. B	10. A

p. 23 | Test 21

1. A	6. C
2. C	7. A
3. D	8. C
4. C	9. B
5. B	10. C

p. 24 | Test 22

1. A	6. A
2. A	7. C
3. D	8. B
4. B	9. B
5. C	10. A

p. 25 | Test 23

1. B	6. A
2. D	7. B
3. C	8. A
4. D	9. A
5. C	10. A

p. 26 | Test 24

1. A	6. B
2. A	7. B
3. A	8. C
4. D	9. B
5. C	10. A

Tests Answer Key *(continued)*

p. 27 | Test 25

1. C	6. D
2. C	7. A
3. B	8. D
4. C	9. D
5. B	10. D

p. 28 | Test 26

1. A	6. C
2. A	7. D
3. D	8. D
4. C	9. D
5. A	10. B

p. 29 | Test 27

1. C	6. C
2. D	7. A
3. B	8. C
4. B	9. B
5. B	10. C

p. 30 | Test 28

1. B	6. C
2. A	7. B
3. D	8. A
4. B	9. C
5. C	10. B

p. 31 | Test 29

1. C	6. B
2. A	7. D
3. B	8. A
4. B	9. A
5. A	10. D

p. 32 | Test 30

1. B	6. B
2. A	7. D
3. A	8. C
4. C	9. C
5. D	10. C

Summative Assessment

p. 35 | Test 1 Part A

1. enhance	11. ecology
2. customary	12. harmonious
3. attain	13. fragile
4. confederation	14. foresight
5. convert	15. inherit
6. assumption	16. posterity
7. folklore	17. basis
8. badger	18. baffle
9. calamity	19. deceased
10. nourish	20. feasible

21. B	36. C
22. D	37. D
23. A	38. C
24. A	39. A
25. C	40. A
26. B	41. B
27. C	42. B
28. B	43. D
29. D	44. C
30. A	45. B
31. D	46. C
32. A	47. B
33. A	48. D
34. C	49. D
35. A	50. C

p. 41 | Test 1 Part B

51. potential	61. impel
52. adapt	62. romantic
53. controversy	63. strategy
54. discord	64. bewilder
55. appalling	65. inflexible
56. menace	66. pacify
57. epidemic	67. defy
58. restore	68. inevitable
59. immense	69. sincerity
60. probable	70. creative

86

Second Course | *Vocabulary Workshop*

Tests Answer Key *(continued)*

71. B
72. A
73. D
74. C
75. C
76. A
77. A
78. D
79. C
80. C
81. D
82. A
83. C
84. B
85. D

86. C
87. B
88. C
89. C
90. D
91. C
92. D
93. C
94. B
95. B
96. C
97. C
98. A
99. D
100. B

p. 47 | Test 2 Part A

1. multitude
2. nationalities
3. aristocrat
4. refuge
5. haven
6. persistent
7. immigrated
8. accommodations
9. exaggeration
10. morale
11. optimism
12. anxiety
13. urban
14. resolute
15. hospitable
16. impulsive
17. acceptance
18. fraudulent
19. thrifty
20. thrive

21. B
22. D
23. A
24. A
25. C
26. B
27. C
28. B
29. D
30. A
31. D
32. D
33. A
34. C
35. A

36. C
37. D
38. C
39. D
40. A
41. C
42. B
43. D
44. C
45. B
46. C
47. D
48. D
49. A
50. D

p. 53 | Test 2 Part B

51. provision
52. marooned
53. burly
54. notified
55. rigid
56. gracious
57. jubilation
58. grieve
59. memento
60. humidity
61. saturated
62. adept
63. predicament
64. recuperate
65. dingy
66. aroma
67. embarrassed
68. diminish
69. naturalization
70. privilege

71. B
72. A
73. D
74. C
75. C
76. A
77. A
78. D
79. C
80. C
81. D
82. A
83. C
84. B
85. D

86. C
87. B
88. C
89. B
90. A
91. C
92. D
93. C
94. B
95. D
96. C
97. B
98. C
99. B
100. A

p. 59 | Test 3 Part A

1. articulate
2. contemporary
3. quaint
4. climax
5. intrigued
6. superficial
7. condemn
8. indelible
9. extensive
10. arrogant
11. fictitious
12. unique
13. literal
14. eccentric
15. category
16. modify
17. dilute
18. distraction
19. demolished
20. emphasize

21. B	**36.** C	**71.** B	**86.** C
22. D	**37.** D	**72.** A	**87.** B
23. A	**38.** D	**73.** D	**88.** C
24. A	**39.** D	**74.** C	**89.** B
25. C	**40.** A	**75.** C	**90.** A
26. B	**41.** B	**76.** A	**91.** C
27. C	**42.** B	**77.** A	**92.** D
28. B	**43.** D	**78.** D	**93.** C
29. D	**44.** C	**79.** C	**94.** B
30. A	**45.** B	**80.** D	**95.** D
31. D	**46.** C	**81.** D	**96.** C
32. A	**47.** D	**82.** A	**97.** D
33. A	**48.** D	**83.** C	**98.** D
34. C	**49.** B	**84.** D	**99.** C
35. A	**50.** C	**85.** D	**100.** C

p. 65 | Test 3 Part B

51. agenda	**61.** imply
52. essay	**62.** confide
53. generated	**63.** colossal
54. miscellaneous	**64.** pewter
55. proposal	**65.** pious
56. falter	**66.** sable
57. tangible	**67.** denial
58. testify	**68.** secluded
59. inclination	**69.** satire
60. erosion	**70.** deduction

Making New Words Your Own

Lesson 1

p. 3 | Exercise 1: Wordbusting

> **NOTES**
> - For each Vocabulary Word, students should fill in at least one of the **context, structure,** and **sound** boxes.
> - Check that students vary the boxes they use throughout the exercise.
> - Make sure students look up each word in the dictionary and fill in the dictionary box; answers will vary depending on the dictionary used.

p. 5 | Exercise 2: Context Clues

11. I extremity
12. A epic
13. G replenish
14. H negotiate
15. C inconspicuous
16. B intact
17. F demoralize
18. D disperse
19. E landlocked
20. J annals

p. 6 | Exercise 3: Sentence Completion

21. D
22. A
23. D
24. B
25. E
26. B
27. A
28. C
29. D
30. A

Lesson 2

p. 7 | Exercise 1: Wordbusting

> **NOTES**
> - For each Vocabulary Word, students should fill in at least one of the **context, structure,** and **sound** boxes.
> - Check that students vary the boxes they use throughout the exercise.
> - Make sure students look up each word in the dictionary and fill in the dictionary box; answers will vary depending on the dictionary used.

p. 9 | Exercise 2: Context Clues

11. J eradicate
12. A meander
13. H havoc
14. I dexterity
15. E manifest
16. F recede
17. G fervent
18. D inflamma-
tion
19. C belligerent
20. B hideous

p. 10 | Exercise 3: Sentence Completion

21. A
22. E
23. C
24. A
25. D
26. E
27. B
28. B
29. D
30. A

Lesson 3

p. 11 | Exercise 1: Wordbusting

> **NOTES**
> - For each Vocabulary Word, students should fill in at least one of the **context, structure,** and **sound** boxes.
> - Check that students vary the boxes they use throughout the exercise.
> - Make sure students look up each word in the dictionary and fill in the dictionary box; answers will vary depending on the dictionary used.

p. 13 | Exercise 2: Context Clues

11. D prowess
12. J venerable
13. F medieval
14. G hereditary
15. B amity
16. C potion
17. H devout
18. I chivalry
19. A sovereign
20. E quest

p. 14 | Exercise 3: Sentence Completion

21. B
22. C
23. D
24. D
25. A
26. E
27. E
28. B
29. C
30. B

Workshop Answer Key (continued)

Lesson 4

p. 15 | Exercise 1: Wordbusting

NOTES

- For each Vocabulary Word, students should fill in at least one of the **context, structure,** and **sound** boxes.
- Check that students vary the boxes they use throughout the exercise.
- Make sure students look up each word in the dictionary and fill in the dictionary box; answers will vary depending on the dictionary used.

p. 17 | Exercise 2: Context Clues

11. D	defile	**16.** C	citadel
12. E	entice	**17.** G	retrieve
13. J	meditate	**18.** B	emissary
14. H	undergo	**19.** A	herald
15. I	omen	**20.** F	garb

p. 18 | Exercise 3: Sentence Completion

21. C		**26.** D	
22. C		**27.** B	
23. B		**28.** E	
24. A		**29.** D	
25. A		**30.** E	

Lesson 5

p. 19 | Exercise 1: Wordbusting

NOTES

- For each Vocabulary Word, students should fill in at least one of the **context, structure,** and **sound** boxes.
- Check that students vary the boxes they use throughout the exercise.
- Make sure students look up each word in the dictionary and fill in the dictionary box; answers will vary depending on the dictionary used.

p. 21 | Exercise 2: Context Clues

11. A	agitation	**16.** J	plaintive
12. E	apparition	**17.** C	obsession
13. H	cope	**18.** B	genealogy
14. G	moor	**19.** F	benefactor
15. D	palatial	**20.** I	aloof

p. 22 | Exercise 3: Sentence Completion

21. B		**26.** D	
22. C		**27.** D	
23. A		**28.** A	
24. E		**29.** E	
25. B		**30.** C	

Lesson 6

p. 23 | Exercise 1: Wordbusting

NOTES

- For each Vocabulary Word, students should fill in at least one of the **context, structure,** and **sound** boxes.
- Check that students vary the boxes they use throughout the exercise.
- Make sure students look up each word in the dictionary and fill in the dictionary box; answers will vary depending on the dictionary used.

p. 25 | Exercise 2: Context Clues

11. F	docile	**16.** J	yearn
12. A	sinister	**17.** C	kindle
13. D	unscrupulous	**18.** H	spurn
14. E	seethe	**19.** B	smug
15. G	arrogance	**20.** I	frivolous

p. 26 | Exercise 3: Sentence Completion

21. D		**26.** A	
22. A		**27.** B	
23. D		**28.** B	
24. E		**29.** D	
25. C		**30.** C	

Lesson 7

p. 27 | Exercise 1: Wordbusting

> **NOTES**
> - For each Vocabulary Word, students should fill in at least one of the **context**, **structure**, and **sound** boxes.
> - Check that students vary the boxes they use throughout the exercise.
> - Make sure students look up each word in the dictionary and fill in the dictionary box; answers will vary depending on the dictionary used.

p. 29 | Exercise 2: Context Clues

11. E	granular	16. I	centrifugal
12. D	flora	17. B	upheaval
13. F	metamorphosis	18. H	sparse
14. J	sectors	19. G	stagnant
15. A	carnivorous	20. C	fauna

p. 30 | Exercise 3: Sentence Completion

21. B	26. C
22. A	27. E
23. D	28. A
24. D	29. B
25. C	30. E

Lesson 8

p. 31 | Exercise 1: Wordbusting

> **NOTES**
> - For each Vocabulary Word, students should fill in at least one of the **context**, **structure**, and **sound** boxes.
> - Check that students vary the boxes they use throughout the exercise.
> - Make sure students look up each word in the dictionary and fill in the dictionary box; answers will vary depending on the dictionary used.

p. 33 | Exercise 2: Context Clues

11. I	irony	16. E	humanoid
12. A	attribute	17. F	tolerate
13. B	infest	18. H	relevant
14. C	bizarre	19. G	horde
15. D	predatory	20. J	humanitarian

p. 34 | Exercise 3: Sentence Completion

21. E	26. D
22. A	27. E
23. C	28. B
24. B	29. D
25. B	30. A

Lesson 9

p. 35 | Exercise 1: Wordbusting

> **NOTES**
> - For each Vocabulary Word, students should fill in at least one of the **context**, **structure**, and **sound** boxes.
> - Check that students vary the boxes they use throughout the exercise.
> - Make sure students look up each word in the dictionary and fill in the dictionary box; answers will vary depending on the dictionary used.

p. 37 | Exercise 2: Context Clues

11. H	conspiracy	16. G	ominous
12. D	lethal	17. B	misconstrue
13. J	advocate	18. C	culmination
14. I	preposterous	19. A	alleged
15. E	manipulate	20. F	uncanny

p. 38 | Exercise 3: Sentence Completion

21. A	26. E
22. C	27. C
23. E	28. A
24. D	29. B
25. B	30. D

Lesson 10

p. 39 | Exercise 1: Wordbusting

> **NOTES**
> - For each Vocabulary Word, students should fill in at least one of the **context, structure,** and **sound** boxes.
> - Check that students vary the boxes they use throughout the exercise.
> - Make sure students look up each word in the dictionary and fill in the dictionary box; answers will vary depending on the dictionary used.

p. 41 | Exercise 2: Context Clues

11. F plaintiff	16. H prospective
12. A credentials	17. C morbid
13. G larceny	18. J superfluous
14. I quorum	19. B genial
15. D cumbersome	20. E hoax

p. 42 | Exercise 3: Sentence Completion

21. A	26. C
22. B	27. D
23. E	28. D
24. A	29. E
25. D	30. B

Lesson 11

p. 43 | Exercise 1: Wordbusting

> **NOTES**
> - For each Vocabulary Word, students should fill in at least one of the **context, structure,** and **sound** boxes.
> - Check that students vary the boxes they use throughout the exercise.
> - Make sure students look up each word in the dictionary and fill in the dictionary box; answers will vary depending on the dictionary used.

p. 45 | Exercise 2: Context Clues

11. B contemptible	16. H impertinent
12. F obtuse	17. A bland
13. J ideally	18. I pessimistic
14. C chronic	19. E malicious
15. D incomprehensible	20. G diligent

p. 46 | Exercise 3: Sentence Completion

21. C	26. D
22. E	27. D
23. E	28. B
24. C	29. A
25. B	30. A

Lesson 12

p. 47 | Exercise 1: Wordbusting

> **NOTES**
> - For each Vocabulary Word, students should fill in at least one of the **context, structure,** and **sound** boxes.
> - Check that students vary the boxes they use throughout the exercise.
> - Make sure students look up each word in the dictionary and fill in the dictionary box; answers will vary depending on the dictionary used.

p. 49 | Exercise 2: Context Clues

11. F gaudy	16. B congeniality
12. C jovial	17. I dupe
13. A extrovert	18. E tycoon
14. D abhor	19. H cynic
15. J quota	20. G intimate

p. 50 | Exercise 3: Sentence Completion

21. B	26. E
22. B	27. B
23. C	28. C
24. D	29. D
25. E	30. D

Lesson 13

p. 51 | Exercise 1: Wordbusting

> **Notes**
> - For each Vocabulary Word, students should fill in at least one of the **context, structure,** and **sound** boxes.
> - Check that students vary the boxes they use throughout the exercise.
> - Make sure students look up each word in the dictionary and fill in the dictionary box; answers will vary depending on the dictionary used.

p. 53 | Exercise 2: Context Clues

11. B implement	17. F acknowledge
12. J surmount	
13. C adversary	18. G objective
14. A wrangle	19. E elude
15. I homage	20. D exploit
16. H precedent	

p. 54 | Exercise 3: Sentence Completion

21. B	26. B
22. E	27. C
23. C	28. D
24. D	29. C
25. A	30. E

Lesson 14

p. 55 | Exercise 1: Wordbusting

> **Notes**
> - For each Vocabulary Word, students should fill in at least one of the **context, structure,** and **sound** boxes.
> - Check that students vary the boxes they use throughout the exercise.
> - Make sure students look up each word in the dictionary and fill in the dictionary box; answers will vary depending on the dictionary used.

p. 57 | Exercise 2: Context Clues

11. H lax	16. C subsequent
12. A evict	17. I formidable
13. E ostracize	18. F addicted
14. B incompatible	19. J radical
15. D solvent	20. G defraud

p. 58 | Exercise 3: Sentence Completion

21. A	26. A
22. B	27. D
23. C	28. E
24. C	29. D
25. B	30. E

Lesson 15

p. 59 | Exercise 1: Wordbusting

> **Notes**
> - For each Vocabulary Word, students should fill in at least one of the **context, structure,** and **sound** boxes.
> - Check that students vary the boxes they use throughout the exercise.
> - Make sure students look up each word in the dictionary and fill in the dictionary box; answers will vary depending on the dictionary used.

p. 61 | Exercise 2: Context Clues

11. A jaunt	16. H cascade
12. B apathy	17. G ravenous
13. J tantalizing	18. C pungent
14. I inverse	19. D induction
15. F repast	20. E sage

p. 62 | Exercise 3: Sentence Completion

21. A	26. D
22. C	27. A
23. E	28. B
24. B	29. B
25. A	30. E

Workshop Answer Key (continued)

Lesson 16

p. 63 | Exercise 1: Wordbusting

NOTES

- For each Vocabulary Word, students should fill in at least one of the **context, structure,** and **sound** boxes.

- Check that students vary the boxes they use throughout the exercise.

- Make sure students look up each word in the dictionary and fill in the dictionary box; answers will vary depending on the dictionary used.

p. 65 | Exercise 2: Context Clues

11. E	buoyant	16. G	invigorating
12. J	incandescent	17. F	opaque
13. B	benign	18. C	oppressive
14. I	murky	19. H	animated
15. D	incessant	20. A	congruent

p. 66 | Exercise 3: Sentence Completion

21. A	26. E
22. D	27. D
23. B	28. A
24. C	29. C
25. A	30. B

Lesson 17

p. 67 | Exercise 1: Wordbusting

NOTES

- For each Vocabulary Word, students should fill in at least one of the **context, structure,** and **sound** boxes.

- Check that students vary the boxes they use throughout the exercise.

- Make sure students look up each word in the dictionary and fill in the dictionary box; answers will vary depending on the dictionary used.

p. 69 | Exercise 2: Context Clues

11. F	passive	16. A	hindrance
12. I	abrasive	17. B	turbulent
13. E	reconcile	18. J	irreducible
14. H	denote	19. D	ultimate
15. C	somber	20. G	necessitate

p. 70 | Exercise 3: Sentence Completion

21. C	26. D
22. D	27. B
23. A	28. C
24. A	29. A
25. A	30. E

Lesson 18

p. 71 | Exercise 1: Wordbusting

NOTES

- For each Vocabulary Word, students should fill in at least one of the **context, structure,** and **sound** boxes.

- Check that students vary the boxes they use throughout the exercise.

- Make sure students look up each word in the dictionary and fill in the dictionary box; answers will vary depending on the dictionary used.

p. 73 | Exercise 2: Context Clues

11. H	figurative	16. D	authenticity
12. I	intensive	17. A	simile
13. G	metaphor	18. E	cadence
14. J	adage	19. C	allusion
15. B	potency	20. F	fallacy

p. 74 | Exercise 3: Sentence Completion

21. A	26. C
22. D	27. A
23. E	28. A
24. B	29. C
25. B	30. E

Lesson 19

p. 75 | Exercise 1: Wordbusting

> **NOTES**
> - For each Vocabulary Word, students should fill in at least one of the **context, structure,** and **sound** boxes.
> - Check that students vary the boxes they use throughout the exercise.
> - Make sure students look up each word in the dictionary and fill in the dictionary box; answers will vary depending on the dictionary used.

p. 77 | Exercise 2: Context Clues

11. D oratory		**16.** C rostrum
12. J ovation		**17.** E inventory
13. F replica		**18.** H soliloquy
14. I encore		**19.** B tripod
15. G intonation		**20.** A ingenuous

p. 78 | Exercise 3: Sentence Completion

21. B	**26.** A
22. A	**27.** B
23. A	**28.** D
24. B	**29.** E
25. C	**30.** B

Lesson 20

p. 79 | Exercise 1: Wordbusting

> **NOTES**
> - For each Vocabulary Word, students should fill in at least one of the **context, structure,** and **sound** boxes.
> - Check that students vary the boxes they use throughout the exercise.
> - Make sure students look up each word in the dictionary and fill in the dictionary box; answers will vary depending on the dictionary used.

p. 81 | Exercise 2: Context Clues

11. C inaudible	**16.** A panorama
12. B predominant	**17.** G resourceful
13. E mimic	**18.** I orthodox
14. F discretion	**19.** H nominal
15. D hectic	**20.** J lavish

p. 82 | Exercise 3: Sentence Completion

21. D	**26.** C
22. B	**27.** B
23. A	**28.** C
24. B	**29.** B
25. E	**30.** D

Lesson 21

p. 83 | Exercise 1: Wordbusting

> **NOTES**
> - For each Vocabulary Word, students should fill in at least one of the **context, structure,** and **sound** boxes.
> - Check that students vary the boxes they use throughout the exercise.
> - Make sure students look up each word in the dictionary and fill in the dictionary box; answers will vary depending on the dictionary used.

p. 85 | Exercise 2: Context Clues

11. I statute	**16.** E hypothetical
12. B asterisk	**17.** H thesis
13. C brochure	**18.** G perspective
14. F discredit	**19.** J jurisdiction
15. D recession	**20.** A bibliography

p. 86 | Exercise 3: Sentence Completion

21. C	**26.** D
22. E	**27.** D
23. B	**28.** B
24. D	**29.** B
25. A	**30.** E

Lesson 22

p. 87 | **Exercise 1: Wordbusting**

NOTES

- For each Vocabulary Word, students should fill in at least one of the **context, structure,** and **sound** boxes.

- Check that students vary the boxes they use throughout the exercise.

- Make sure students look up each word in the dictionary and fill in the dictionary box; answers will vary depending on the dictionary used.

p. 89 | **Exercise 2: Context Clues**

11. B denounce
12. D galvanize
13. J bilingual
14. F deficient
15. E infamous
16. H biographical
17. G satirical
18. C dissuade
19. I fluent
20. A chronological

p. 90 | **Exercise 3: Sentence Completion**

21. D
22. A
23. C
24. A
25. E
26. C
27. B
28. A
29. B
30. D

Lesson 23

p. 91 | **Exercise 1: Wordbusting**

NOTES

- For each Vocabulary Word, students should fill in at least one of the **context, structure,** and **sound** boxes.

- Check that students vary the boxes they use throughout the exercise.

- Make sure students look up each word in the dictionary and fill in the dictionary box; answers will vary depending on the dictionary used.

p. 93 | **Exercise 2: Context Clues**

11. I ideology
12. G ponderous
13. A applicable
14. E premature
15. B immaterial
16. C tentative
17. J inconvenient
18. D trivial
19. H optimistic
20. F perceptible

p. 94 | **Exercise 3: Sentence Completion**

21. C
22. A
23. D
24. B
25. B
26. D
27. C
28. E
29. E
30. A

Lesson 24

p. 95 | **Exercise 1: Wordbusting**

NOTES

- For each Vocabulary Word, students should fill in at least one of the **context, structure,** and **sound** boxes.

- Check that students vary the boxes they use throughout the exercise.

- Make sure students look up each word in the dictionary and fill in the dictionary box; answers will vary depending on the dictionary used.

p. 97 | **Exercise 2: Context Clues**

11. H clamber
12. J incalculable
13. A acclaim
14. B influential
15. I perennial
16. F affirmation
17. C affected
18. E priority
19. G prominence
20. D circumscribe

p. 98 | **Exercise 3: Sentence Completion**

21. A
22. B
23. A
24. D
25. E
26. C
27. D
28. D
29. C
30. C

Lesson 25

p. 99 | Exercise 1: Wordbusting

> **NOTES**
> - For each Vocabulary Word, students should fill in at least one of the **context, structure,** and **sound** boxes.
> - Check that students vary the boxes they use throughout the exercise.
> - Make sure students look up each word in the dictionary and fill in the dictionary box; answers will vary depending on the dictionary used.

p. 101 | Exercise 2: Context Clues

11. H frenzied	16. G volatile
12. I haphazard	17. F equation
13. C dubious	18. J essence
14. A grueling	19. D liability
15. E unkempt	20. B vanity

p. 102 | Exercise 3: Sentence Completion

21. D	26. D
22. A	27. A
23. E	28. B
24. C	29. E
25. A	30. B

Lesson 26

p. 103 | Exercise 1: Wordbusting

> **NOTES**
> - For each Vocabulary Word, students should fill in at least one of the **context, structure,** and **sound** boxes.
> - Check that students vary the boxes they use throughout the exercise.
> - Make sure students look up each word in the dictionary and fill in the dictionary box; answers will vary depending on the dictionary used.

p. 105 | Exercise 2: Context Clues

11. D functional	16. I disrupt
12. F paramount	17. A autonomous
13. B collaborate	18. E collective
14. C depict	19. J virtual
15. H transcribe	20. G reluctant

p. 106 | Exercise 3: Sentence Completion

21. C	26. A
22. B	27. E
23. B	28. D
24. D	29. B
25. C	30. A

Lesson 27

p. 107 | Exercise 1: Wordbusting

> **NOTES**
> - For each Vocabulary Word, students should fill in at least one of the **context, structure,** and **sound** boxes.
> - Check that students vary the boxes they use throughout the exercise.
> - Make sure students look up each word in the dictionary and fill in the dictionary box; answers will vary depending on the dictionary used.

p. 109 | Exercise 2: Context Clues

11. B nimble	16. J discreet
12. D connive	17. I transpire
13. C raucous	18. H instigate
14. E convey	19. F wry
15. A skeptical	20. G intimidate

p. 110 | Exercise 3: Sentence Completion

21. B	26. A
22. B	27. C
23. A	28. D
24. E	29. A
25. D	30. C

Workshop Answer Key *(continued)*

Lesson 28

p. 111 | Exercise 1: Wordbusting

NOTES

- For each Vocabulary Word, students should fill in at least one of the **context, structure,** and **sound** boxes.
- Check that students vary the boxes they use throughout the exercise.
- Make sure students look up each word in the dictionary and fill in the dictionary box; answers will vary depending on the dictionary used.

p. 113 | Exercise 2: Context Clues

11. F	alteration	**16.** J	medley
12. E	initiative	**17.** C	reprimand
13. B	irretrievable	**18.** G	indivisible
14. I	amends	**19.** A	promenade
15. H	intervention	**20.** D	drastic

p. 114 | Exercise 3: Sentence Completion

21. A		**26.** D	
22. B		**27.** A	
23. C		**28.** C	
24. D		**29.** B	
25. B		**30.** B	

Lesson 29

p. 115 | Exercise 1: Wordbusting

NOTES

- For each Vocabulary Word, students should fill in at least one of the **context, structure,** and **sound** boxes.
- Check that students vary the boxes they use throughout the exercise.
- Make sure students look up each word in the dictionary and fill in the dictionary box; answers will vary depending on the dictionary used.

p. 117 | Exercise 2: Context Clues

11. E	retract	**16.** H	dwindle
12. D	surpass	**17.** F	wary
13. A	agility	**18.** C	exasperate
14. I	susceptible	**19.** B	nonchalant
15. J	veneer	**20.** G	elapse

p. 118 | Exercise 3: Sentence Completion

21. B		**26.** A	
22. D		**27.** C	
23. C		**28.** D	
24. E		**29.** A	
25. B		**30.** B	

Lesson 30

p. 119 | Exercise 1: Wordbusting

NOTES

- For each Vocabulary Word, students should fill in at least one of the **context, structure,** and **sound** boxes.
- Check that students vary the boxes they use throughout the exercise.
- Make sure students look up each word in the dictionary and fill in the dictionary box; answers will vary depending on the dictionary used.

p. 121 | Exercise 2: Context Clues

11. C	collateral	**16.** B	assess
12. H	emerge	**17.** G	contaminate
13. D	comply	**18.** F	immunity
14. I	expend	**19.** E	maintenance
15. A	condolence	**20.** J	depreciate

p. 122 | Exercise 3: Sentence Completion

21. D		**26.** C	
22. C		**27.** E	
23. E		**28.** B	
24. A		**29.** C	
25. B		**30.** D	

Connecting New Words and Patterns

Lesson 1

p. 126 | Analogies

1. (B); Antonym. *Belligerent*, which means quarrelsome, means the opposite of *peaceful*. *Disappointed* and *pleased* have opposite meanings.

2. (A); Synonym. *Manifest*, which means show, means the same as *reveal*. *Endure*, which means to hold out or last, has a meaning similar to *persist*.

3. (B); Synonym. *Meander* and *wander* have similar meanings, as do *wiggle* and *squirm*.

4. (B); Characteristic Quality. A *disciple*, or follower, is characteristically *fervent*, or devoted. An *inventor* is characteristically *creative*.

5. (E); Cause and Effect. *Practice* can result in *dexterity*, or skill. *Study* can result in *knowledge*.

6. (D); Performer and Related Action. A *diplomat negotiates* with other countries, just as a *lawyer settles* a lawsuit.

7. (C); Antonym. *Intact*, or whole, means the opposite of *damaged*. *Valued* means the opposite of *scorned*.

8. (D); Synonym. *Recede* and *withdraw* have similar meanings, as do *predict* and *forecast*.

9. (D); Degree. Something that is *hideous* is extremely *unattractive*, just as someone who is *overjoyed* is extremely *pleased*.

10. (E); Degree. To *replenish* something is to *provide* it again when it runs out. To *refill* something is to *fill* it again.

Lesson 2

p. 127 | Analogies

1. (D); Synonym. An *emissary* is a *messenger*, just as a *doctor* is a *physician*.

2. (C); Characteristic Quality. A *citadel*, or hilltop fortress, is characteristically *elevated*, or high. A *courtyard*, or inner patio, is characteristically *walled*.

3. (D); Performer and Related Object. A *herald*, or messenger, delivers a *message*, just as a *mail carrier* delivers a *letter*.

4. (D); Synonym. *Medieval* and *gothic*, adjectives which refer to the period in Europe's history called the Middle Ages, have similar meanings, as do *intentional* and *purposeful*.

5. (E); Antonym. *Prowess*, which means great ability, means the opposite of *ineptitude*, or incompetence. *Pride* and *humility* are also opposite in meaning.

6. (C); Cause and Effect. Some believe a *potion* can result in *magic*, just as a *sedative* can result in *tranquility*.

7. (C); Synonym. *Garb* and *clothing* have the same meaning, as do *whiskers* and *beard*.

8. (E); Synonym. *Undergo* and *endure* have similar meanings, as do *gratify* and *please*.

9. (E); Synonym. *Amity* and *friendship* have similar meanings, as do *richness* and *wealth*.

10. (B); Function. The function of an *omen* is to *foretell* the future. The function of a *crane* is to *lift* something heavy.

Lesson 3

p. 128 | Analogies

1. (D); Performer and Related Action. A *benefactor* is someone who *helps* the needy, just as a *patron* is someone who *supports* individuals or causes.

2. (E); Synonym. *Moor*, as in to moor a boat, and *secure* have similar meanings, as do *speak* and *talk*.

3. (E); Antonym. *Plaintive*, which means sad, is opposite in meaning to *joyous*. *Moderate* and *excessive* are also opposite in meaning.

4. (B); Characteristic Quality. A *villain* is characteristically *sinister*, just as a *benefactor* is characteristically *kindly*.

5. (E); Synonym. *Cope* and *handle* possess similar meanings, as do *recall* and *remember.*

6. (A); Synonym. *Agitation* and *commotion* are similar in meaning, as are *assault* and *attack.*

7. (C); Part and Whole. A *grandparent*, like all your relatives, is a part of your *genealogy*, or family history, in the same way that an *item* is a part of a *list.*

8. (B); Antonym. *Spurn*, which means reject, is opposite in meaning to *accept. Forbid* and *authorize* also have opposite meanings.

9. (B); Synonym. *Kindle* and *ignite* have similar meanings, as do *conceal* and *hide.*

10. (A); Synonym. *Smug* and *self-satisfied* have similar meanings, as do *hesitant* and *unsure.*

Lesson 4

p. 129 | Analogies

1. (B); Classification. A *rabbit* is classified as *fauna*, or animal life, just as a *rosebush* is classified as *vegetation*, or plant life.

2. (D); Part and Whole. *Larva* is one stage of *metamorphosis*, a dramatic change, just as a *blueprint* is one part of the *construction process.*

3. (E); Synonym. *Sector* and *division* have similar meanings, as do *territory* and *region.*

4. (D); Characteristic Quality. A *tiger* is characteristically *carnivorous*, or meat-eating, just as a *monkey* is characteristically *acrobatic.*

5. (D); Classification. A *daffodil* is classified as *flora*, or plant life, just as a *beaver* is classified as an *animal.*

6. (D); Performer and Related Action. One expects a *horde* of people to *wander*, just as one expects a *cast* to *perform.*

7. (D); Synonym. *Centrifugal*, which means moving out from the center, has a meaning similar to *outward. Heated* and *warm* also have similar meanings.

8. (B); Antonym. *Stagnant* and *moving* have opposite meanings, as do *still* and *active.*

9. (C); Part and Whole. *Contrast* is an element of *irony*, just as *conflict* is an element of *drama.*

10. (D); Degree. *Tolerate* and *endure* have similar meanings but differ in degree: Endure implies withstanding much greater suffering. *Torment* and *torture* are also similar, but to torture is more severe than to torment.

Lesson 5

p. 130 | Analogies

1. (D); Synonym. *Culmination*, which means the highest point, has a meaning similar to *peak. Elevation* and *height* also have similar meanings.

2. (A); Synonym. *Superfluous* and *excessive* have similar meanings, as do *changeless* and *monotonous.*

3. (C); Characteristic Quality. A *host* is characteristically *genial*, or pleasant, just as a *guest* is characteristically *polite.*

4. (E); Characteristic Quality. *Credentials* are characteristically *written*, just as a *speech* is characteristically *uttered.*

5. (C); Antonym. *Preposterous*, which means senseless or ridiculous, is opposite in meaning to *sensible. Harmless* and *destructive* also have opposite meanings.

6. (A); Classification. *Larceny*, or theft, is classified as a *crime*. An *apple* is classified as a *fruit.*

7. (A); Performer and Related Action. An *advocate* is someone who *supports* someone else. An *opponent* is someone who *opposes.*

8. (D); Synonym. *Hoax* and *trick* have similar meanings, as do *sport* and *game.*

9. (A); Synonym. *Lethal* and *deadly* have the same meaning, as do *vital* and *essential.*

10. (E); Performer and Related Action. A *plaintiff* is someone who *sues*, or files a lawsuit. A *tailor* is someone who *sews* clothing.

Workshop Answer Key *(continued)*

THIRD COURSE

Lesson 6

p. 131 | Analogies

1. (D); Degree. *Abhor*, which means hate, is stronger in meaning than *dislike*. *Idolize*, which means worship, is stronger in meaning than *admire*.

2. (E); Synonym. All four words mean ongoing.

3. (E); Characteristic Quality. An *ant* is characteristically *diligent*, or hard-working, just as a *bee* is characteristically *busy*.

4. (B); Antonym. *Contemptible* and *admirable* have opposite meanings, as do *handsome* and *ugly*.

5. (A); Synonym. *Impertinent*, which means rude, has a meaning similar to *impolite*. *Reverent* and *respectful* also have similar meanings.

6. (A); Synonym. *Jovial* and *jolly* have similar meanings, as do *valuable* and *precious*.

7. (A); Antonym. *Malicious*, or mean, is opposite in meaning to *kind*. *Scarce* and *abundant* are also opposite in meaning.

8. (D); Synonym. *Obtuse*, or dense, has a meaning similar to *dull*. *Common* and *ordinary* also have similar meanings.

9. (E); Synonym. *Quota* and *share* have similar meanings, as do *portion* and *part*.

10. (A); Synonym. *Dupe* and *deceive* have similar meanings, as do *fool* and *trick* when they are used as verbs.

Lesson 7

p. 132 | Analogies

1. (C); Performer and Related Action. An *adversary*, or opponent, is someone who *opposes*. A *teammate* is someone who *plays*.

2. (E); Antonym. *Acknowledge* and *ignore* are opposite in meaning, as are *write* and *erase*.

3. (A); Synonym. *Subsequent*, which means next, has the same meaning as *following*

when following is used as an adjective. *Last* and *final* also have the same meaning.

4. (B); Antonym. *Ostracize*, which means to keep out, is opposite in meaning to *include*. *Enter* and *exit* also have opposite meanings.

5. (E); Antonym. *Lax* and *strict* are opposite in meaning, as are *gentle* and *harsh*.

6. (D); Degree. To *exploit* is to *use* to the degree of abusing, just as to *exaggerate* is to *describe* to the degree of distorting facts.

7. (E); Action and Related Object. One *surmounts* an *obstacle*, just as one *overcomes* a *difficulty*.

8. (A); Synonym. *Elude* and *escape* have similar meanings, as do *trap* and *catch*.

9. (D); Synonym. *Defraud*, or cheat, has a meaning similar to *swindle*. *Begin* and *start* also have similar meanings.

10. (C); Degree. To *wrangle* is to *disagree* to the extent of an argument. To *adore* is to *like* to an extreme extent.

Lesson 8

p. 133 | Analogies

1. (D); Synonym. *Pungent* and *sharp* have similar meanings, as do *lively* and *active*.

2. (D); Degree. *Incandescent* is similar in meaning to *bright*, but much stronger, just as *gigantic* implies greater size than *big* does.

3. (B); Classification. *Breakfast* is classified as a *repast*, or meal. *Gray* is classified as a *color*.

4. (C); Synonym. *Congruent*, which means in agreement or corresponding, has a meaning similar to *harmonious*. *Precise* and *exact* also have similar meanings.

5. (A); Antonym. *Animated*, which means lively, is opposite in meaning to *depressed*. *Curious* and *disinterested* are also opposite in meaning.

ANSWER KEY

101

6. (A); Antonym. *Apathy,* a lack of interest or feeling, is opposite in meaning to *concern,* just as *tension* is opposite in meaning to *relaxation.*

7. (B); Synonym. *Incessant,* or never ending, has a meaning similar to *constant. Earnest* and *sincere* also have similar meanings.

8. (E); Antonym. *Opaque* and *transparent* have opposite meanings, as do *plentiful* and *scarce.*

9. (A); Synonym. *Inverse* and *opposite* have similar meanings, as do *difficult* and *hard.*

10. (D); Antonym. *Tantalizing* and *repulsive* are opposite in meaning, as are *calming* and *upsetting.*

Lesson 9

p. 134 | Analogies

1. (A); Synonym. *Denote,* which means signify, has the same meaning as *mean* when mean is a verb. *Create* and *invent* also have the same meaning.

2. (C); Function. The function of a *simile* is to *compare* two dissimilar things. The function of an *adjective* is to *modify* a noun.

3. (E); Synonym. *Authenticity,* the state of being real or true, has a meaning similar to *genuineness,* just as *magnificence* and *splendor* have similar meanings.

4. (B); Antonym. *Ultimate,* or final, means the opposite of *initial,* or first. *Fictitious,* or imaginary, means the opposite of *actual.*

5. (A); Part and Whole. *Metaphor* is a literary device used in *poetry,* just as *shading* is a technique used in *drawing.*

6. (B); Synonym. *Cadence* and *beat* have the same meaning, as do *melody* and *tune.*

7. (A); Antonym. *Hindrance,* which means obstacle, means the opposite of *help. Creation* and *destruction* also have opposite meanings.

8. (A); Characteristic Quality. *Sandpaper* is characteristically *abrasive,* or gritty, just as *water* is characteristically *wet.*

9. (B); Characteristic Quality. A *waterfall* is characteristically *turbulent,* just as the *sunshine* is characteristically *warm.*

10. (E); Characteristic Quality. An *adage* is characteristically an *old* saying. *Rain* is characteristically *wet.*

Lesson 10

p. 135 | Analogies

1. (E); Part and Whole. A *soliloquy,* or monologue, is part of a *drama.* A *song* is part of a *musical comedy.*

2. (B); Antonym. *Inaudible,* which means unable to be heard, is opposite in meaning to *loud. Obscure* and *prominent* are also opposite in meaning.

3. (E); Characteristic Quality. A *panorama,* which is a broad vista or view, is characteristically *wide,* just as *lace* is characteristically *delicate.*

4. (D); Antonym. *Discretion,* which means freedom to make decisions and choices, is nearly opposite in meaning to *restriction. Enthusiasm,* which means intense interest, is opposite in meaning to *disinterest.*

5. (E); Antonym. *Hectic* and *calm* have opposite meanings, as do *relaxed* and *tense.*

6. (D); Antonym. *Lavish,* or extravagant, is opposite in meaning to *meager,* which means sparse or spare. *Expensive* and *cheap* are also opposite in meaning.

7. (A); Synonym. To *inventory* items in a store is the same thing as to *list* them, just as to *remark* is to *comment.*

8. (E); Synonym. *Predominant,* which means of first importance, is similar in meaning to *supreme,* just as *present* and *now* have similar meanings.

9. (B); Part and Whole. *Intonation* is an element of *speech,* just as *melody* is an element of *music.*

10. (D); Characteristic Quality. A *tripod* is characteristically *three-legged,* just as a *bicycle* is characteristically *two-wheeled.*

Lesson 11

p. 136 | Analogies

1. (A); Part and Whole. *Titles* of books make up a *bibliography*, just as *entries* of words make up a *dictionary*.

2. (D); Synonym. *Infamous* and *scandalous* have similar meanings, as do *heroic* and *brave*.

3. (C); Location. A *judge* works in a *jurisdiction*, just as a *salesperson* works in a *territory*.

4. (C); Antonym. *Dissuade*, or discourage, is opposite in meaning to *encourage*. *Occupy* and *vacate* are also opposite in meaning.

5. (E); Synonym. *Discredit* also means *disbelief* and therefore the two are similar in meaning, just as *famous* is similar in meaning to *well-known*.

6. (D); Classification. *Recession*, or a temporary business slump, is considered a classification of *economics*, just as a *doctor* is classified as a *professional*.

7. (A); Antonym. *Chronological*, which means in time order, is opposite in meaning to *random*. *Chaotic*, which can mean unsettled and disorderly, is opposite in meaning to *orderly*.

8. (D); Classification. An *asterisk* is a type of *mark*, just as a *period* is a type of *punctuation*.

9. (D); Antonym. *Denounce* and *praise* are nearly opposite in meaning, as are *avoid* and *encounter*.

10. (D); Classification. A *statute* is classified as a *law*, just as a *fine* is classified as a *penalty*.

Lesson 12

p. 137 | Analogies

1. (C); Synonym. *Applicable* and *appropriate* have similar meanings, as do *strange* and *odd*.

2. (A); Antonym. *Influential* and *powerless* are opposite in meaning, as are *eternal* and *temporary*.

3. (D); Synonym. *Trivial*, or unimportant, means nearly the same as *insignificant*. *Complicated* means nearly the same as *complex*.

4. (C); Antonym. *Optimistic* and *negative* are opposite in meaning, as are *safe* and *dangerous*.

5. (D); Synonym. *Ponderous*, which means massive, has a meaning similar to *bulky*. *Heavy* and *weighty* also have similar meanings.

6. (D); Synonym. *Perceptible* and *noticeable* have nearly the same meaning, as do *necessary* and *needed*.

7. (C); Classification. A *perennial* is classified as a *plant*, just as a *sofa* is classified as *furniture*.

8. (B); Degree. To *acclaim* is to *approve* with enthusiasm. To adore something is to *like* it intensely.

9. (B); Performer and Related Object. *Affirmation*, meaning testimony by one who cannot conscientiously swear an oath, is performed by a *witness*. In the same way, an *author* performs, or writes *books*.

10. (A); Synonym. *Clamber* and *climb* have nearly the same meaning, as do *sprint* and *run*.

Lesson 13

p. 138 | Analogies

1. (C); Antonym. *Haphazard*, or disorderly, means the opposite of *systematic*, just as *hostile* means the opposite of *friendly*.

2. (D); Synonym. *Paramount*, which means ranking higher than any other, has the same meaning as *supreme*. *Practiced* has the same meaning as *rehearsed*.

3. (A); Synonym. *Unkempt* and *untidy* have the same meaning, as do *unorganized* and *disorderly*.

4. (A); Antonym. *Volatile*, which means changeable or shifting, means the opposite of *stable*. *Exciting* and *dull* also have opposite meanings.

Workshop Answer Key (continued)

5. (B); Action and Related Object. You *transcribe notes*, just as you *translate* a *language*.

6. (A); Part and Whole. An *equation* is part of *mathematics*, just as a *sentence* is part of *language*.

7. (A); Degree. *Frenzied* and *upset* are similar in meaning, but frenzied suggests rushed activity. In the same way, *ecstatic* suggests a stronger degree of response than *pleased*.

8. (E); Antonym. *Liability* and *advantage* have nearly opposite meanings, as do *debt* and *credit*.

9. (D); Synonym. *Dubious* and *questionable* have nearly the same meaning, as do *rough* and *uneven*.

10. (E); Synonym. *Grueling* and *exhausting* have similar meanings, as do *thrilling* and *exciting*.

Lesson 14

p. 139 | Analogies

1. (E); Synonym. *Drastic* and *severe* have nearly the same meaning, as do *stormy* and *violent*.

2. (A); Performer and Related Action. *Thugs intimidate* their victims, just as *champs celebrate* their victories.

3. (B); Synonym. To *promenade* is to *walk,* just as to *lounge* is to *lie*.

4. (D); Antonym. *Instigate,* or start, means the opposite of *halt*. *Oppose* and *promote* are also opposite in meaning.

5. (B); Characteristic Quality. A *gymnast* is characteristically *nimble,* or agile, just as an *antelope* is characteristically *speedy*.

6. (E); Synonym. Taking the *initiative* in a situation is the same as taking the *first step,* just as a *regulation* is the same thing as a *rule*.

7. (A); Synonym. *Alteration* and *change* have nearly the same meaning, as do *method* and *system*.

8. (C); Part and Whole. *Songs* are part of a *medley,* just as *vegetables* are part of a *salad*.

9. (E); Antonym. *Discreet,* or cautious, means the opposite of *careless*. *Proud* means the opposite of *ashamed*.

10. (A); Synonym. *Indivisible* and *united* have similar meanings, as do *unspoiled* and *fresh*.

Lesson 15

p. 140 | Analogies

1. (A); Cause and Effect. A *vaccination* can result in *immunity* to a disease, just as *exercise* can result in *strength*.

2. (A); Antonym. *Agility* is the opposite of *sluggishness,* just as *angularity* is the opposite of *roundness*.

3. (A); Synonym. *Wary* and *cautious* have the same meaning, as do *funny* and *comic*.

4. (D); Synonym. *Surpass* means nearly the same thing as *excel,* just as *harm* means nearly the same thing as *hurt*.

5. (A); Antonym. *Dwindle,* which means to lessen, is opposite in meaning to *increase*. *Appear* means the opposite of *vanish*.

6. (C); Synonym. *Comply* and *obey* have the same meaning, as do *adjust* and *adapt*.

7. (A); Antonym. *Contaminate,* or pollute, means the opposite of *purify*. *Destroy* and *build* also have opposite meanings.

8. (D); Action and Related Object. You *expend,* or use, *resources,* just as you *spend money*.

9. (A); Antonym. *Nonchalant,* or unconcerned, means the opposite of *concerned*. *Sloppy* and *orderly* also have opposite meanings.

10. (B); Synonym. *Retract,* which means to pull back, means nearly the same as *withdraw*. *Accuse* and *blame* also have nearly the same meaning.

Reading New Words in Context

Lesson 1

p. 144 | Exercise 1: Finding Synonyms

Answers will vary. The following are possible responses.

1. disaster
2. resupply
3. depress
4. severe difficulty
5. angered
6. give out
7. reveal
8. eliminate
9. records
10. story of a hero
11. whole
12. deeply felt
13. surrounded by land
14. aggressive
15. work out
16. skill
17. horrible
18. fade away
19. not noticeable
20. wander

p. 145 | Exercise 2: Reading Strategically

1. D
2. A
3. B
4. D
5. C
6. D
7. E
8. A
9. B
10. E
11. A
12. C
13. D
14. C
15. B
16. A
17. E
18. B
19. B
20. C

Lesson 2

p. 150 | Exercise 1: Finding Synonyms

Answers will vary. The following are possible responses.

1. kings
2. friendship
3. of the Middle Ages
4. pious
5. clothing
6. respectable
7. inherited
8. code of knight-hood
9. skill
10. endure
11. think seriously
12. search
13. bring back
14. fortress
15. tempt
16. damage
17. messenger
18. drink
19. warning
20. person who makes heraldry

p. 151 | Exercise 2: Reading Strategically

1. A
2. C
3. B
4. C
5. E
6. C
7. A
8. E
9. A
10. B
11. B
12. B
13. A
14. C
15. A
16. B
17. E
18. A
19. B
20. E

Lesson 3

p. 156 | Exercise 1: Finding Synonyms

Answers will vary. The following are possible responses.

1. large
2. silly
3. disturbance
4. family history
5. wicked
6. ghost
7. immoral
8. preoccupation
9. marshes
10. deals with
11. obedient
12. sad
13. excessive pride
14. self-righteous
15. distant
16. starts a fire
17. rejects
18. patron
19. desires
20. boils

p. 157 | Exercise 2: Reading Strategically

1. D
2. A
3. B
4. A
5. C
6. E
7. B
8. E
9. B
10. C
11. A
12. C
13. C
14. C
15. B
16. A
17. E
18. A
19. A
20. C

Lesson 4

p. 162 | Exercise 1: Finding Synonyms

Answers will vary. The following are possible responses.

1. characteristic
2. weird
3. related
4. concerned with human beings
5. humanlike being
6. preying
7. moving away from center
8. put up with
9. grainy
10. plants
11. animals
12. violent change
13. dramatic change
14. meat-eating
15. invade
16. opposite of what is expected
17. large group
18. not crowded
19. section
20. stale

p. 163 | Exercise 2: Reading Strategically

1. A
2. B
3. A
4. A
5. E
6. D
7. B
8. C
9. B
10. E
11. D
12. A
13. E
14. D
15. E
16. B
17. C
18. B
19. D
20. E

Lesson 5

p. 168 | Exercise 1: Finding Synonyms

Answers will vary. The following are possible responses.

1. gruesome
2. threatening
3. deadly
4. theft
5. high point
6. misinterpret
7. unimportant
8. control
9. burdensome
10. certification
11. good-natured
12. extraordinary
13. potential
14. complainant
15. ridiculous
16. defender
17. unproven
18. plot
19. sufficient number
20. trick

p. 169 | Exercise 2: Reading Strategically

1. C
2. A
3. B
4. E
5. D
6. D
7. C
8. B
9. E
10. A
11. B
12. D
13. C
14. B
15. C
16. D
17. A
18. E
19. E
20. E

Lesson 6

p. 174 | Exercise 1: Finding Synonyms

Answers will vary. The following are possible responses.

1. impossible to understand
2. negative person
3. dull person
4. expecting the worst
5. hate
6. evil
7. hard-working
8. deserving scorn; despicable
9. trick
10. pleasant
11. stupid
12. showy
13. outgoing person
14. wealthy business person
15. perfectly
16. agreeableness
17. continually
18. limit
19. friendly
20. disrespectful

p. 175 | Exercise 2: Reading Strategically

1. A
2. C
3. A
4. C
5. B
6. B
7. C
8. A
9. A
10. D
11. B
12. C
13. C
14. D
15. E
16. E
17. B
18. A
19. D
20. D

Workshop Answer Key *(continued)*

Lesson 7

p. 180 | Exercise 1: Finding Synonyms

Answers will vary. The following are possible responses.

1. mismatched
2. admit
3. respect
4. later
5. use
6. extreme
7. exclude
8. unprejudiced
9. escape
10. forerunner; example
11. difficult
12. apply
13. overcome
14. enemy
15. throw out
16. careless
17. cheat
18. dependent
19. liquid substance
20. fights

p. 181 | Exercise 2: Reading Strategically

1. C
2. B
3. C
4. A
5. B
6. D
7. E
8. C
9. A
10. E
11. A
12. C
13. D
14. A
15. D
16. C
17. D
18. E
19. D
20. B

Lesson 8

p. 186 | Exercise 1: Finding Synonyms

Answers will vary. The following are possible responses.

1. enlivening
2. in agreement
3. entry
4. sage
5. intimidating
6. trip
7. dark
8. glowing
9. gloomy
10. indifference
11. good
12. in the opposite way
13. shower
14. food
15. tempting
16. sharp
17. hungry
18. lively
19. continuous
20. cheerful

p. 187 | Exercise 2: Reading Strategically

1. C
2. C
3. A
4. E
5. B
6. A
7. D
8. D
9. C
10. D
11. E
12. E
13. E
14. A
15. B
16. A
17. B
18. E
19. D
20. C

Lesson 9

p. 192 | Exercise 1: Finding Synonyms

Answers will vary. The following are possible responses.

1. most
2. old saying
3. difficulty
4. mean
5. inactive
6. bring together
7. genuineness
8. require
9. references
10. deeply
11. mistaken idea
12. stormy
13. irritating
14. not literal
15. direct comparison
16. comparison using words such as *like* or *as*
17. rhythm
18. power
19. basic; can't be made simpler
20. serious

p. 193 | Exercise 2: Reading Strategically

1. B
2. A
3. C
4. A
5. D
6. E
7. C
8. B
9. E
10. B
11. A
12. C
13. A
14. D
15. A
16. D
17. C
18. C
19. B
20. E

Lesson 10

p. 198 | Exercise 1: Finding Synonyms

Answers will vary. The following are possible responses.

1. clever
2. prolonged applause
3. overruling
4. list
5. elaborate
6. platform
7. very small
8. judgment
9. frenzied
10. not hearable
11. public speaking
12. the rise and fall of the voice
13. a speech given in drama, revealing the character's thoughts
14. person who imitates others
15. naive
16. conventional
17. reproduction
18. three-legged stand
19. wide, unbroken scene
20. repeat performance

p. 199 | Exercise 2: Reading Strategically

1. C
2. A
3. A
4. D
5. B
6. E
7. A
8. E
9. D
10. C
11. A
12. D
13. B
14. C
15. C
16. C
17. B
18. B
19. D
20. D

Lesson11

p. 204 | Exercise 1: Finding Synonyms

Answers will vary. The following are possible responses.

1. pamphlet
2. to turn aside
3. cast doubt on
4. point of view
5. notorious
6. put down
7. lacking
8. sarcastic
9. list of books
10. about a person's life
11. arouse
12. law
13. authority
14. a starlike symbol
15. in time order
16. research paper
17. a time of economic trouble
18. proficiency in a language
19. using two languages
20. supposed

p. 205 | Exercise 2: Reading Strategically

1. B
2. A
3. D
4. B
5. C
6. D
7. D
8. A
9. E
10. C
11. D
12. E
13. A
14. B
15. B
16. B
17. D
18. E
19. C
20. C

Workshop Answer Key *(continued)*

Lesson 12

p. 210 | Exercise 1: Finding Synonyms

Answers will vary. The following are possible responses.

1. lasting
2. touched
3. hopeful
4. climb
5. limit
6. doctrine
7. unimportant
8. verifications
9. noticeable
10. having a strong effect
11. most important thing
12. beyond measure
13. state of importance
14. hesitant
15. praises
16. relevant
17. lacking significance
18. heavy
19. awkward
20. too early

p. 211 | Exercise 2: Reading Strategically

1. D
2. E
3. C
4. B
5. A
6. C
7. B
8. D
9. C
10. E
11. D
12. E
13. A
14. A
15. C
16. C
17. D
18. A
19. E
20. B

Lesson 13

p. 216 | Exercise 1: Finding Synonyms

Answers will vary. The following are possible responses.

1. major
2. doubtful
3. show
4. a balanced group of elements
5. most essential part
6. hesitant
7. drawback
8. explosive
9. conceitedness
10. work together
11. group effort
12. independent
13. careless
14. difficult
15. wildly excited
16. write down
17. effective
18. disturb
19. almost
20. messy

p. 217 | Exercise 2: Reading Strategically

1. A
2. B
3. B
4. C
5. C
6. D
7. C
8. B
9. A
10. D
11. E
12. E
13. D
14. B
15. E
16. D
17. A
18. E
19. C
20. D

Lesson 14

p. 222 | Exercise 1: Finding Synonyms

Answers will vary. The following are possible responses.

1. disbelieving
2. close
3. scold
4. plot something
5. enterprise
6. changes
7. major
8. occur
9. secretive
10. make afraid
11. start
12. action to stop
13. cannot be recovered
14. ironic
15. rowdy
16. march
17. graceful
18. give
19. collection
20. something given to make up for something done

p. 223 | Exercise 2: Reading Strategically

1. C
2. B
3. C
4. A
5. A
6. B
7. C
8. B
9. D
10. C
11. A
12. C
13. C
14. B
15. B
16. A
17. C
18. D
19. E
20. B

Workshop Answer Key *(continued)*

Lesson 15

p. 228 | **Exercise 1: Finding Synonyms**

Answers will vary. The following are possible responses.

1. facade
2. casual
3. frustrate
4. vulnerable
5. cautious
6. evaluate
7. use
8. security
9. exceed
10. decrease
11. protection
12. pass
13. expression of sorrow
14. pollute
15. take back
16. upkeep
17. fell in value
18. nimbleness
19. exit
20. go along with

p. 229 | **Exercise 2: Reading Strategically**

1. E
2. E
3. A
4. B
5. C
6. C
7. A
8. C
9. D
10. B
11. A
12. A
13. B
14. C
15. E
16. B
17. C
18. C
19. C
20. A

p. 3 | Test 1

1. C		**6.** E	
2. C		**7.** D	
3. B		**8.** A	
4. E		**9.** D	
5. C		**10.** D	

p. 4 | Test 2

1. A	**6.** A
2. B	**7.** E
3. E	**8.** D
4. C	**9.** C
5. D	**10.** B

p. 5 | Test 3

1. E	**6.** E
2. B	**7.** A
3. D	**8.** C
4. B	**9.** D
5. B	**10.** D

p. 6 | Test 4

1. D	**6.** E
2. A	**7.** C
3. B	**8.** C
4. D	**9.** C
5. B	**10.** B

p. 7 | Test 5

1. B	**6.** D
2. D	**7.** D
3. C	**8.** E
4. C	**9.** B
5. C	**10.** A

p. 8 | Test 6

1. A	**6.** C
2. A	**7.** B
3. D	**8.** E
4. C	**9.** C
5. B	**10.** A

p. 9 | Test 7

1. B	**6.** C
2. A	**7.** C
3. D	**8.** E
4. B	**9.** E
5. C	**10.** A

p. 10 | Test 8

1. E	**6.** A
2. B	**7.** D
3. D	**8.** C
4. B	**9.** C
5. C	**10.** A

p. 11 | Test 9

1. D	**6.** C
2. B	**7.** A
3. E	**8.** B
4. A	**9.** E
5. D	**10.** C

p. 12 | Test 10

1. D	**6.** C
2. E	**7.** C
3. D	**8.** C
4. A	**9.** A
5. C	**10.** A

p. 13 | Test 11

1. D	**6.** C
2. A	**7.** A
3. D	**8.** D
4. E	**9.** C
5. A	**10.** B

p. 14 | Test 12

1. D	**6.** E
2. B	**7.** B
3. D	**8.** B
4. E	**9.** D
5. C	**10.** A

Tests Answer Key *(continued)*

p. 15 | Test 13

1. A	**6.** B
2. C	**7.** E
3. B	**8.** A
4. C	**9.** C
5. D	**10.** C

p. 16 | Test 14

1. D	**6.** B
2. C	**7.** D
3. A	**8.** C
4. E	**9.** B
5. B	**10.** B

p. 17 | Test 15

1. D	**6.** B
2. E	**7.** C
3. A	**8.** A
4. B	**9.** E
5. C	**10.** D

p. 18 | Test 16

1. C	**6.** B
2. E	**7.** C
3. B	**8.** E
4. C	**9.** D
5. B	**10.** A

p. 19 | Test 17

1. B	**6.** A
2. D	**7.** B
3. A	**8.** E
4. C	**9.** C
5. A	**10.** D

p. 20 | Test 18

1. A	**6.** C
2. E	**7.** C
3. A	**8.** C
4. D	**9.** E
5. B	**10.** D

p. 21 | Test 19

1. A	**6.** E
2. C	**7.** A
3. E	**8.** A
4. A	**9.** D
5. B	**10.** C

p. 22 | Test 20

1. D	**6.** A
2. C	**7.** C
3. A	**8.** B
4. D	**9.** D
5. C	**10.** D

p. 23 | Test 21

1. C	**6.** A
2. A	**7.** D
3. C	**8.** C
4. E	**9.** D
5. B	**10.** D

p. 24 | Test 22

1. D	**6.** D
2. B	**7.** C
3. D	**8.** D
4. C	**9.** D
5. E	**10.** A

p. 25 | Test 23

1. A	**6.** B
2. D	**7.** A
3. B	**8.** A
4. B	**9.** C
5. E	**10.** D

p. 26 | Test 24

1. B	**6.** C
2. A	**7.** C
3. B	**8.** C
4. A	**9.** B
5. D	**10.** E

Tests Answer Key *(continued)*

p. 27 | Test 25

1. C	6. C
2. A	7. C
3. B	8. D
4. E	9. B
5. A	10. D

p. 28 | Test 26

1. C	6. C
2. C	7. E
3. D	8. D
4. A	9. B
5. B	10. D

p. 29 | Test 27

1. E	6. B
2. A	7. D
3. C	8. B
4. D	9. A
5. E	10. B

p. 30 | Test 28

1. C	6. E
2. B	7. A
3. C	8. A
4. C	9. A
5. B	10. D

p. 31 | Test 29

1. B	6. A
2. C	7. D
3. B	8. B
4. E	9. B
5. C	10. A

p. 32 | Test 30

1. C	6. D
2. A	7. C
3. D	8. A
4. A	9. D
5. C	10. E

Summative Assessment

p. 35 | Test 1 Part A

1. D	11. C
2. B	12. E
3. D	13. C
4. A	14. B
5. C	15. D
6. A	16. D
7. B	17. C
8. E	18. A
9. B	19. E
10. C	20. B

p. 39 | Test 1 Part B

21. A	46. D
22. B	47. C
23. E	48. E
24. D	49. E
25. D	50. A
26. C	51. C
27. B	52. B
28. B	53. C
29. E	54. B
30. C	55. A
31. A	56. D
32. D	57. E
33. A	58. E
34. B	59. C
35. C	60. C
36. A	61. B
37. E	62. A
38. D	63. D
39. C	64. B
40. B	65. B
41. E	66. A
42. A	67. A
43. C	68. C
44. B	69. D
45. A	70. E

p. 44 | Test 1 Part C

71. (E); Synonym. *Amity* and *friendship* have similar meanings, as do *richness* and *wealth*.

72. (A); Synonym. *Assault* and *attack* are similar in meaning, as are *agitation* and *commotion*.

73. (D); Characteristic Quality. A *tiger* is characteristically *carnivorous*, or meat-eating, just as a *monkey* is characteristically *acrobatic*.

74. (D); Performer and Related Action. One expects a *cast* to *perform*, just as one expects a *horde* of people to *wander*.

75. (D); Synonym. *Centrifugal*, which means moving out from the center, has a meaning similar to *outward*. *Heated* and *warm* also have similar meanings.

76. (A); Synonym. *Changeless* and *monotonous* have similar meanings, as do *superfluous* and *excessive*.

77. (E); Characteristic Quality. *Credentials* are characteristically *written*, just as a *speech* is characteristically *uttered*.

78. (C); Part and Whole. *Conflict* is an element of *drama*, just as *contrast* is an element of *irony*.

79. (B); Classification. A *rabbit* is classified as *fauna*, or animal life, just as a *tree* is classified as *vegetation*, or plant life.

80. (A); Classification. A *tree* is classified as *flora*, or plant life, just as *yellow* is classified as a *color*.

81. (C); Part and Whole. A *grandparent*, like all your relatives, is a part of your *genealogy*, or family history, in the same way that an *item* is a part of a *list*.

82. (C); Characteristic Quality. *Sugar* is characteristically *granular*, just as *mayonnaise* is characteristically *smooth*.

83. (C); Cause and Effect. An *infection* can cause an *inflammation*, just as a *virus* can cause a *disease*.

84. (A); Classification. *Larceny*, or theft, is classified as a *crime*. An *apple* is classified as a *fruit*.

85. (C); Synonym. *Makeup* and *cosmetics* have the same meaning, as do *garb* and *clothing*.

86. (A); Synonym. *Manifest*, which means show, means the same thing as *reveal*. *Endure*, which means to hold out or last, has a meaning similar to *persist*.

87. (E); Synonym. *Meander* and *wander* have similar meanings, as do *wiggle* and *squirm*.

88. (D); Performer and Related Action. A *diplomat negotiates* with other countries, just as a *lawyer settles* a lawsuit.

89. (E); Performer and Related Action. A *plaintiff* is someone who *sues*, or files a lawsuit. A *tailor* is someone who *sews* clothing.

90. (D); Synonym. *Predict* and *forecast* have similar meanings, as do *recede* and *withdraw*.

91. (D); Performer and Related Action. One expects a *quorum* of people to *decide*, just as one expects a *senate* to *debate*.

92. (E); Degree. To *replenish* something is to *provide* it again when it runs out. To *refill* something is to *fill* it again.

93. (D); Antonym. *Sparse*, which means thinly spread, is opposite in meaning to *dense*. In the same way, *joyous* and *sad* are opposite in meaning.

94. (E); Synonym. *Speak* and *talk* have similar meanings, as do *moor* (as in to *moor* a boat) and *secure*.

95. (B); Antonym. *Still* and *active* have opposite meanings, as do *stagnant* and *moving*.

96. (E); Synonym. *Territory* and *region* have similar meanings, as do *sector* and *division*.

97. (D); Degree. *Tolerate* and *endure* have similar meanings but differ in degree: *Endure* implies withstanding much greater suffering than does *tolerate*. *Torment* and *torture* are also similar, but to *torture* is more severe than to *torment*.

98. (C); Antonym.   *Valued* means the opposite of *scorned*. *Intact*, or whole, means the opposite of *damaged*.

99. (B); Synonym.   *Vital* and *essential* have the same meaning, as do *lethal* and *deadly*.

100. (B); Performer and Related Action.   A *winner* is someone who *triumphs*. An *advocate* is someone who *supports* someone else.

p. 47 | Test 2 Part A

1. D	**11.** A
2. B	**12.** D
3. A	**13.** E
4. B	**14.** C
5. C	**15.** C
6. E	**16.** A
7. E	**17.** D
8. D	**18.** B
9. B	**19.** A
10. B	**20.** D

p. 51 | Test 2 Part B

21. D	**46.** B
22. D	**47.** D
23. B	**48.** D
24. C	**49.** A
25. B	**50.** E
26. D	**51.** E
27. A	**52.** C
28. B	**53.** B
29. B	**54.** A
30. D	**55.** C
31. B	**56.** C
32. A	**57.** B
33. B	**58.** C
34. A	**59.** C
35. A	**60.** C
36. B	**61.** A
37. D	**62.** B
38. D	**63.** E
39. E	**64.** E
40. E	**65.** E
41. A	**66.** D
42. E	**67.** C
43. E	**68.** A
44. C	**69.** A
45. E	**70.** B

p. 56 | Test 2 Part C

71. (C); Characteristic Quality.   *Sandpaper* is characteristically *abrasive*, or gritty, just as *milk* is characteristically *wet*.

72. (C); Degree.   To *adore* is to *like* to an extreme extent. To *wrangle* is to *disagree* to the extent of an argument.

73. (A); Classification.   *Beard* is a type of *hair*, just as *sage* is a type of *herb*.

74. (E); Characteristic Quality.   A *bee* is characteristically *busy*, just as an *ant* is characteristically *diligent*, or hard-working.

75. (B); Synonym.   *Cadence* and *beat* have the same meaning, as do *melody* and *tune*.

76. (D); Antonym.   *Calming* and *upsetting* are opposite in meaning, as are *tantalizing* and *repulsive*.

77. (E); Synonym.   All four words have the meaning of ongoing.

78. (B); Classification.   *Yellow* is classified as a *color*, just as *breakfast* is classified as a *repast*, or meal.

79. (D); Synonym.   *Common* and *ordinary* have similar meanings. *Obtuse*, or dense, has a meaning similar to *dull*.

80. (C); Synonym.   *Congruent*, which means in agreement or corresponding, has a meaning similar to *harmonious*. *Precise* and *exact* also have similar meanings.

81. (A); Synonym.   *Create* and *invent* have the same meaning. *Denote*, which means signify, has the same meaning as *mean* when used as a verb.

82. (A); Antonym.   *Curious* and *disinterested* are opposite in meaning. *Animated*, which means lively, is opposite in meaning to *depressed*.

83. (A); Synonym.   *Elude* and *escape* have similar meanings, as do *trap* and *catch*.

84. (E); Synonym.   *Impartial* and *fair* have the same meaning, as do *unbroken* and *whole*.

Tests Answer Key *(continued)*

85. (D); Degree. *Incandescent* is similar in meaning to *bright*, but much stronger, just as *gigantic* implies greater size than *big*.

86. (B); Synonym. *Incessant*, or never-ending, has a meaning similar to *constant*. *Earnest* and *sincere* also have similar meanings.

87. (E); Synonym. *Inverse* and *opposite* have similar meanings, as do *cautious* and *careful*.

88. (A); Synonym. *Jovial* and *jolly* have similar meanings, as do *valuable* and *precious*.

89. (E); Antonym. *Lax* and *strict* are opposite in meaning, as are *gentle* and *harsh*.

90. (E); Synonym. *Magnetic* and *fascinating* have similar meanings, just as *ingenuous*, or naive, has a meaning similar to *unsophisticated*.

91. (A); Antonym. *Malicious*, or mean, is opposite in meaning to *kind*. *Scarce* and *abundant* are also opposite in meaning.

92. (D); Synonym. *Objective* is similar in meaning to *detached*. In the same way, *obvious* and *clear* have similar meanings.

93. (D); Antonym. *Opaque* and *transparent* have opposite meanings, as do *common* and *rare*.

94. (E); Characteristic Quality. A *panorama*, which is a broad vista or view, is characteristically *wide*, just as *lace* is characteristically *delicate*.

95. (E); Synonym. *Portion* and *part* have similar meanings, as do *quota* and *share* (the noun form).

96. (A); Antonym. *Problem* means the opposite of *solution*. *Hindrance*, which means obstacle, means the opposite of *help*.

97. (D); Synonym. *Pungent* and *sharp* have similar meanings, as do *lively* and *active*.

98. (A); Synonym. *Reverent* and *respectful* have similar meanings. *Impertinent*, which means not showing proper respect, has a meaning similar to *rude*.

99. (D); Characteristic Quality. A *tripod* is characteristically *three-legged*, just as a *bicycle* is characteristically *two-wheeled*.

100. (E); Synonym. To be *victorious* is to be *triumphant*, just as to be *predominant* is to be *supreme*.

p. 59 | Test 3 Part A

1. C	11. A
2. B	12. E
3. A	13. C
4. C	14. B
5. A	15. C
6. B	16. B
7. D	17. D
8. E	18. D
9. D	19. C
10. E	20. A

p. 63 | Test 3 Part B

21. C	46. B
22. B	47. D
23. A	48. E
24. C	49. D
25. A	50. E
26. B	51. A
27. D	52. E
28. E	53. C
29. D	54. B
30. E	55. D
31. A	56. B
32. E	57. C
33. C	58. B
34. B	59. D
35. D	60. A
36. B	61. C
37. C	62. B
38. B	63. A
39. D	64. C
40. A	65. A
41. C	66. B
42. B	67. D
43. A	68. D
44. C	69. D
45. A	70. E

p. 69 | Test 3 Part C

71. (E); Antonym. *Ashamed* means the opposite of *proud*, just as *discreet*, or careful, means the opposite of *careless*.

72. (B); Classification. An *asterisk* is classified as a *symbol*, just as a *house* is classified as a *building*.

73. (A); Synonym. *Clamber* and *climb* have nearly the same meaning, as do *scamper* and *run*.

74. (C); Synonym. *Comply* and *obey* have the same meaning, as do *adjust* and *adapt*.

75. (B); Action and Related Object. Someone might *compose* a *song*, just as someone might *convey land*.

76. (A); Antonym. *Contaminate*, or pollute, means the opposite of *purify*. *Destroy* and *build* also have opposite meanings.

77. (E); Synonym. *Feeling* and *emotion* have similar meanings, as do *ideology* and *beliefs*.

78. (A); Degree. *Frenzied*, or frantic, is stronger in degree than *upset*. *Ecstatic* is stronger in degree than *pleased*.

79. (D); Synonym. *Heroic* and *brave* have similar meanings, as do *infamous* and *scandalous*.

80. (C): Antonym. *Hostile* means the opposite of *friendly*, just as *haphazard*, or disorderly, means the opposite of *systematic*.

81. (A); Cause and Effect. A *vaccination* can result in *immunity* to a disease, just as *exercise* can result in *strength*.

82. (B); Synonym. *Initiative* and *enterprise* have similar meanings, as do *calm* and *tranquility*.

83. (A); Performer and Related Action. A *thug* *intimidates* a victim, just as a *champ* *celebrates* a victory.

84. (C); Location. A *judge* works in a *jurisdiction*, just as a *salesperson* works in a *territory*.

85. (C); Synonym. To *lounge* is to *lie*, just as to *promenade* is to *walk*.

86. (C); Part and Whole. *Songs* are part of a *medley*, just as *vegetables* are part of a *salad*.

87. (B); Characteristic Quality. A *gymnast* is characteristically *nimble*, just as a *tiger* is characteristically *wild*.

88. (C); Antonym. *Occupy* and *vacate* have opposite meanings. *Dissuade*, or discourage, is opposite in meaning to *encourage*.

89. (D); Antonym. *Oppose* and *promote* are opposite in meaning. *Instigate*, or start, means the opposite of *halt*.

90. (E); Synonym. *Original* and *fresh* have similar meanings. *Ponderous*, which means massive, has a meaning similar to *bulky*.

91. (D); Synonym. *Perceptible* and *noticeable* have nearly the same meaning, as do *necessary* and *needed*.

92. (D); Synonym. *Rough* and *uneven* have nearly the same meaning, as do *dubious* and *questionable*.

93. (C); Classification. A *sofa* is classified as a type of *furnishings*, just as a *perennial* is classified as a *plant*.

94. (A); Part and Whole. A *statement* is part of *language*, just as an *equation* is part of *mathematics*.

95. (D); Classification. A *statute* is classified as a *law*, just as a *fine* is classified as a *penalty*.

96. (E); Synonym. *Stormy* and *violent* have nearly the same meaning, as do *drastic* and *severe*.

97. (C); Antonym. *Strange* and *familiar* have opposite meanings, as do *collective* and *separate*.

98. (B); Action and Related Object. You *transcribe notes*, just as you *translate a language*.

99. (A); Synonym. *Unorganized* and *disorderly* have the same meaning, as do *unkempt* and *untidy*.

100. (D); Action and Related Object. You *write* a *thesis*, just as you *mail a letter*.

Workshop Answer Key

Making New Words Your Own

Lesson 1

p. 3 | Exercise 1: Wordbusting

> **NOTES**
> - For each Vocabulary Word, students should fill in at least one of the **context, structure,** and **sound** boxes.
> - Check that students vary the boxes they use throughout the exercise.
> - Make sure students look up each word in the dictionary and fill in the dictionary box; answers will vary depending on the dictionary used.

p. 5 | Exercise 2: Context Clues

11. E	fortitude	**17.** H	elite
12. G	condescend	**18.** B	mentor
13. D	evolve	**19.** C	inarticulate
14. I	notoriety	**20.** F	contemptu-
15. A	assert		ous
16. J	acquittal		

p. 6 | Exercise 3: Sentence Completion

21. E	**26.** C
22. D	**27.** E
23. C	**28.** D
24. B	**29.** A
25. A	**30.** B

Lesson 2

p. 7 | Exercise 1: Wordbusting

> **NOTES**
> - For each Vocabulary Word, students should fill in at least one of the **context, structure,** and **sound** boxes.
> - Check that students vary the boxes they use throughout the exercise.
> - Make sure students look up each word in the dictionary and fill in the dictionary box; answers will vary depending on the dictionary used.

p. 9 | Exercise 2: Context Clues

11. H	pauper	**16.** I	heresy
12. C	excerpt	**17.** A	paternal
13. E	analogy	**18.** F	antiquity
14. B	ethical	**19.** J	posthumous
15. D	prophetic	**20.** G	electorate

p. 10 | Exercise 3: Sentence Completion

21. D	**26.** C
22. C	**27.** C
23. E	**28.** A
24. D	**29.** D
25. E	**30.** B

Lesson 3

p. 11 | Exercise 1: Wordbusting

> **NOTES**
> - For each Vocabulary Word, students should fill in at least one of the **context, structure,** and **sound** boxes.
> - Check that students vary the boxes they use throughout the exercise.
> - Make sure students look up each word in the dictionary and fill in the dictionary box; answers will vary depending on the dictionary used.

p. 13 | Exercise 2: Context Clues

11. C	malleable	**16.** F	indomitable
12. G	amiable	**17.** H	succumb
13. D	vibrant	**18.** A	bayou
14. J	melodramatic	**19.** I	whimsical
15. B	grimace	**20.** E	visage

p. 14 | Exercise 3: Sentence Completion

21. C	**26.** D
22. E	**27.** B
23. B	**28.** C
24. D	**29.** B
25. A	**30.** E

Lesson 4

p. 15 | Exercise 1: Wordbusting

NOTES
- For each Vocabulary Word, students should fill in at least one of the **context, structure,** and **sound** boxes.
- Check that students vary the boxes they use throughout the exercise.
- Make sure students look up each word in the dictionary and fill in the dictionary box; answers will vary depending on the dictionary used.

p. 17 | Exercise 2: Context Clues

11. I callous
12. J mystic
13. H indignant
14. G verbatim
15. F paraphrase
16. B commendable
17. D judicious
18. A personification
19. E ineffectual
20. C apprehensive

p. 18 | Exercise 3: Sentence Completion

21. C
22. B
23. D
24. A
25. E
26. C
27. E
28. D
29. B
30. A

Lesson 5

p. 19 | Exercise 1: Wordbusting

NOTES
- For each Vocabulary Word, students should fill in at least one of the **context, structure,** and **sound** boxes.
- Check that students vary the boxes they use throughout the exercise.
- Make sure students look up each word in the dictionary and fill in the dictionary box; answers will vary depending on the dictionary used.

p. 21 | Exercise 2: Context Clues

11. A invariably
12. I proximity
13. C affiliate
14. J rejuvenate
15. E portly
16. H encumber
17. D unprecedented
18. B exalted
19. F pompous
20. G plausible

p. 22 | Exercise 3: Sentence Completion

21. A
22. E
23. B
24. E
25. D
26. C
27. D
28. B
29. A
30. C

Lesson 6

p. 23 | Exercise 1: Wordbusting

NOTES
- For each Vocabulary Word, students should fill in at least one of the **context, structure,** and **sound** boxes.
- Check that students vary the boxes they use throughout the exercise.
- Make sure students look up each word in the dictionary and fill in the dictionary box; answers will vary depending on the dictionary used.

p. 25 | Exercise 2: Context Clues

11. E insipid
12. D painstaking
13. I deteriorate
14. B lament
15. J compassion
16. H discern
17. C repress
18. G loathe
19. A composure
20. F atrocious

p. 26 | Exercise 3: Sentence Completion

21. B
22. D
23. C
24. E
25. A
26. D
27. C
28. B
29. A
30. E

Lesson 7

p. 27 | Exercise 1: Wordbusting

> **NOTES**
> - For each Vocabulary Word, students should fill in at least one of the **context, structure,** and **sound** boxes.
> - Check that students vary the boxes they use throughout the exercise.
> - Make sure students look up each word in the dictionary and fill in the dictionary box; answers will vary depending on the dictionary used.

p. 29 | Exercise 2: Context Clues

11. C	martial	**16.** I	charisma
12. D	cliché	**17.** J	recipient
13. A	prolific	**18.** G	emphatically
14. F	wan	**19.** E	paradox
15. H	aesthetic	**20.** B	conceive

p. 30 | Exercise 3: Sentence Completion

21. E	**26.** D
22. C	**27.** C
23. A	**28.** E
24. B	**29.** A
25. D	**30.** B

Lesson 8

p. 31 | Exercise 1: Wordbusting

> **NOTES**
> - For each Vocabulary Word, students should fill in at least one of the **context, structure,** and **sound** boxes.
> - Check that students vary the boxes they use throughout the exercise.
> - Make sure students look up each word in the dictionary and fill in the dictionary box; answers will vary depending on the dictionary used.

p. 33 | Exercise 2: Context Clues

11. B	aura	**16.** C	mediocre
12. E	qualm	**17.** I	reactionary
13. G	zealous	**18.** F	fabricate
14. A	impediment	**19.** J	stamina
15. H	zephyr	**20.** D	opportune

p. 34 | Exercise 3: Sentence Completion

21. D	**26.** A
22. C	**27.** B
23. E	**28.** E
24. C	**29.** C
25. B	**30.** D

Lesson 9

p. 35 | Exercise 1: Wordbusting

> **NOTES**
> - For each Vocabulary Word, students should fill in at least one of the **context, structure,** and **sound** boxes.
> - Check that students vary the boxes they use throughout the exercise.
> - Make sure students look up each word in the dictionary and fill in the dictionary box; answers will vary depending on the dictionary used.

p. 37 | Exercise 2: Context Clues

11. D	innate	**16.** H	prevalent
12. J	recourse	**17.** I	compatible
13. B	mutable	**18.** A	perception
14. E	compliance	**19.** F	axiom
15. C	indestructible	**20.** G	inanimate

p. 38 | Exercise 3: Sentence Completion

21. D	**26.** E
22. B	**27.** D
23. E	**28.** C
24. A	**29.** A
25. C	**30.** B

Workshop Answer Key *(continued)*

Lesson 10

p. 39 | Exercise 1: Wordbusting

NOTES

- For each Vocabulary Word, students should fill in at least one of the **context, structure,** and **sound** boxes.

- Check that students vary the boxes they use throughout the exercise.

- Make sure students look up each word in the dictionary and fill in the dictionary box; answers will vary depending on the dictionary used.

p. 41 | Exercise 2: Context Clues

11. H militant		**16.** J stringent
12. G transitory		**17.** D implacable
13. A incentive		**18.** I retribution
14. B encompass		**19.** C pivotal
15. E postulate		**20.** F transcend

p. 42 | Exercise 3: Sentence Completion

21. A	**26.** B
22. C	**27.** C
23. E	**28.** D
24. D	**29.** A
25. E	**30.** E

Lesson 11

p. 43 | Exercise 1: Wordbusting

NOTES

- For each Vocabulary Word, students should fill in at least one of the **context, structure,** and **sound** boxes.

- Check that students vary the boxes they use throughout the exercise.

- Make sure students look up each word in the dictionary and fill in the dictionary box; answers will vary depending on the dictionary used.

p. 45 | Exercise 2: Context Clues

11. E precarious		**17.** D autonomy
12. G devastation		**18.** J wane
13. C vulnerable		**19.** H inclement
14. A besiege		**20.** B latitude
15. F wreak		
16. I perseverance		

p. 46 | Exercise 3: Sentence Completion

21. B	**26.** C
22. D	**27.** C
23. A	**28.** E
24. E	**29.** B
25. D	**30.** A

Lesson 12

p. 47 | Exercise 1: Wordbusting

NOTES

- For each Vocabulary Word, students should fill in at least one of the **context, structure,** and **sound** boxes.

- Check that students vary the boxes they use throughout the exercise.

- Make sure students look up each word in the dictionary and fill in the dictionary box; answers will vary depending on the dictionary used.

p. 49 | Exercise 2: Context Clues

11. J balmy		**16.** H invincible
12. A facsimile		**17.** F beguile
13. D vigilant		**18.** C appease
14. B commence		**19.** G pretext
15. I archaic		**20.** E espionage

p. 50 | Exercise 3: Sentence Completion

21. B	**26.** E
22. D	**27.** C
23. A	**28.** B
24. D	**29.** D
25. C	**30.** A

Workshop Answer Key (continued)

Lesson 13

p. 51 | Exercise 1: Wordbusting

NOTES

- For each Vocabulary Word, students should fill in at least one of the **context, structure,** and **sound** boxes.
- Check that students vary the boxes they use throughout the exercise.
- Make sure students look up each word in the dictionary and fill in the dictionary box; answers will vary depending on the dictionary used.

p. 53 | Exercise 2: Context Clues

11. D	juncture	**16.** J	coffer
12. I	tawny	**17.** F	rivulet
13. E	hieroglyphic	**18.** H	edifice
14. A	subsidize	**19.** G	retainer
15. C	inaccessible	**20.** B	innovation

p. 54 | Exercise 3: Sentence Completion

21. B	**26.** C
22. D	**27.** D
23. E	**28.** A
24. B	**29.** C
25. C	**30.** B

Lesson 14

p. 55 | Exercise 1: Wordbusting

NOTES

- For each Vocabulary Word, students should fill in at least one of the **context, structure,** and **sound** boxes.
- Check that students vary the boxes they use throughout the exercise.
- Make sure students look up each word in the dictionary and fill in the dictionary box; answers will vary depending on the dictionary used.

p. 57 | Exercise 2: Context Clues

11. B	canine	**16.** G	defunct
12. C	ossify	**17.** A	perceive
13. I	meager	**18.** H	bourgeois
14. E	ravage	**19.** J	influx
15. D	apex	**20.** F	obliterate

p. 58 | Exercise 3: Sentence Completion

21. E	**26.** C
22. C	**27.** A
23. A	**28.** E
24. B	**29.** B
25. D	**30.** D

Lesson 15

p. 59 | Exercise 1: Wordbusting

NOTES

- For each Vocabulary Word, students should fill in at least one of the **context, structure,** and **sound** boxes.
- Check that students vary the boxes they use throughout the exercise.
- Make sure students look up each word in the dictionary and fill in the dictionary box; answers will vary depending on the dictionary used.

p. 61 | Exercise 2: Context Clues

11. B	ensue	**16.** J	expedient
12. F	succulent	**17.** I	palatable
13. E	facilitate	**18.** C	buffet
14. G	steppe	**19.** H	lapse
15. A	hors d'oeuvre	**20.** D	delectable

p. 62 | Exercise 3: Sentence Completion

21. E	**26.** A
22. A	**27.** D
23. C	**28.** C
24. B	**29.** B
25. E	**30.** D

Lesson 16

p. 63 | Exercise 1: Wordbusting

> **NOTES**
> - For each Vocabulary Word, students should fill in at least one of the **context, structure,** and **sound** boxes.
> - Check that students vary the boxes they use throughout the exercise.
> - Make sure students look up each word in the dictionary and fill in the dictionary box; answers will vary depending on the dictionary used.

p. 65 | Exercise 2: Context Clues

11. C	quantitative	16. D	erratic
12. A	zenith	17. I	mosque
13. F	astute	18. J	pastoral
14. H	recur	19. E	requisite
15. B	conducive	20. G	aptitude

p. 66 | Exercise 3: Sentence Completion

21. E		26. C	
22. C		27. E	
23. A		28. C	
24. D		29. A	
25. B		30. D	

Lesson 17

p. 67 | Exercise 1: Wordbusting

> **NOTES**
> - For each Vocabulary Word, students should fill in at least one of the **context, structure,** and **sound** boxes.
> - Check that students vary the boxes they use throughout the exercise.
> - Make sure students look up each word in the dictionary and fill in the dictionary box; answers will vary depending on the dictionary used.

p. 69 | Exercise 2: Context Clues

11. F	insolence	16. E	moderation
12. H	prone	17. C	concession
13. B	diversion	18. I	flagrant
14. G	annihilate	19. J	decimate
15. D	purge	20. A	evade

p. 70 | Exercise 3: Sentence Completion

21. B		26. D	
22. D		27. E	
23. E		28. B	
24. A		29. D	
25. C		30. C	

Lesson 18

p. 71 | Exercise 1: Wordbusting

> **NOTES**
> - For each Vocabulary Word, students should fill in at least one of the **context, structure,** and **sound** boxes.
> - Check that students vary the boxes they use throughout the exercise.
> - Make sure students look up each word in the dictionary and fill in the dictionary box; answers will vary depending on the dictionary used.

p. 73 | Exercise 2: Context Clues

11. J	protocol	16. H	mannerism
12. B	dissent	17. F	inhibition
13. D	pacifist	18. E	meticulous
14. I	ultimatum	19. A	submission
15. C	clemency	20. G	mandatory

p. 74 | Exercise 3: Sentence Completion

21. D		26. E	
22. A		27. A	
23. C		28. C	
24. E		29. D	
25. B		30. C	

Lesson 19

p. 75 | Exercise 1: Wordbusting

> **NOTES**
> - For each Vocabulary Word, students should fill in at least one of the **context, structure,** and **sound** boxes.
> - Check that students vary the boxes they use throughout the exercise.
> - Make sure students look up each word in the dictionary and fill in the dictionary box; answers will vary depending on the dictionary used.

p. 77 | Exercise 2: Context Clues

11. D censure	**16.** I inalienable
12. H abound	**17.** G bias
13. B amnesty	**18.** C timorous
14. A rift	**19.** F affidavit
15. E admirably	**20.** J diminutive

p. 78 | Exercise 3: Sentence Completion

21. C	**26.** B
22. E	**27.** D
23. B	**28.** C
24. B	**29.** C
25. A	**30.** A

Lesson 20

p. 79 | Exercise 1: Wordbusting

> **NOTES**
> - For each Vocabulary Word, students should fill in at least one of the **context, structure,** and **sound** boxes.
> - Check that students vary the boxes they use throughout the exercise.
> - Make sure students look up each word in the dictionary and fill in the dictionary box; answers will vary depending on the dictionary used.

p. 81 | Exercise 2: Context Clues

11. I ornate	**16.** J exultant
12. B constituent	**17.** C bedlam
13. H destitute	**18.** A curtail
14. D prelude	**19.** G consolidate
15. F colloquial	**20.** E emancipate

p. 82 | Exercise 3: Sentence Completion

21. C	**26.** C
22. E	**27.** E
23. A	**28.** B
24. B	**29.** D
25. D	**30.** C

Lesson 21

p. 83 | Exercise 1: Wordbusting

> **NOTES**
> - For each Vocabulary Word, students should fill in at least one of the **context, structure,** and **sound** boxes.
> - Check that students vary the boxes they use throughout the exercise.
> - Make sure students look up each word in the dictionary and fill in the dictionary box; answers will vary depending on the dictionary used.

p. 85 | Exercise 2: Context Clues

11. B documentary	**16.** A debut
12. E reprieve	**17.** D melancholy
13. J fluctuate	**18.** I requiem
14. H casement	**19.** F theoretical
15. C vehement	**20.** G bestride

p. 86 | Exercise 3: Sentence Completion

21. A	**26.** C
22. D	**27.** D
23. C	**28.** E
24. B	**29.** A
25. E	**30.** C

Lesson 22

p. 87 | Exercise 1: Wordbusting

> **NOTES**
> - For each Vocabulary Word, students should fill in at least one of the **context, structure,** and **sound** boxes.
> - Check that students vary the boxes they use throughout the exercise.
> - Make sure students look up each word in the dictionary and fill in the dictionary box; answers will vary depending on the dictionary used.

p. 89 | Exercise 2: Context Clues

11. I	gloat	**16.** D	indict
12. A	legacy	**17.** J	patriarch
13. H	clangor	**18.** C	mortify
14. G	wheedle	**19.** E	enjoin
15. F	patent	**20.** B	livid

p. 90 | Exercise 3: Sentence Completion

21. E	**26.** A
22. C	**27.** E
23. D	**28.** D
24. B	**29.** C
25. E	**30.** A

Lesson 23

p. 91 | Exercise 1: Wordbusting

> **NOTES**
> - For each Vocabulary Word, students should fill in at least one of the **context, structure,** and **sound** boxes.
> - Check that students vary the boxes they use throughout the exercise.
> - Make sure students look up each word in the dictionary and fill in the dictionary box; answers will vary depending on the dictionary used.

p. 93 | Exercise 2: Context Clues

11. J	closure	**16.** H	impartial
12. A	indifferent	**17.** C	condole
13. I	crony	**18.** F	stipulate
14. G	convene	**19.** E	clientele
15. B	botch	**20.** D	momentum

p. 94 | Exercise 3: Sentence Completion

21. D	**26.** A
22. C	**27.** D
23. B	**28.** E
24. E	**29.** B
25. C	**30.** C

Lesson 24

p. 95 | Exercise 1: Wordbusting

> **NOTES**
> - For each Vocabulary Word, students should fill in at least one of the **context, structure,** and **sound** boxes.
> - Check that students vary the boxes they use throughout the exercise.
> - Make sure students look up each word in the dictionary and fill in the dictionary box; answers will vary depending on the dictionary used.

p. 97 | Exercise 2: Context Clues

11. D	oblivious	**17.** J	arbiter
12. C	subsidiary	**18.** F	stratagem
13. H	cant	**19.** B	disconcert-
14. E	equilibrium		ing
15. I	rectify	**20.** G	breach
16. A	substantially		

p. 98 | Exercise 3: Sentence Completion

21. E	**26.** B
22. C	**27.** D
23. A	**28.** C
24. C	**29.** E
25. E	**30.** A

Workshop Answer Key (continued)

Lesson 25

p. 99 | Exercise 1: Wordbusting

> **NOTES**
> - For each Vocabulary Word, students should fill in at least one of the **context**, **structure**, and **sound** boxes.
> - Check that students vary the boxes they use throughout the exercise.
> - Make sure students look up each word in the dictionary and fill in the dictionary box; answers will vary depending on the dictionary used.

p. 101 | Exercise 2: Context Clues

11. C mull	16. B resonant
12. H imposition	17. D explicate
13. F synthesis	18. I immaculate
14. A effervescent	19. E quibble
15. J debase	20. G sporadic

p. 102 | Exercise 3: Sentence Completion

21. B	26. C
22. E	27. B
23. A	28. E
24. D	29. A
25. C	30. D

Lesson 26

p. 103 | Exercise 1: Wordbusting

> **NOTES**
> - For each Vocabulary Word, students should fill in at least one of the **context**, **structure**, and **sound** boxes.
> - Check that students vary the boxes they use throughout the exercise.
> - Make sure students look up each word in the dictionary and fill in the dictionary box; answers will vary depending on the dictionary used.

p. 105 | Exercise 2: Context Clues

11. J translucent	16. F inadvertent
12. B itinerary	17. A naive
13. H stimulant	18. I abdicate
14. D infallible	19. E rankle
15. C sardonic	20. G episode

p. 106 | Exercise 3: Sentence Completion

21. A	26. C
22. D	27. D
23. B	28. B
24. C	29. A
25. E	30. C

Lesson 27

p. 107 | Exercise 1: Wordbusting

> **NOTES**
> - For each Vocabulary Word, students should fill in at least one of the **context**, **structure**, and **sound** boxes.
> - Check that students vary the boxes they use throughout the exercise.
> - Make sure students look up each word in the dictionary and fill in the dictionary box; answers will vary depending on the dictionary used.

p. 109 | Exercise 2: Context Clues

11. I pallid	16. B irrelevant
12. F intermittent	17. D synopsis
13. A redundant	18. E edify
14. J sequel	19. G intuition
15. C demure	20. H reminiscent

p. 110 | Exercise 3: Sentence Completion

21. C	26. D
22. B	27. E
23. E	28. C
24. A	29. B
25. C	30. A

Lesson 28

p. 111 | Exercise 1: Wordbusting

> **NOTES**
> - For each Vocabulary Word, students should fill in at least one of the **context, structure,** and **sound** boxes.
> - Check that students vary the boxes they use throughout the exercise.
> - Make sure students look up each word in the dictionary and fill in the dictionary box; answers will vary depending on the dictionary used.

p. 113 | Exercise 2: Context Clues

11. E lexicon	**16.** F daunt
12. J simulate	**17.** D irrational
13. B eject	**18.** C contend
14. I rendezvous	**19.** A jostle
15. G detonate	**20.** H throng

p. 114 | Exercise 3: Sentence Completion

21. D	**26.** E
22. B	**27.** B
23. A	**28.** C
24. D	**29.** D
25. C	**30.** E

Lesson 29

p. 115 | Exercise 1: Wordbusting

> **NOTES**
> - For each Vocabulary Word, students should fill in at least one of the **context, structure,** and **sound** boxes.
> - Check that students vary the boxes they use throughout the exercise.
> - Make sure students look up each word in the dictionary and fill in the dictionary box; answers will vary depending on the dictionary used.

p. 117 | Exercise 2: Context Clues

11. C irksome	**16.** F rebuke
12. A malignant	**17.** B decrepit
13. G farce	**18.** J pertinent
14. H parody	**19.** I inconsistent
15. D jargon	**20.** E obligatory

p. 118 | Exercise 3: Sentence Completion

21. C	**26.** A
22. E	**27.** D
23. D	**28.** E
24. B	**29.** C
25. C	**30.** B

Lesson 30

p. 119 | Exercise 1: Wordbusting

> **NOTES**
> - For each Vocabulary Word, students should fill in at least one of the **context, structure,** and **sound** boxes.
> - Check that students vary the boxes they use throughout the exercise.
> - Make sure students look up each word in the dictionary and fill in the dictionary box; answers will vary depending on the dictionary used.

p. 121 | Exercise 2: Context Clues

11. A negligible	**16.** I caustic
12. J sordid	**17.** C scenario
13. D protrude	**18.** G transition
14. E carp	**19.** B odious
15. F incendiary	**20.** H coincidental

p. 122 | Exercise 3: Sentence Completion

21. C	**26.** A
22. D	**27.** D
23. E	**28.** C
24. B	**29.** E
25. B	**30.** B

Workshop Answer Key *(continued)*

Connecting New Words and Patterns

Lesson 1

p. 126 | Analogies

1. (D); Performer and Related Action. You expect a *snob* to *condescend*, or look down on others, just as you expect an *assistant* to *help*.

2. (A); Synonym. *Contemptuous* and *scornful* have the same meaning, as do *careful* and *cautious*.

3. (C); Characteristic Quality. The *elite*, or members of a distinguished group, are often considered to be characteristically *superior*, just as *heroes* are characteristically *brave*.

4. (B); Synonym. *Evolve* and *change* have the same meaning, as do *spin* and *twirl*. This is true when change, spin, and twirl are used as verbs.

5. (D); Characteristic Quality. An *excerpt*, or something taken out of a larger whole, is characteristically *selected*, just as a *play* is characteristically *performed*.

6. (B); Antonym. *Fortitude*, or strength, is opposite in meaning to *weakness*, just as *anxiety* is opposite in meaning to *calm*.

7. (D); Performer and Related Action. A *mentor*, or teacher, is someone who *advises* others, just as a *critic* is someone who *reviews* performances and other creative works.

8. (C); Synonym. *Notoriety* and *fame* have similar meanings, as do *merit* and *worth*.

9. (C); Characteristic Quality. A *pauper*, or very poor person, is characteristically *impoverished*, just as a *convict* is characteristically *imprisoned*.

10. (C); Synonym. *Prophetic* and *predictive* have similar meanings, as do *remarkable* and *outstanding*.

Lesson 2

p. 127 | Analogies

1. (D); Synonym. *Amiable*, which means friendly, has a meaning similar to *pleasant*. *Inviting* and *appealing* also have similar meanings.

2. (D); Antonym. *Apprehensive*, which means uneasy, is opposite in meaning to *calm*. *Tranquil* and *stormy* also have opposite meanings.

3. (B); Location. A *bayou*, or marshy inlet, can be found in *Louisiana*, just as a *glacier*, or enormous sheet of ice, can be found in *Alaska*.

4. (C); Characteristic Quality. A *dictator*, or tyrant, is characteristically *callous*, or unfeeling, just as a *glutton* is characteristically *greedy*.

5. (B); Synonym. *Commendable* and *praiseworthy* have similar meanings, as do *horrible* and *awful*.

6. (C); Cause and Effect. *Pain* can result in a *grimace*, just as a *joke* can result in *laughter*.

7. (A); Characteristic Quality. *Clay* is characteristically *malleable*, or easily formed, just as *rubber* is characteristically *flexible*.

8. (D); Characteristic Quality. A *soap opera* is characteristically *melodramatic*, just as a *comedy* is characteristically *funny*.

9. (C); Performer and Related Action. A *patient* is someone who may *succumb*, or give in, to illness, just as a *terrorist* is someone who may *threaten* people in order to achieve a political goal.

10. (E); Synonym. *Whimsical* and *fanciful* have similar meanings, as do *tired* and *weary*.

Lesson 3

p. 128 | Analogies

1. (D); Degree. Something that is *atrocious*, or awful, is much worse than something that is *bad*, just as something that is *wonderful* is much better than something that is *good*.

2. (A); Cause and Effect. *Suffering* can result in *compassion*, just as a *crime* can result in *outrage*.

3. (B); Antonym. *Deteriorate* and *improve* have opposite meanings, as do *succeed* and *fail*.

4. (C); Synonym. *Insipid*, which means tasteless, has a meaning similar to *flavorless*. *Amazing* and *astonishing* also have similar meanings.

5. (E); Degree. To *loathe* means to have stronger feelings of distaste than does to *dislike*. To *adore* means to have stronger positive feelings than does to *like*.

6. (C); Characteristic Quality. *Embroidering* is characteristically *painstaking*, requiring great care. *Parachuting* is characteristically *thrilling*.

7. (C); Degree. Something that is *plausible*, or possible, is not as positive as something that is *certain*. In the same way, someone who is *afraid* may not be afraid to the extent of being *terrified*.

8. (D); Antonym. *Pompous*, which means pretentious and self-important, is opposite in meaning to *humble*. *Knowledgeable* and *ignorant* are also opposite in meaning.

9. (D); Synonym. *Portly* and *stout* have the same meaning, as do *rigid* and *stiff*.

10. (C); Function. The function of a *vacation* is to *rejuvenate* a person, making him or her refreshed. The function of *armor* is to *protect* its wearer.

Lesson 4

p. 129 | Analogies

1. (C); Synonym. *Emphatically* and *forcefully* have similar meanings, as do *severely* and *sternly*.

2. (C); Action and Related Object. You *fabricate*, or make up, an *excuse*, just as you *tell* a *story*.

3. (C); Synonym. An *impediment* is the same thing as an *obstacle*. *Device* is similar in meaning to *machine*.

4. (D); Characteristic Quality. *Weaponry* is characteristically *martial*, or military, just as *wool* is characteristically *soft*.

5. (B); Degree. Something that is *mediocre* is inferior to something that is *good*. In the same way, something that is *adequate* is inferior to something that is *superb*, or excellent.

6. (C); Synonym. *Qualm* and *doubt* (when used as a noun) have the same meaning, as do *trembling* and *quaking*.

7. (C); Antonym. A *recipient*, or someone who receives, is opposite in meaning to a *donor*, someone who gives. *Buyer* and *seller* are also opposite in meaning.

8. (A); Cause and Effect. *Exercise* can result in *stamina*, or endurance, just as *difficulty* can result in *stress*.

9. (E); Antonym. *Zealous*, which means extremely enthusiastic, is opposite in meaning to *unenthusiastic*. *Timid* and *courageous* are also opposite in meaning.

10. (D); Characteristic Quality. A *zephyr*, or soft breeze, is characteristically *gentle*, just as a *bird* is characteristically *feathered*.

Workshop Answer Key (continued)

Lesson 5

p. 130 | Analogies

1. **(B); Characteristic Quality.** *Friends* are characteristically *compatible*, or well-matched, just as *enemies* are characteristically *hostile*, or belligerent.

2. **(C); Synonym.** *Encompass*, which means to encircle and contain, has a meaning similar to *include*. *Gather* and *collect* also have similar meanings.

3. **(C); Characteristic Quality.** A *rock* is characteristically *inanimate*, or nonliving, just as *water* is characteristically *wet*.

4. **(A); Synonym.** An *incentive* is the same thing as a *motive*, just as a *fee* is the same thing as a *payment*.

5. **(C); Antonym.** *Indestructible* is opposite in meaning to *fragile*. *Quarrelsome* and *agreeable* are also opposite in meaning.

6. **(B); Characteristic Quality.** A *soldier* is characteristically *militant*, or aggressive, just as a *volunteer* is characteristically *charitable*, or generous.

7. **(C); Synonym.** *Prevalent* and *widespread* have similar meanings, as do *ordinary* and *usual*.

8. **(B); Cause and Effect.** *Retribution*, or punishment, can be a result of *wrongdoing*, just as *wages* are usually the result of *work*.

9. **(C); Antonym.** *Stringent*, which means strict, is opposite in meaning to *lax*. *Frequent* and *rare* are also opposite in meaning.

10. **(E); Synonym.** *Transcend*, which means to go beyond something, is similar in meaning to *surpass*. *Recall* means the same as *recollect*.

Lesson 6

p. 131 | Analogies

1. **(E); Action and Related Object.** You *appease*, or satisfy, *hunger*, just as you *toss* a *coin* in the air.

2. **(B); Characteristic Quality.** A *suit of armor* is characteristically *archaic*, or old-fashioned, just as an *artist* is characteristically *creative*.

3. **(C); Characteristic Quality.** A *breeze* is characteristically *balmy*, just as a *jalapeño pepper* is characteristically *hot*.

4. **(D); Antonym.** *Commence*, which means start, is opposite in meaning to *finish*. *Waste* and *save* are also opposite in meaning.

5. **(E); Degree.** *Devastation* is a severe degree of *damage*. *Luxury*, a standard of living usually associated with the wealthy, includes *comfort* but to a much greater degree.

6. **(C); Performer and Related Action.** You expect a *spy* to practice *espionage*, just as you expect to find a *minister* engaged in *preaching*.

7. **(D); Synonym.** *Inclement* and *stormy* have similar meanings, as do *remarkable* and *noteworthy*.

8. **(D); Characteristic Quality.** A *superhero* is characteristically *invincible*, just as *exercise* is characteristically *invigorating*.

9. **(E); Synonym.** *Vigilant* and *watchful* have similar meanings, as do *observant* and *attentive*.

10. **(C); Antonym.** *Vulnerable*, which means easily hurt or attacked, is opposite in meaning to *strong*. *Rough* and *smooth* also have opposite meanings.

Lesson 7

p. 132 | Analogies

1. (E); Classification. A *wolf* is classified as a *canine*, or member of the dog family, just as a *snake* is classified as a *reptile*.

2. (C); Synonym. *Defunct* and *extinct* have similar meanings. *Active* means the same as *lively*.

3. (B); Location. A *hieroglyphic,* or symbol from an alphabet of pictures, can be found in *Egypt.* In the same way, a *cactus* can be found in the *desert.*

4. (C); Characteristic Quality. An *innovation* is characteristically *new,* just as an *antique* is characteristically *old.*

5. (C); Antonym. *Meager,* which means inadequate or of a small amount, means the opposite of *abundant. Awkward* and *graceful* are also opposite in meaning.

6. (C); Antonym. *Obliterate,* which means to destroy or wipe out, is opposite in meaning to *create. Demolish* and *construct* are also opposite in meaning.

7. (B); Performer and Related Action. You expect *locusts* to *ravage* vegetation, just as you expect *bees* to *pollinate* flowers.

8. (C); Degree. A *rivulet,* which is a little stream or a brook, is a much smaller body of water than a *river,* just as a *footpath,* for the use of pedestrians only, is a much smaller trailway than a *road.*

9. (D); Function. The function of a *grant* is to *subsidize,* or provide financial support, just as the function of *money* is to *buy* goods and services.

10. (A); Synonym. *Tawny* and *tan* have similar meanings, as do *misty* and *hazy.*

Lesson 8

p. 133 | Analogies

1. (A); Synonym. *Aptitude,* or skill, means the same thing as *ability. Talent* and *gift* also have the same meaning.

2. (B); Synonym. *Astute,* which means cunning or shrewd, is similar in meaning to *keen,* which means sharp-witted. *Persuasive* and *convincing* have the same meaning.

3. (D); Location. A *buffet,* or sideboard, can be found in a *dining room,* just as a *sink* can be found in a *kitchen.*

4. (E); Antonym. *Delectable,* which means very pleasing or delicious, is opposite in meaning to *displeasing. Delightful* and *disgusting* are also opposite in meaning.

5. (D); Part and whole. An *hors d'oeuvre* is a part of a *meal* that is served in the beginning as an appetizer. An *overture* is the opening segment of an *opera* that is performed before the first act.

6. (A); Characteristic Quality. *Food* is characteristically *palatable,* or tasty and edible, just as *perfume* is characteristically *fragrant.*

7. (C); Antonym. *Pastoral,* or characteristic of rural life, means the opposite of *urban,* or characteristic of city life. *Private* and *public* also have opposite meanings.

8. (E); Characteristic Quality. *Economics,* the study of wealth and labor, is characteristically *quantitative,* having to do with measurement. In the same way, a *safari* is characteristically *adventurous.*

9. (B); Classification. A *succulent* is classified as a kind of *plant life,* just as *granite* is classified as a kind of *rock.*

10. (B); Synonym. *Zenith* and *peak* have the same meaning. A *violin* is the same as a *fiddle.*

Workshop Answer Key *(continued)*

p. 134 | Analogies

1. (B); Degree. *Annihilate*, which means to demolish or destroy completely, has a much stronger meaning than *defeat* (when used as a verb). *Torment*, which means to torture or cause anguish, has a much stronger meaning than *bother*, which means to annoy or trouble.

2. (C); Action and Related Object. One can *grant clemency*, or mercy. In the same way, someone can *toss horseshoes*.

3. (C); Antonym. *Dissent*, or disagreement, is the opposite in meaning of *agree*. In the same way, *maturity* is the opposite of *childishness*.

4. (C); Classification. *Golf* can be classified as a *diversion*, or form of amusement, just as *carpentry* can be classified as an *occupation*.

5. (C); Characteristic Quality. *Insolence*, or rude behavior, is characteristically *disrespectful*, just as a *celebration* is characteristically *joyous*.

6. (B); Antonym. *Mandatory*, or required, means the opposite of *optional*. *Hesitant* and *certain* have opposite meanings.

7. (C); Degree. *Meticulous* means scrupulous, or excessively *careful*. Something that is *fatal* is not only *harmful* but also deadly.

8. (D) Synonym. To be *prone* to something is the same as being *inclined* to something. In the same way, *curious* and *inquisitive* are similar in meaning.

9. (E); Synonym. *Purge* (the verb form) and *rid* have similar meanings, as do *show* and *display* when they are used as verbs.

10. (C); Performer and Related Object. An *ultimatum* is a final demand stated by a *diplomat*, who represents his or her country in negotiations. A *cross-examination* of a witness is conducted by a *lawyer* to discredit previous testimony.

Lesson 10

p. 135 | Analogies

1. (D); Performer and Related Object. An *affidavit*, or sworn statement, is given by a *witness*. A *law* is passed by *legislators* in Congress.

2. (D); Characteristic Quality. *Bedlam*, a state of noisy disorder, is characteristically *chaotic*, just as a *riot* is characteristically *violent*.

3. (C); Antonym. *Destitute*, or extremely poor, means the opposite of *wealthy*, or extremely rich. *Shy* and *bold* also have opposite meanings.

4. (B); Synonym. *Diminutive* and *tiny* have the same meaning, as do *ragged* and *tattered*.

5. (C); Degree. *Exultant*, which means exuberantly triumphant, is much stronger in meaning than *pleased*, which means satisfied. *Shocked* is similar in meaning to *surprised* but suggests a much more violent and troubled reaction.

6. (C); Location. *Worshipers* can be found in a *mosque*, or Muslim place of worship. *Fish* can be found in an *aquarium*.

7. (E); Synonym. *Ornate* and *fancy* have similar meanings, as do *organized* and *orderly*.

8. (C); Function. The function of a *prelude* is to *introduce* something. In the same way, the function of a *ruler* (in the sense of a measuring stick) is to *measure* something.

9. (A); Cause and Effect. A *rift*, or a break in a previously friendly relationship, can be the result of a *disagreement*, just as *suffering* can be the result of a *war*.

10. (D); Antonym. *Timorous*, or fearful, is opposite in meaning to *courageous*. *Elderly*, or old, is opposite in meaning to *youthful*.

Fourth Course | *Vocabulary Workshop*

Lesson 11

p. 136 | Analogies

1. (C); Characteristic Quality. A *clangor* is a characteristically *loud* sound, just as a *rose* is a characteristically *fragrant* flower.

2. (C); Performer and Related Action. You expect an inexperienced *actress* to *debut* (the verb form), or give a first public performance, just as you expect a *comedian* to *amuse* an audience.

3. (E); Classification. A *documentary* is classified as *film*, just as a *ballet* is classified as *dance*.

4. (B); Degree. To *gloat* means to *enjoy* something but with a degree of malicious pleasure. When used as verbs, *glare* and *look* have similar meanings. However, glare means to look with a fierce, angry stare.

5. (A); Performer and Related Action. A *grand jury* acts to *indict*, or charge a defendant with a crime, just as a *monarch* acts to *rule*.

6. (B); Synonym. *Melancholy* and *gloom* have similar meanings, as do *tradition* and *custom*.

7. (D); Action and Related Object. You *patent* an *invention* by being granted an exclusive right to it, just as you *insure valuables* by paying to have them replaced should they be lost or stolen.

8. (C); Performer and Related Action. You expect a *patriarch*, the male leader of a group or family, to *lead* his people, just as you expect a *patron*, a person who benefits and protects others, to *support* his or her dependents.

9. (A); Performer and Related Object. A *requiem* is written by a *composer*, just as a *novel* is written by an *author*.

10. (C); Synonym. *Vehement*, which means impetuous or impassioned, has the same meaning as *passionate*. *Earnest* and *sincere* are also similar in meaning.

Lesson 12

p. 137 | Analogies

1. (C); Performer and Related Action. You expect an *arbiter*, or judge, to *decide* a dispute, just as you expect an *architect* to *design* buildings.

2. (C); Synonym. *Botch* and *spoil* have similar meanings, as do *neglect* and *ignore*.

3. (B); Characteristic Quality. *Cant* is characteristically *insincere* talk, just as a *conjunction* is characteristically *connective*, joining different parts of a sentence.

4. (E); Synonym. One's *clientele* is the same as one's *customers*, just as *replacements* are *substitutes*.

5. (D); Performer and Related Action. You expect *members* of a group to *convene*, or meet, just as you expect *citizens* to *vote*.

6. (C); Synonym. A *crony* is a *buddy*, just as a *duty* is an *obligation*.

7. (D); Antonym. *Indifferent*, or uninterested, is opposite in meaning to *interested*. In the same way, *vague*, or unclear, is the opposite of *clear*.

8. (C); Characteristic Quality. A *sleeper* is characteristically *oblivious*, or unaware, just as a *guard* is characteristically *watchful*.

9. (B); Antonym. *Rectify*, which means to correct or fix, means the opposite of *upset*. *Nourish* and *starve* are also opposite in meaning.

10. (B); Function. The function of a *stratagem*, or trick, is to *deceive*, just as the function of an *outline* is to *organize* information.

Workshop Answer Key *(continued)*

Lesson 13

p. 138 | Analogies

1. (C); Action and Related Object. A ruler *abdicates*, or formally gives up, a *throne*, just as legislators *pass* a *law*.

2. (A); Antonym. *Effervescent*, as in having a bubbly personality, means the opposite of *listless*. *Brilliant* and *dull* also have opposite meanings.

3. (D); Synonym. *Immaculate* and *pure* have similar meanings, as do *convinced* and *certain*.

4. (D); Antonym. *Inadvertent*, which means unintended, is opposite in meaning to *intentional*. *Unconcerned* and *worried* are also opposite in meaning.

5. (B); Antonym. *Infallible*, which means incapable of error, is opposite in meaning to *unreliable*. *Ferocious* and *gentle* are also opposite in meaning.

6. (E); Performer and Related Object. Before traveling, a *traveler* develops an *itinerary*, or plan of travel. A *coach* uses a *game plan* during a contest.

7. (C); Antonym. One meaning of *naive* is innocent, which means the opposite of *sophisticated*. *Perfect* and *flawed* are also opposite in meaning.

8. (B); Characteristic Quality. A *cello* is characteristically *resonant*, or vibrating with sound, just as a *breeze* is characteristically *gentle*.

9. (D); Function. The function of a *stimulant* is to *activate*, just as the function of *meditation* is to *relax*.

10. (C); Characteristic Quality. *Frosted glass* is characteristically *translucent*, or partially clear, just as *frost* is characteristically *white*.

Lesson 14

p. 139 | Analogies

1. (B); Antonym. One of the definitions of *demure*, reserved, is opposite in meaning to *flashy*. *Plain* and *fancy* are also opposite in meaning.

2. (D); Action and Related Object. You *detonate*, or set off, an *explosive*, just as you *strike* a *match*.

3. (C); Degree. *Jostle* is similar in meaning to *bump* but implies much rougher contact. In the same way, *beg* is similar in meaning to *ask*, but to beg is to ask in a pleading way.

4. (D); Classification. A *lexicon*, or dictionary, is classified as a *reference book*, just as *Judaism* is classified as a *religion*.

5. (B); Synonym. *Pallid* and *pale* have the same meaning, as do *quiet* and *hushed*.

6. (D); Synonym. *Redundant*, which means unnecessarily repeated, has a meaning similar to *repetitive*. *Basic* and *elementary* also have similar meanings.

7. (C); Performer and Related Action. You expect *troops* to *rendezvous*, or meet at a designated time and place, just as you expect a group's *members* to *congregate*, or gather together.

8. (C); Function. The function of a *sequel*, one phase of a literary work, is to *continue* a story, just as the function of a *foreword*, an introductory statement, is to *introduce* a story.

9. (D); Function. The function of a *synopsis*, which means a condensation or summary, is to *summarize* something, just as the function of a *videotape* is to *record* something.

10. (B); Antonym. *Throng*, or a crowd, is the opposite in meaning to *few*. In the same way, *spacious* and *cramped* are opposite in meaning.

Lesson 15

p. 140 | Analogies

1. (D); Synonym. *Carp* and *nag* have the same meaning, as do *offend* and *insult*.

2. (C); Characteristic Quality. *Sarcasm*, which means making cutting remarks, is characteristically *caustic*, or corrosive. In the same way, a *cavity*, or hole, is characteristically *hollow*.

3. (E); Degree. *Decrepit* is similar in meaning to *worn* but means even more broken down or worn out. In the same way, *eager* is similar in meaning to *willing* but implies much greater enthusiasm.

4. (C); Characteristic Quality. A *farce*, an exaggerated, humorous play, is characteristically *funny*, just as a *tragedy*, a serious play with an unhappy ending, is characteristically *sad*.

5. (A); Characteristic Quality. *Jargon* is characteristically *unintelligible*, or gibberish, just as a *plateau* is characteristically *elevated*, or raised above sea level.

6. (C); Degree. Something that is *malignant* is much more dangerous or likely to cause death than something that is *harmful*. Similarly, someone who is *evil* has much more wicked intentions than someone who is *mischievous*.

7. (B); Synonym. *Negligible*, which means unimportant and easily disregarded, has a meaning similar to *insignificant*. *Critical* and *serious* also have similar meanings.

8. (C); Antonym. *Odious*, which means disgusting and offensive, is opposite in meaning to *appealing*. *Realistic* and *fantastic* are also opposite in meaning.

9. (C); Synonym. *Pertinent*, or relevant, is similar in meaning to *appropriate*. *Tiresome* and *annoying* also have similar meanings.

10. (B); Antonym. When used as verbs, *rebuke*, which means scold, and *praise* have opposite meanings. When used as verbs, *hamper* and *help* also have opposite meanings.

Reading New Words in Context

Lesson 1

p. 144 | Exercise 1: Finding Synonyms

Answers will vary. The following are possible responses.

1. ancient times
2. from the father
3. a poor person
4. having to do with right and wrong
5. an unorthodox view
6. teacher or advisor
7. widespread but poor reputation
8. firmly declares
9. selection
10. unable to speak clearly
11. scornful
12. voters
13. comparisons
14. wealthy, powerful group
15. stooped
16. verdict of not guilty
17. moral strength
18. predictive
19. grew from
20. after death

p. 145 | Exercise 2: Reading Strategically

1. C
2. B
3. D
4. A
5. E
6. C
7. E
8. A
9. B
10. E
11. B
12. D
13. C
14. D
15. A
16. B
17. E
18. B
19. C
20. D

Workshop Answer Key *(continued)*

Lesson 2

p. 150 | Exercise 1: Finding Synonyms

Answers will vary. The following are possible responses.

1. mysterious
2. marshy inlet
3. angry
4. made disapproving faces
5. faces
6. human qualities applied to non-human entities
7. to retell in one's own words
8. word for word
9. friendly
10. easily formed
11. wise
12. fanciful
13. not producing a desired effect
14. unyielding
15. cruel; unfeeling
16. to give in to
17. lively
18. exciting and sensational
19. anxious words
20. deserving praise

p. 151 | Exercise 2: Reading Strategically

1. A
2. D
3. E
4. C
5. B
6. B
7. A
8. D
9. C
10. C
11. E
12. B
13. B
14. A
15. A
16. C
17. A
18. B
19. E
20. D

Lesson 3

p. 156 | Exercise 1: Finding Synonyms

Answers will vary. The following are possible responses.

1. constantly
2. detests
3. determines
4. careful
5. burdened
6. original or new
7. grieves
8. stout
9. sympathy
10. calmness
11. nearness
12. grows worse
13. arrogant, self-important
14. appalling
15. joyful
16. dull
17. restores youth
18. acceptable
19. associated with
20. controlled

p. 157 | Exercise 2: Reading Strategically

1. B
2. E
3. B
4. D
5. A
6. C
7. C
8. E
9. A
10. D
11. B
12. C
13. B
14. B
15. E
16. D
17. A
18. B
19. C
20. D

136

Fourth Course | *Vocabulary Workshop*

Lesson 4

p. 162 | Exercise 1: Finding Synonyms

Answers will vary. The following are possible responses.

1. gentle breeze
2. artistic
3. pale
4. eager
5. forcefully
6. create
7. well-timed
8. obstacle
9. productive
10. average
11. receiver
12. military
13. vigor, strength, and endurance
14. overused expression
15. appearance and bearing
16. charm; allure
17. apparent contradiction
18. formed
19. one who wants to return to earlier ways
20. doubts

p. 163 | Exercise 2: Reading Strategically

1. D
2. C
3. E
4. A
5. D
6. B
7. E
8. D
9. A
10. C
11. B
12. E
13. B
14. D
15. A
16. B
17. A
18. C
19. D
20. E

Lesson 5

p. 168 | Exercise 1: Finding Synonyms

Answers will vary. The following are possible responses.

1. widespread
2. basic principles
3. relentlessly
4. agreeable
5. self-evident truths
6. contains; encircles
7. cannot be destroyed
8. punishment
9. pass beyond
10. nonliving
11. central or crucial
12. obedience
13. aggressive or violent
14. inborn; inner
15. chance for help
16. understanding
17. temporary; ever-changing
18. encouragement
19. strict
20. changeable

p. 169 | Exercise 2: Reading Strategically

1. C
2. E
3. B
4. A
5. C
6. D
7. C
8. D
9. B
10. A
11. D
12. C
13. A
14. C
15. B
16. E
17. B
18. D
19. A
20. C

Lesson 6

p. 174 | Exercise 1: Finding Synonyms

Answers will vary. The following are possible responses.

1. freedom
2. persistence
3. destruction
4. begins
5. cause or inflict
6. independent
7. spying
8. overwhelm or surround
9. tricked
10. weak
11. false story
12. unbeatable
13. uncertain and dangerous
14. reproduction
15. mild and pleasant
16. severe
17. alert
18. pacified
19. ancient
20. fade

p. 175 | Exercise 2: Reading Strategically

1. C
2. A
3. E
4. B
5. B
6. D
7. E
8. A
9. B
10. D
11. B
12. E
13. A
14. C
15. C
16. D
17. A
18. C
19. B
20. B

Lesson 7

p. 180 | Exercise 1: Finding Synonyms

Answers will vary. The following are possible responses.

1. crossroads
2. see
3. financed
4. unreachable
5. a flowing in
6. buildings
7. highest point
8. streams
9. middle class
10. servants
11. invention
12. dog
13. extinct
14. picture writing
15. tan
16. changed into bone
17. destroyed
18. inadequate
19. violently destroying
20. chests

p. 181 | Exercise 2: Reading Strategically

1. E
2. A
3. B
4. B
5. D
6. B
7. C
8. D
9. E
10. B
11. A
12. C
13. D
14. A
15. C
16. E
17. D
18. C
19. A
20. B

Lesson 8

p. 186 | Exercise 1: Finding Synonyms

Answers will vary. The following are possible responses.

1. leading to
2. Muslim place of worship
3. high point
4. followed
5. passed
6. plain
7. irregular
8. rural
9. assisted
10. shrewd
11. talent
12. necessary
13. related to quantity; measurable
14. appetizers
15. self-serve meal
16. efficient
17. tasty
18. moist and flavorful
19. delicious
20. happen again

p. 187 | Exercise 2: Reading Strategically

1. B
2. D
3. D
4. C
5. E
6. C
7. A
8. D
9. B
10. A
11. C
12. D
13. E
14. B
15. B
16. D
17. C
18. D
19. A
20. A

Lesson 9

p. 192 | Exercise 1: Finding Synonyms

Answers will vary. The following are possible responses.

1. required
2. total obedience
3. disrespect
4. style or behavior
5. carefully
6. restraints
7. grants
8. expel
9. code of conduct
10. disagree; differ
11. destroy completely
12. avoid
13. crush, destroy
14. avoidance of extremes
15. distraction
16. mercy or forgiveness
17. inclined
18. nonviolence
19. outrageous
20. final demand

p. 193 | Exercise 2: Reading Strategically

1. E
2. B
3. D
4. C
5. A
6. B
7. C
8. D
9. B
10. A
11. C
12. E
13. A
14. E
15. B
16. A
17. D
18. A
19. E
20. C

Lesson 10

p. 198 | Exercise 1: Finding Synonyms

Answers will vary. The following are possible responses.

1. jubilant
2. influenced; swayed
3. deserving of praise
4. can't be taken away
5. fearful
6. free
7. criticized
8. tiny
9. introduction
10. be plentiful
11. loud; confusing place
12. informal
13. penniless
14. elaborately decorated
15. unified
16. voters
17. separation
18. pardon
19. a sworn statement
20. shortened

p. 199 | Exercise 2: Reading Strategically

1. C
2. D
3. D
4. A
5. E
6. B
7. C
8. D
9. A
10. D
11. B
12. B
13. E
14. D
15. C
16. A
17. B
18. D
19. E
20. D

Workshop Answer Key (continued)

Lesson 11

p. 204 | Exercise 1: Finding Synonyms

Answers will vary. The following are possible responses.

1. first public appearance
2. inheritance
3. coaxed
4. window frame with hinges
5. loud, ringing sound
6. straddling
7. hypothetical
8. obvious
9. male leader
10. prevent
11. charged with a crime
12. exult
13. shamed
14. temporary relief
15. furious
16. gloom
17. film of or about actual events
18. funeral hymn
19. passionately
20. vary

p. 205 | Exercise 2: Reading Strategically

1. D
2. B
3. C
4. C
5. A
6. E
7. A
8. B
9. E
10. C
11. B
12. A
13. D
14. E
15. C
16. B
17. D
18. A
19. C
20. B

Lesson 12

p. 210 | Exercise 1: Finding Synonyms

Answers will vary. The following are possible responses.

1. confusing
2. without bias
3. companies owned by larger companies
4. customers
5. friends
6. judge
7. bungle
8. ending
9. unaware
10. balance
11. growing force; movement
12. solidly; mostly
13. met
14. schemes
15. mourn
16. violation
17. correct
18. arrange; specify
19. insincere talk
20. lack of concern

p. 211 | Exercise 2: Reading Strategically

1. A
2. D
3. C
4. A
5. E
6. D
7. A
8. E
9. A
10. C
11. B
12. D
13. A
14. A
15. E
16. B
17. C
18. B
19. C
20. D

Lesson 13

p.216 | Exercise 1: Finding Synonyms

Answers will vary. The following are possible responses.

1. explain
2. thought about
3. combination
4. inexperienced
5. sarcastic
6. irritates
7. renounce office
8. make petty objections
9. route; travel plan
10. deep; rich in tone
11. never wrong
12. event
13. irregular
14. unintentionally
15. bubbly
16. something causing excitement
17. letting some light through
18. clean; pure
19. lowers worth
20. something forced

p.217 | Exercise 2: Reading Strategically

1. E
2. B
3. C
4. A
5. D
6. D
7. E
8. C
9. A
10. B
11. B
12. E
13. A
14. A
15. C
16. B
17. A
18. D
19. C
20. A

Lesson 14

p.222 | Exercise 1: Finding Synonyms

Answers will vary. The following are possible responses.

1. insight
2. enlighten
3. dictionary
4. summary
5. senseless
6. assert
7. not applicable
8. suggestive
9. repetitive
10. discouraging; intimidating
11. explode
12. reserved
13. occasionally
14. crowd; large number of people
15. throw out
16. shoving
17. imitated
18. pale
19. continuation
20. prearranged meeting

p.223 | Exercise 2: Reading Strategically

1. B
2. C
3. E
4. A
5. C
6. C
7. E
8. B
9. B
10. C
11. D
12. A
13. B
14. C
15. D
16. E
17. B
18. C
19. A
20. C

Workshop Answer Key *(continued)*

Lesson 15

p. 228 | Exercise 1: Finding Synonyms

Answers will vary. The following are possible responses.

1. annoying
2. changeable
3. outline of proposed events
4. something ridiculous
5. occurring together by accident
6. relevant
7. scold
8. disgusting
9. dirty and degrading
10. complain
11. worn-out
12. stick out
13. insignificant
14. humorous, satirical imitation
15. life-threatening
16. required
17. change
18. corrosive
19. flammable; causing fire
20. specialized language of a group

p. 229 | Exercise 2: Reading Strategically

1. D
2. A
3. C
4. E
5. B
6. C
7. C
8. D
9. E
10. A
11. D
12. C
13. B
14. B
15. A
16. D
17. B
18. B
19. A
20. B

Tests Answer Key

Formative Assessment

p.3 | Test 1

1. B	6. D
2. A	7. B
3. C	8. E
4. A	9. C
5. C	10. A

p.4 | Test 2

1. D	6. D
2. B	7. E
3. A	8. C
4. D	9. B
5. C	10. E

p.5 | Test 3

1. B	6. D
2. B	7. A
3. C	8. B
4. D	9. E
5. E	10. A

p.6 | Test 4

1. B	6. A
2. D	7. C
3. C	8. A
4. A	9. D
5. E	10. B

p.7 | Test 5

1. B	6. A
2. C	7. C
3. A	8. B
4. E	9. D
5. C	10. C

p.8 | Test 6

1. D	6. E
2. C	7. B
3. A	8. D
4. D	9. B
5. A	10. A

p.9 | Test 7

1. E	6. A
2. A	7. D
3. B	8. B
4. B	9. D
5. D	10. C

p.10 | Test 8

1. E	6. B
2. A	7. B
3. D	8. E
4. A	9. C
5. C	10. D

p.11 | Test 9

1. A	6. A
2. C	7. D
3. C	8. D
4. E	9. D
5. B	10. B

p.12 | Test 10

1. D	6. B
2. E	7. A
3. E	8. C
4. D	9. D
5. A	10. B

p.13 | Test 11

1. A	6. A
2. B	7. C
3. A	8. C
4. D	9. C
5. B	10. E

p.14 | Test 12

1. C	6. E
2. D	7. B
3. D	8. C
4. A	9. E
5. A	10. B

p. 15 | Test 13

1. C	**6.** B
2. B	**7.** A
3. D	**8.** C
4. E	**9.** B
5. C	**10.** D

p. 16 | Test 14

1. D	**6.** B
2. B	**7.** E
3. C	**8.** A
4. D	**9.** A
5. A	**10.** C

p. 17 | Test 15

1. C	**6.** C
2. D	**7.** B
3. A	**8.** A
4. E	**9.** E
5. D	**10.** D

p. 18 | Test 16

1. C	**6.** B
2. B	**7.** A
3. D	**8.** C
4. D	**9.** C
5. B	**10.** A

p. 19 | Test 17

1. D	**6.** E
2. B	**7.** C
3. D	**8.** A
4. A	**9.** C
5. C	**10.** C

p. 20 | Test 18

1. B	**6.** E
2. C	**7.** C
3. E	**8.** A
4. D	**9.** D
5. B	**10.** C

p. 21 | Test 19

1. E	**6.** C
2. A	**7.** C
3. A	**8.** A
4. C	**9.** B
5. E	**10.** D

p. 22 | Test 20

1. B	**6.** D
2. D	**7.** A
3. E	**8.** A
4. B	**9.** C
5. B	**10.** E

p. 23 | Test 21

1. D	**6.** E
2. D	**7.** C
3. A	**8.** D
4. B	**9.** C
5. B	**10.** D

p. 24 | Test 22

1. D	**6.** C
2. B	**7.** C
3. B	**8.** D
4. D	**9.** E
5. B	**10.** A

p. 25 | Test 23

1. E	**6.** A
2. B	**7.** A
3. C	**8.** B
4. D	**9.** A
5. B	**10.** D

p. 26 | Test 24

1. D	**6.** B
2. E	**7.** A
3. D	**8.** A
4. E	**9.** D
5. B	**10.** C

Tests Answer Key *(continued)*

p. 27 | Test 25

1. C
2. A
3. D
4. E
5. D
6. C
7. D
8. B
9. D
10. B

p. 28 | Test 26

1. C
2. B
3. C
4. E
5. A
6. D
7. C
8. B
9. C
10. A

p. 29 | Test 27

1. B
2. E
3. C
4. C
5. B
6. A
7. A
8. C
9. D
10. E

p. 30 | Test 28

1. D
2. D
3. C
4. A
5. B
6. D
7. E
8. B
9. B
10. C

p. 31 | Test 29

1. A
2. A
3. B
4. E
5. E
6. B
7. C
8. D
9. D
10. D

p. 32 | Test 30

1. C
2. E
3. D
4. A
5. C
6. A
7. B
8. D
9. B
10. C

Summative Assessment

p. 35 | Test 1 Part A

1. D
2. B
3. C
4. C
5. D
6. E
7. B
8. B
9. A
10. E
11. E
12. A
13. B
14. C
15. E
16. A
17. C
18. D
19. C
20. D

p. 39 | Test 1 Part B

21. D
22. C
23. B
24. D
25. A
26. C
27. B
28. B
29. B
30. A
31. A
32. E
33. D
34. C
35. C
36. E
37. D
38. B
39. C
40. E
41. A
42. C
43. C
44. D
45. A
46. D
47. B
48. D
49. E
50. A
51. A
52. D
53. E
54. A
55. E
56. B
57. C
58. C
59. E
60. B
61. D
62. C
63. A
64. A
65. E
66. C
67. E
68. B
69. C
70. E

Tests Answer Key *(continued)*

p. 44 | Test 1 Part C

71. (E); Degree. To *adore* means to love or worship someone or something. To *like* someone or something means to have less intense positive feelings. To *loathe* someone or something means to have stronger feelings of distaste than to *dislike*.

72. (C); Synonym. *Analogy* and *comparison* have similar meanings, as do *similarity* and *sameness*.

73. (D); Antonym. *Apprehensive,* which means uneasy, is opposite in meaning to *calm. Tranquil* and *stormy* also have opposite meanings.

74. (C); Antonym. *Buyer* and *seller* are opposite in meaning. A *recipient,* or someone who receives, is opposite in meaning to a *donor,* someone who gives.

75. (A); Synonym. *Careful* and *cautious* have the same meaning, as do *contemptuous* and *scornful.*

76. (B); Synonym. *Charisma* and *charm* have similar meanings, as do *talent* and *ability.*

77. (B); Antonym; *Deteriorate* and *improve* have opposite meanings, as do *succeed* and *fail.*

78. (D); Performer and Related Action. You expect an *electorate,* or the voting population, to *vote,* just as you would expect an *audience* to *applaud.*

79. (C); Synonym. An *impediment* is the same thing as an *obstacle. Device* is similar in meaning to *machine.*

80. (E); Synonym. *Inarticulate* and *mute* have similar meanings, as do *willing* and *eager.*

81. (B); Synonym. *Insipid,* which means tasteless, has a meaning similar to *flavorless. Amazing* and *astonishing* also have similar meanings.

82. (E); Antonym. *Judicious,* which means wise, is opposite in meaning to *unwise. Trustworthy* and *unreliable* also have opposite meanings.

83. (B); Performer and Related Action. You expect a *mourner* to *lament,* or grieve, just as you expect a *sleeper* to *dream.*

84. (A); Characteristic Quality. *Clay* is characteristically *malleable,* just as *rubber* is characteristically *flexible.*

85. (D); Performer and Related Action. A *mentor,* or teacher, is someone who *advises* others, just as a *critic* is someone who *reviews* performances and other creative works.

86. (B); Synonym. *Notoriety* and *fame* have similar meanings, as do *merit* and *worth.*

87. (E); Classification. *Personification* may be classified as a *figure of speech,* just as a *sneaker* may be classified as *footwear.*

88. (D); Antonym. *Pompous,* or self-important, is opposite in meaning to *humble. Knowledgeable* and *ignorant* are also opposite in meaning.

89. (C); Synonym. *Prophetic* and *predictive* have nearly the same meaning, as do *remarkable* and *outstanding.*

90. (D); Performer and Related Action. You expect a *reactionary* to *react,* just as you expect a *novelist* to *write.*

91. (B); Synonym. *Repress* and *restrain* have similar meanings, as do *bicker* and *quarrel.*

92. (B); Cause and Effect. *Retribution,* or punishment, can be a result of *wrongdoing,* just as *wages* are usually the result of *work.*

93. (C); Performer and Related Action. A *terrorist* is someone who may *threaten* people in order to achieve a political goal, just as a *lawyer* is someone who may *argue* a case in order to achieve a legal goal.

94. (C); Characteristic Quality. *Parachuting* is characteristically *thrilling*, just as *embroidering*, or ornamental needlework, is characteristically *painstaking*.

95. (A); Characteristic Quality. A *moment* is characteristically *transitory*, just as *ice* is characteristically *cold*.

96. (E); Antonym. *Vibrant*, meaning full of life, is the opposite in meaning of *lifeless*. In the same way, *vague*, meaning unclear, is the opposite of *clear*.

97. (C); Performer and Related Action. A *waiter serves* food to customers, just as a *pauper*, or penniless person, may sometimes *beg* for money.

98. (E); Synonym. *Whimsical* and *fanciful* have similar meanings, as do *tired* and *weary*.

99. (E); Antonym. *Zealous*, meaning extremely eager, is the opposite of *unenthusiastic*. *Timid* and *courageous* are also opposite in meaning.

100. (D); Characteristic Quality. A *zephyr*, or soft breeze, is characteristically *gentle*, just as a *bird* is characteristically *feathered*.

p. 47 | Test 2 Part A

1. E	**11.** B
2. B	**12.** D
3. E	**13.** E
4. B	**14.** D
5. C	**15.** A
6. C	**16.** D
7. D	**17.** B
8. C	**18.** A
9. A	**19.** B
10. C	**20.** E

p. 51 | Test 2 Part B

21. D	**46.** C
22. D	**47.** D
23. C	**48.** C
24. E	**49.** E
25. A	**50.** E
26. C	**51.** C
27. B	**52.** A
28. C	**53.** D
29. A	**54.** A
30. C	**55.** E
31. E	**56.** C
32. D	**57.** B
33. B	**58.** E
34. A	**59.** B
35. E	**60.** D
36. D	**61.** B
37. C	**62.** C
38. C	**63.** A
39. B	**64.** D
40. A	**65.** C
41. D	**66.** E
42. E	**67.** A
43. C	**68.** D
44. E	**69.** C
45. D	**70.** C

p. 56 | Test 2 Part C

71. (D); Performer and Related Object. An *affidavit*, or sworn statement, is given by a *witness*, just as a *law* is passed by *legislators*.

72. (C); Location. *Fish* can be found in an *aquarium*, just as *worshippers* can be found in a *mosque*.

73. (C); Characteristic Quality. A *breeze* is characteristically *balmy*, just as *sleet* is characteristically *cold*.

74. (D); Characteristic Quality. *Bedlam*, a state of chaos, is characteristically *chaotic*, just as a *riot* is characteristically *violent*.

75. (B); Action and Related Object. You *besiege* a *fort*, just as you *plan* a *trip*.

76. (C); Synonym. *Bias* and *prejudice* have the same meaning, as do *violin* and *fiddle*.

77. (A); Antonym. *Bourgeois* means the opposite of *unconventional*, just as *colloquial* means the opposite of *formal*.

78. (D); Location. A *buffet*, or sideboard, can be found in a *dining room*, just as a *tub* can be found in a *bathroom*.

79. (D); Synonym. *Clemency* and *mercy* have the same meaning. *Essay* and *theme* are also similar in meaning.

80. (A); Function. The function of a *coffer*, or chest, is to *safeguard* valuables, just as one function of a *calculator* is to *multiply* numbers.

81. (E); Characteristic Quality. *Slang* is characteristically *colloquial*, just as an *artist* is characteristically *creative*.

82. (D); Classification. A *concession* is a type of *privilege*, just as a *fork* is a type of *utensil*.

83. (E); Cause and Effect. A *hurricane* can cause *devastation*, which means complete ruin or destruction, just as *medicine* can cause *healing*.

84. (B); Cause and Effect. One meaning of *dissent* is disagreement, which perhaps could lead to an *argument*, just as *praise* could cause one to have *pride*.

85. (C); Action and Related Object. You *build* an *edifice*, or building, just as you *direct* a *film*.

86. (B); Performer and Related Action. You expect a *liberator* to *emancipate*, or to set free, just as you expect a *pacifist* to *placate*.

87. (C); Antonym. *Erratic* means the opposite of *regular*, just as *hesitant* means the opposite of *certain*.

88. (E); Performer and Related Action. You expect a *frog* to *leap*, just as you expect a *canine* to *howl*.

89. (B); Location. *Hieroglyphics*, pictures used to express language, can be found in *Egypt*. An *oasis* can be found in the *desert*.

90. (B); Antonym. *Latitude*, which means lack of restriction, means the opposite of *restriction*, just as *introduction* means the opposite of *conclusion*.

91. (D); Performer and Related Object. You expect an *actor* to use *mannerisms*, just as you expect a *nurse* to use a *thermometer*.

92. (C); Degree. *Meticulous* means extremely careful. Something that is *fatal* is *harmful* to the point of being deadly.

93. (B); Antonym. *Moderation*, or lack of excess, is opposite in meaning of *excess*. In the same way, *kindness* and *meanness* have opposite meanings.

94. (C); Antonym. *Obliterate*, which means to wipe out, is opposite in meaning to *create*. *Demolish* and *construct* are also opposite in meaning.

95. (A); Synonym. One meaning of *prone* is lying *flat*. *Lethal* and *fatal* also have similar meanings.

96. (C); Synonym. *Purge* and *rid* have the same meaning, as do *notify* and *inform*.

97. (E); Characteristic Quality. *Economics*, the science of wealth and labor, is characteristically *quantitative*, just as a *trek*, or journey, is characteristically *adventurous*.

98. (C); Degree. A *rivulet*, which is a little stream or brook, is a much smaller body of water than a *river*, just as a *path* is much smaller than a *road*.

99. (C); Location. A *steppe* can be found in *Russia*, just as a *coat* can be found in a *closet*.

100. (A); Performer and Related Object. An *ultimatum* is a final demand that might be stated by a *diplomat*, who represents his or her country in negotiations. A game *strategy* is offered by a *coach*.

p. 59 | Test 3 Part A

1. E	**11.** E
2. C	**12.** C
3. B	**13.** A
4. D	**14.** D
5. A	**15.** A
6. E	**16.** B
7. C	**17.** B
8. A	**18.** E
9. C	**19.** C
10. B	**20.** B

p. 63 | Test 3 Part B

21. B	**46.** C
22. E	**47.** D
23. A	**48.** B
24. E	**49.** E
25. D	**50.** B
26. C	**51.** E
27. B	**52.** A
28. E	**53.** D
29. A	**54.** C
30. C	**55.** B
31. D	**56.** A
32. D	**57.** C
33. C	**58.** A
34. C	**59.** D
35. D	**60.** B
36. E	**61.** C
37. A	**62.** A
38. C	**63.** E
39. D	**64.** D
40. E	**65.** C
41. C	**66.** C
42. D	**67.** D
43. C	**68.** E
44. B	**69.** D
45. D	**70.** D

p. 68 | Test 3 Part C

71. (C); Performer and Related Action. You expect an *arbiter,* or judge, to *decide* a dispute, just as you expect an *architect* to *design* a building.

72. (B); Classification. A *casement* is a type of *window,* and a *cafeteria* is a type of *restaurant.*

73. (E); Characteristic Quality. *Sarcasm,* which means cutting remarks, is characteristically *caustic.* In the same way, a *cavity,* or hole, is characteristically *hollow.*

74. (B); Performer and Related Action. A *sympathizer condoles,* just as a *winner celebrates.*

75. (D); Synonym. *Convinced* and *certain* have similar meanings, as do *immaculate* and *pure.*

76. (C); Synonym. A *crony* is a *buddy,* just as a *duty* is an *obligation.*

77. (D); Antonym. To *debase,* or lower in some way, means the opposite of *elevate,* just as *criticize* means the opposite of *praise.*

78. (B); Antonym. *Demure* is opposite in meaning to *flashy. Plain* and *fancy* are also opposite in meaning.

79. (C); Synonym. *Earnest* and *sincere* have similar meanings. *Vehement,* which means impassioned, and *passionate* also have similar meanings.

80. (A); Antonym. *Effervescent,* or active and bubbly, means the opposite of *listless. Brilliant* and *dull* also have opposite meanings.

81. (B); Characteristic Quality. A *breeze* is characteristically *gentle,* just as a *cello* is characteristically *resonant,* or vibrating with sound.

82. (B); Degree. To *gloat* means to *enjoy* something with a great degree of malicious pleasure. To *glare* means to *look* with a fierce, angry stare.

83. (A); Performer and Related Action. A *grand jury* may *indict,* or charge a defendant with a crime, just as a *monarch* may *rule* a country.

84. (B); Characteristic Quality. A *pest* is characteristically *irksome,* or annoying, just as a *clown* is characteristically *amusing.*

85. (E); Synonym. *Journalists* and *reporters* have nearly the same meaning, as do *clientele* and *customers.*

86. (D); Classification. A *lexicon,* or dictionary, is classified as a *reference book,* just as *Judaism* is classified as a *religion.*

87. (E); Synonym. *Locate* and *find* have similar meanings, as do *carp* and *complain*.

88. (B); Synonym. *Melancholy* and *gloom* have similar meanings, as do *tradition* and *custom*.

89. (B); Synonym. *Pallid* and *pale* have the same meaning, as do *quiet* and *hushed*.

90. (A); Characteristic Quality. A *plateau* is characteristically *elevated*, just as *jargon* is characteristically *unintelligible*.

91. (D); Synonym. *Protrude* and *jut out* have similar meanings, as do *remember* and *recall*.

92. (E); Antonym. *Rankle*, meaning to irritate, is the opposite of *smooth*. *Enjoy* and *dislike* are also opposite in meaning.

93. (C); Antonym. *Realistic* is opposite in meaning to *fantastic*. *Odious* and *appealing* are also opposite in meaning.

94. (A); Function. A *requiem*, a mass or dirge performed for the dead, is meant to *honor*, just as a *novel* is meant to *entertain*.

95. (E); Synonym. *Sardonic* and *sarcastic* have similar meanings, as do *cheerful* and *glad*.

96. (B); Synonym. *Sporadic* and *occasional* have the same meaning, as do *considerate* and *thoughtful*.

97. (D); Synonym. One meaning of *subsidiary* is being in a *secondary*, or subordinate, relationship. *Strange* and *odd* also have similar meanings.

98. (B); Performer and Related Object. A *chemist* may use *synthesis*, the combining of elements, just as an *artist* may work on a *statue*.

99. (D); Synonym. One meaning of *throng* is a *crowd*. In the same way, *melody* and *tune* are similar in meaning.

100. (C); Characteristic Quality. A *tragedy*, a serious play with an unhappy ending, is characteristically *sad*. In the same way, a *farce* is characteristically *funny*.

Making New Words Your Own

Lesson 1

p. 3 | **Exercise 1: Wordbusting**

> **NOTES**
> - For each Vocabulary Word, students should fill in at least one of the **context, structure,** and **sound** boxes.
> - Check that students vary the boxes they use throughout the exercise.
> - Make sure students look up each word in the dictionary and fill in the dictionary box; answers will vary depending on the dictionary used.

p. 5 | **Exercise 2: Context Clues**

11. J	vernacular	**17.** A	felicitous
12. D	rhetorical	**18.** F	usurp
13. C	provocative	**19.** H	comprehensive
14. B	accentuate		
15. G	intricacy	**20.** I	ambiguous
16. E	introspective		

p. 6 | **Exercise 3: Sentence Completion**

21. D	**26.** C
22. B	**27.** D
23. B	**28.** C
24. E	**29.** E
25. E	**30.** B

Lesson 2

p. 7 | **Exercise 1: Wordbusting**

> **NOTES**
> - For each Vocabulary Word, students should fill in at least one of the **context, structure,** and **sound** boxes.
> - Check that students vary the boxes they use throughout the exercise.
> - Make sure students look up each word in the dictionary and fill in the dictionary box; answers will vary depending on the dictionary used.

p. 9 | **Exercise 2: Context Clues**

11. J	prologue	**16.** A	dissolute
12. H	conjecture	**17.** B	protagonist
13. C	terse	**18.** D	despicable
14. G	misanthrope	**19.** F	incongruous
15. E	allegory	**20.** I	ferocity

p. 10 | **Exercise 3: Sentence Completion**

21. B	**26.** A
22. D	**27.** C
23. A	**28.** E
24. D	**29.** B
25. E	**30.** B

Lesson 3

p. 11 | **Exercise 1: Wordbusting**

> **NOTES**
> - For each Vocabulary Word, students should fill in at least one of the **context, structure,** and **sound** boxes.
> - Check that students vary the boxes they use throughout the exercise.
> - Make sure students look up each word in the dictionary and fill in the dictionary box; answers will vary depending on the dictionary used.

p. 13 | **Exercise 2: Context Clues**

11. C	symposium	**16.** D	lucid
12. E	foreshadow	**17.** I	perpetuate
13. G	scrutinize	**18.** F	evoke
14. J	evasive	**19.** A	epithet
15. B	infer	**20.** H	laudable

p. 14 | **Exercise 3: Sentence Completion**

21. C	**26.** E
22. A	**27.** B
23. B	**28.** E
24. B	**29.** A
25. D	**30.** D

Workshop Answer Key *(continued)*

Lesson 4

p. 15 | Exercise 1: Wordbusting

> **NOTES**
> - For each Vocabulary Word, students should fill in at least one of the **context, structure,** and **sound** boxes.
> - Check that students vary the boxes they use throughout the exercise.
> - Make sure students look up each word in the dictionary and fill in the dictionary box; answers will vary depending on the dictionary used.

p. 17 | Exercise 2: Context Clues

11.	D novice	**16.**	E affluent
12.	H banter	**17.**	B reiterate
13.	I connotation	**18.**	C embellish
14.	A nostalgic	**19.**	F brevity
15.	J stipend	**20.**	G imbibe

p. 18 | Exercise 3: Sentence Completion

21.	D	**26.**	E
22.	E	**27.**	B
23.	D	**28.**	C
24.	A	**29.**	A
25.	C	**30.**	D

Lesson 5

p. 19 | Exercise 1: Wordbusting

> **NOTES**
> - For each Vocabulary Word, students should fill in at least one of the **context, structure,** and **sound** boxes.
> - Check that students vary the boxes they use throughout the exercise.
> - Make sure students look up each word in the dictionary and fill in the dictionary box; answers will vary depending on the dictionary used.

p. 21 | Exercise 2: Context Clues

11.	J anagram	**16.**	C coherent
12.	I goad	**17.**	E fulminate
13.	G noncommittal	**18.**	H proboscis
14.	A assertion	**19.**	B inexplicable
15.	F quixotic	**20.**	D surmise

p. 22 | Exercise 3: Sentence Completion

21.	B	**26.**	C
22.	C	**27.**	C
23.	D	**28.**	B
24.	E	**29.**	E
25.	B	**30.**	A

Lesson 6

p. 23 | Exercise 1: Wordbusting

> **NOTES**
> - For each Vocabulary Word, students should fill in at least one of the **context, structure,** and **sound** boxes.
> - Check that students vary the boxes they use throughout the exercise.
> - Make sure students look up each word in the dictionary and fill in the dictionary box; answers will vary depending on the dictionary used.

p. 25 | Exercise 2: Context Clues

11.	I climactic	**17.**	G epilogue
12.	H fidelity	**18.**	A stigma
13.	F anecdote	**19.**	B hypochon-driac
14.	E staunch		
15.	C prodigy	**20.**	J extempora-neous
16.	D forte		

p. 26 | Exercise 3: Sentence Completion

21.	C	**26.**	B
22.	C	**27.**	A
23.	E	**28.**	D
24.	D	**29.**	A
25.	D	**30.**	C

Workshop Answer Key *(continued)*

Lesson 7

p. 27 | Exercise 1: Wordbusting

NOTES
- For each Vocabulary Word, students should fill in at least one of the **context, structure,** and **sound** boxes.
- Check that students vary the boxes they use throughout the exercise.
- Make sure students look up each word in the dictionary and fill in the dictionary box; answers will vary depending on the dictionary used.

p. 29 | Exercise 2: Context Clues

11. A subservient
12. G rudiment
13. I gibe
14. H bumptious
15. J repartee
16. E consonant
17. D satiate
18. B sanction
19. C vivacious
20. F cite

p. 30 | Exercise 3: Sentence Completion

21. C
22. D
23. E
24. B
25. B
26. D
27. B
28. B
29. A
30. D

Lesson 8

p. 31 | Exercise 1: Wordbusting

NOTES
- For each Vocabulary Word, students should fill in at least one of the **context, structure,** and **sound** boxes.
- Check that students vary the boxes they use throughout the exercise.
- Make sure students look up each word in the dictionary and fill in the dictionary box; answers will vary depending on the dictionary used.

p. 32 | Exercise 2: Context Clues

11. G comely
12. E miscreant
13. I flaunt
14. C erroneous
15. H decadence
16. B stereotype
17. J pretentious
18. F ostentatious
19. A hypercritical
20. D irascible

p. 34 | Exercise 3: Sentence Completion

21. C
22. E
23. B
24. E
25. A
26. B
27. C
28. D
29. E
30. C

Lesson 9

p. 35 | Exercise 1: Wordbusting

NOTES
- For each Vocabulary Word, students should fill in at least one of the **context, structure,** and **sound** boxes.
- Check that students vary the boxes they use throughout the exercise.
- Make sure students look up each word in the dictionary and fill in the dictionary box; answers will vary depending on the dictionary used.

p. 37 | Exercise 2: Context Clues

11. F shrew
12. H lucrative
13. D garrulous
14. B abridge
15. I verbose
16. E invoke
17. J finality
18. A impromptu
19. G supercilious
20. C emendation

p. 38 | Exercise 3: Sentence Completion

21. C
22. A
23. E
24. D
25. C
26. A
27. D
28. B
29. E
30. A

Workshop Answer Key *(continued)*

Lesson 10

p. 39 | Exercise 1: Wordbusting

> **NOTES**
> - For each Vocabulary Word, students should fill in at least one of the **context**, **structure**, and **sound** boxes.
> - Check that students vary the boxes they use throughout the exercise.
> - Make sure students look up each word in the dictionary and fill in the dictionary box; answers will vary depending on the dictionary used.

p. 41 | Exercise 2: Context Clues

11. G intangible	**16.** C reciprocate
12. J idiomatic	**17.** H wistful
13. D expletive	**18.** E furor
14. B affable	**19.** I subterfuge
15. A bolster	**20.** F tawdry

p. 42 | Exercise 3: Sentence Completion

21. C	**26.** E
22. B	**27.** B
23. E	**28.** D
24. B	**29.** C
25. B	**30.** D

Lesson 11

p. 43 | Exercise 1: Wordbusting

> **NOTES**
> - For each Vocabulary Word, students should fill in at least one of the **context**, **structure**, and **sound** boxes.
> - Check that students vary the boxes they use throughout the exercise.
> - Make sure students look up each word in the dictionary and fill in the dictionary box; answers will vary depending on the dictionary used.

p. 45 | Exercise 2: Context Clues

11. E congenital	**16.** D sortie
12. A consensus	**17.** H betrothed
13. F interminable	**18.** C intrepid
14. J sallow	**19.** G beneficent
15. B repugnant	**20.** I ambivalent

p. 46 | Exercise 3: Sentence Completion

21. D	**26.** A
22. E	**27.** B
23. B	**28.** C
24. E	**29.** B
25. D	**30.** D

Lesson 12

p. 47 | Exercise 1: Wordbusting

> **NOTES**
> - For each Vocabulary Word, students should fill in at least one of the **context**, **structure**, and **sound** boxes.
> - Check that students vary the boxes they use throughout the exercise.
> - Make sure students look up each word in the dictionary and fill in the dictionary box; answers will vary depending on the dictionary used.

p. 49 | Exercise 2: Context Clues

11. C supplication	**16.** A frustrate
12. J resilient	**17.** H adamant
13. E factious	**18.** B procrastinate
14. G autocrat	**19.** F antagonize
15. I archives	**20.** D peremptory

p. 50 | Exercise 3: Sentence Completion

21. D	**26.** E
22. B	**27.** D
23. A	**28.** B
24. C	**29.** E
25. B	**30.** A

Lesson 13

p. 51 | Exercise 1: Wordbusting

> **NOTES**
> - For each Vocabulary Word, students should fill in at least one of the **context, structure,** and **sound** boxes.
> - Check that students vary the boxes they use throughout the exercise.
> - Make sure students look up each word in the dictionary and fill in the dictionary box; answers will vary depending on the dictionary used.

p. 53 | Exercise 2: Context Clues

11. D	incoherent	**16.** I	exonerate
12. G	provocation	**17.** J	secular
13. E	plebeian	**18.** C	expedite
14. A	incredulous	**19.** F	shibboleth
15. H	query	**20.** B	forgo

p. 54 | Exercise 3: Sentence Completion

21. B	**26.** C
22. E	**27.** D
23. B	**28.** A
24. D	**29.** E
25. B	**30.** D

Lesson 14

p. 55 | Exercise 1: Wordbusting

> **NOTES**
> - For each Vocabulary Word, students should fill in at least one of the **context, structure,** and **sound** boxes.
> - Check that students vary the boxes they use throughout the exercise.
> - Make sure students look up each word in the dictionary and fill in the dictionary box; answers will vary depending on the dictionary used.

p. 57 | Exercise 2: Context Clues

11. G	filial	**16.** J	remission
12. D	chagrin	**17.** B	interpose
13. H	cede	**18.** E	debonair
14. I	proficient	**19.** A	blithe
15. C	precipitate	**20.** F	intrinsic

p. 58 | Exercise 3: Sentence Completion

21. E	**26.** B
22. C	**27.** E
23. B	**28.** B
24. A	**29.** C
25. D	**30.** A

Lesson 15

p. 59 | Exercise 1: Wordbusting

> **NOTES**
> - For each Vocabulary Word, students should fill in at least one of the **context, structure,** and **sound** boxes.
> - Check that students vary the boxes they use throughout the exercise.
> - Make sure students look up each word in the dictionary and fill in the dictionary box; answers will vary depending on the dictionary used.

p. 61 | Exercise 2: Context Clues

11. E	palliate	**16.** B	acquiesce
12. G	assail	**17.** C	deprecate
13. D	altercation	**18.** A	beleaguer
14. H	phalanx	**19.** F	brunt
15. J	predecessor	**20.** I	redress

p. 62 | Exercise 3: Sentence Completion

21. C	**26.** B
22. B	**27.** E
23. E	**28.** D
24. A	**29.** A
25. D	**30.** C

Workshop Answer Key *(continued)*

Lesson 16

p. 63 | Exercise 1: Wordbusting

> **NOTES**
> - For each Vocabulary Word, students should fill in at least one of the **context, structure,** and **sound** boxes.
> - Check that students vary the boxes they use throughout the exercise.
> - Make sure students look up each word in the dictionary and fill in the dictionary box; answers will vary depending on the dictionary used.

p. 65 | Exercise 2: Context Clues

11. E coalition	**16.** D bulwark
12. I insidious	**17.** B exodus
13. A repression	**18.** J invidious
14. G peripheral	**19.** F waive
15. H martyr	**20.** C heinous

p. 66 | Exercise 3: Sentence Completion

21. B	**26.** C
22. D	**27.** C
23. C	**28.** E
24. E	**29.** E
25. A	**30.** B

Lesson 17

p. 67 | Exercise 1: Wordbusting

> **NOTES**
> - For each Vocabulary Word, students should fill in at least one of the **context, structure,** and **sound** boxes.
> - Check that students vary the boxes they use throughout the exercise.
> - Make sure students look up each word in the dictionary and fill in the dictionary box; answers will vary depending on the dictionary used.

p. 69 | Exercise 2: Context Clues

11. E derogatory	**16.** C oscillate
12. B convivial	**17.** D audacious
13. G deign	**18.** I epicure
14. A affinity	**19.** H ingratiate
15. F fastidious	**20.** J array

p. 70 | Exercise 3: Sentence Completion

21. C	**26.** A
22. A	**27.** E
23. D	**28.** B
24. B	**29.** C
25. D	**30.** D

Lesson 18

p. 71 | Exercise 1: Wordbusting

> **NOTES**
> - For each Vocabulary Word, students should fill in at least one of the **context, structure,** and **sound** boxes.
> - Check that students vary the boxes they use throughout the exercise.
> - Make sure students look up each word in the dictionary and fill in the dictionary box; answers will vary depending on the dictionary used.

p. 73 | Exercise 2: Context Clues

11. G flay	**16.** F imperious
12. B felony	**17.** J relent
13. C efficacious	**18.** E malevolent
14. D rationalize	**19.** I equestrian
15. A degenerate	**20.** H bandy

p. 74 | Exercise 3: Sentence Completion

21. C	**26.** B
22. D	**27.** A
23. A	**28.** D
24. E	**29.** E
25. D	**30.** C

Lesson 19

p. 75 | Exercise 1: Wordbusting

> **NOTES**
> - For each Vocabulary Word, students should fill in at least one of the **context, structure,** and **sound** boxes.
> - Check that students vary the boxes they use throughout the exercise.
> - Make sure students look up each word in the dictionary and fill in the dictionary box; answers will vary depending on the dictionary used.

p. 77 | Exercise 2: Context Clues

11. J purport	16. I allure
12. F demeanor	17. E auspicious
13. D syndicate	18. A immemorial
14. C abash	19. H deference
15. G guise	20. B integral

p. 78 | Exercise 3: Sentence Completion

21. B	26. B
22. D	27. C
23. B	28. C
24. A	29. A
25. D	30. C

Lesson 20

p. 79 | Exercise 1: Wordbusting

> **NOTES**
> - For each Vocabulary Word, students should fill in at least one of the **context, structure,** and **sound** boxes.
> - Check that students vary the boxes they use throughout the exercise.
> - Make sure students look up each word in the dictionary and fill in the dictionary box; answers will vary depending on the dictionary used.

p. 81 | Exercise 2: Context Clues

11. G contraband	16. C arbitrary
12. E politic	17. I transient
13. F inane	18. B premeditated
14. J proxy	19. D browbeat
15. A bureaucracy	20. H scapegoat

p. 82 | Exercise 3: Sentence Completion

21. D	26. E
22. B	27. B
23. C	28. A
24. E	29. C
25. C	30. B

Lesson 21

p. 83 | Exercise 1: Wordbusting

> **NOTES**
> - For each Vocabulary Word, students should fill in at least one of the **context, structure,** and **sound** boxes.
> - Check that students vary the boxes they use throughout the exercise.
> - Make sure students look up each word in the dictionary and fill in the dictionary box; answers will vary depending on the dictionary used.

p. 85 | Exercise 2: Context Clues

11. H vogue	16. C inherent
12. D faction	17. E fiord
13. G assay	18. I unremitting
14. F taint	19. B augment
15. A diverge	20. J subside

p. 86 | Exercise 3: Sentence Completion

21. D	26. A
22. C	27. D
23. E	28. C
24. B	29. A
25. E	30. E

Workshop Answer Key *(continued)*

Lesson 22

p. 87 | Exercise 1: Wordbusting

NOTES

- For each Vocabulary Word, students should fill in at least one of the **context, structure,** and **sound** boxes.
- Check that students vary the boxes they use throughout the exercise.
- Make sure students look up each word in the dictionary and fill in the dictionary box; answers will vary depending on the dictionary used.

p. 89 | Exercise 2: Context Clues

11. C	abstain	**16.** A	omnivorous
12. H	entomology	**17.** B	idyll
13. J	tepid	**18.** D	catharsis
14. I	prototype	**19.** G	dissipate
15. F	credence	**20.** E	entity

p. 90 | Exercise 3: Sentence Completion

21. E	**26.** D
22. B	**27.** A
23. C	**28.** E
24. C	**29.** C
25. B	**30.** C

Lesson 23

p. 91 | Exercise 1: Wordbusting

NOTES

- For each Vocabulary Word, students should fill in at least one of the **context, structure,** and **sound** boxes.
- Check that students vary the boxes they use throughout the exercise.
- Make sure students look up each word in the dictionary and fill in the dictionary box; answers will vary depending on the dictionary used.

p. 93 | Exercise 2: Context Clues

11. E	enormity	**16.** B	undermine
12. C	camaraderie	**17.** H	elation
13. A	apprise	**18.** D	austere
14. I	recrimination	**19.** F	correlate
15. J	exhaustive	**20.** G	bestow

p. 94 | Exercise 3: Sentence Completion

21. C	**26.** B
22. D	**27.** C
23. A	**28.** D
24. E	**29.** A
25. D	**30.** E

Lesson 24

p. 95 | Exercise 1: Wordbusting

NOTES

- For each Vocabulary Word, students should fill in at least one of the **context, structure,** and **sound** boxes.
- Check that students vary the boxes they use throughout the exercise.
- Make sure students look up each word in the dictionary and fill in the dictionary box; answers will vary depending on the dictionary used.

p. 97 | Exercise 2: Context Clues

11. H	furtive	**16.** D	rapacious
12. B	mercenary	**17.** E	recalcitrant
13. F	permeate	**18.** J	appraisal
14. I	accost	**19.** C	proletarian
15. A	populace	**20.** G	pernicious

p. 98 | Exercise 3: Sentence Completion

21. B	**26.** B
22. B	**27.** B
23. D	**28.** C
24. E	**29.** D
25. E	**30.** C

Workshop Answer Key *(continued)*

FIFTH COURSE

Lesson 25

p. 99 | Exercise 1: Wordbusting

NOTES
- For each Vocabulary Word, students should fill in at least one of the **context, structure,** and **sound** boxes.
- Check that students vary the boxes they use throughout the exercise.
- Make sure students look up each word in the dictionary and fill in the dictionary box; answers will vary depending on the dictionary used.

p. 101 | Exercise 2: Context Clues

11. E brusque
12. B microcosm
13. A acquisition
14. D debacle
15. G wily
16. J ulterior
17. I alleviate
18. F tenacity
19. H thwart
20. C rigorous

p. 102 | Exercise 3: Sentence Completion

21. B
22. A
23. B
24. D
25. D
26. A
27. A
28. B
29. D
30. C

Lesson 26

p. 103 | Exercise 1: Wordbusting

NOTES
- For each Vocabulary Word, students should fill in at least one of the **context, structure,** and **sound** boxes.
- Check that students vary the boxes they use throughout the exercise.
- Make sure students look up each word in the dictionary and fill in the dictionary box; answers will vary depending on the dictionary used.

p. 105 | Exercise 2: Context Clues

11. I impetuous
12. G synchronize
13. F arduous
14. A platitude
15. J insatiable
16. C grandiose
17. H enthrall
18. E sluice
19. B oracular
20. D deluge

p. 106 | Exercise 3: Sentence Completion

21. D
22. B
23. E
24. A
25. D
26. B
27. D
28. D
29. A
30. B

Lesson 27

p. 107 | Exercise 1: Wordbusting

NOTES
- For each Vocabulary Word, students should fill in at least one of the **context, structure,** and **sound** boxes.
- Check that students vary the boxes they use throughout the exercise.
- Make sure students look up each word in the dictionary and fill in the dictionary box; answers will vary depending on the dictionary used.

p. 109 | Exercise 2: Context Clues

11. B indolence
12. H wrest
13. G propagate
14. I contrition
15. C stint
16. J abate
17. D presumptuous
18. A protract
19. E effete
20. F inure

p. 110 | Exercise 3: Sentence Completion

21. C
22. E
23. E
24. C
25. E
26. B
27. A
28. C
29. E
30. B

ANSWER KEY

159

Workshop Answer Key *(continued)*

Lesson 28

p. 111 | Exercise 1: Wordbusting

NOTES
- For each Vocabulary Word, students should fill in at least one of the **context, structure,** and **sound** boxes.
- Check that students vary the boxes they use throughout the exercise.
- Make sure students look up each word in the dictionary and fill in the dictionary box; answers will vary depending on the dictionary used.

p. 113 | Exercise 2: Context Clues

11. H panacea		**16.** I innocuous
12. D fallible		**17.** F abominable
13. B concerted		**18.** C insular
14. J vilify		**19.** E vegetate
15. G encroach		**20.** A defile

p. 114 | Exercise 3: Sentence Completion

21. A	**26.** D
22. D	**27.** E
23. C	**28.** E
24. B	**29.** D
25. E	**30.** C

Lesson 29

p. 115 | Exercise 1: Wordbusting

NOTES
- For each Vocabulary Word, students should fill in at least one of the **context, structure,** and **sound** boxes.
- Check that students vary the boxes they use throughout the exercise.
- Make sure students look up each word in the dictionary and fill in the dictionary box; answers will vary depending on the dictionary used.

p. 117 | Exercise 2: Context Clues

11. G flail	**16.** F somnolent
12. I stoic	**17.** A entourage
13. B haggard	**18.** E bilateral
14. D vanquish	**19.** C impunity
15. J baleful	**20.** H attrition

p. 118 | Exercise 3: Sentence Completion

21. B	**26.** C
22. E	**27.** B
23. B	**28.** D
24. E	**29.** B
25. A	**30.** C

Lesson 30

p. 119 | Exercise 1: Wordbusting

NOTES
- For each Vocabulary Word, students should fill in at least one of the **context, structure,** and **sound** boxes.
- Check that students vary the boxes they use throughout the exercise.
- Make sure students look up each word in the dictionary and fill in the dictionary box; answers will vary depending on the dictionary used.

p. 121 | Exercise 2: Context Clues

11. H arable	**16.** I abut
12. G gird	**17.** C oriental
13. E incise	**18.** F indigenous
14. A gradation	**19.** B nurture
15. J askew	**20.** D solstice

p. 122 | Exercise 3: Sentence Completion

21. E	**26.** A
22. B	**27.** E
23. D	**28.** C
24. B	**29.** D
25. C	**30.** B

Connecting New Words and Patterns

Lesson 1

p. 126 | Analogies

1. (C); Classification. An *allegory* is classified as a *story*, just as a *ballad* is classified as a *song*.

2. (D); Antonym. *Comprehensive*, or complete, means the opposite of *limited*. *Narrow* and *wide* also have opposite meanings.

3. (C); Synonym. *Felicitous* and *appropriate* have similar meanings, as do *affluent* and *wealthy*.

4. (A); Characteristic Quality. A *lion* is characteristically *ferocious*, just as a *mouse* is characteristically *timid*.

5. (E); Antonym. *Incongruous*, which means lacking in harmony or agreement, means the opposite of *harmonious*, just as *reluctant*, or unwilling, means the opposite of *enthusiastic*.

6. (C); Synonym. *Intricacy* and *complexity* have nearly the same meaning, as do *commendation* and *praise*.

7. (C); Characteristic Quality. *Self-analysis* is by nature characteristically *introspective*, or inward-looking. A *mirror* is characteristically *reflective*.

8. (C); Part and Whole. A *prologue* is the first part of a *play*, as a *preamble* is the first part of a *constitution*.

9. (E); Classification. A *protagonist* is a type of *character* in a story, just as a *beagle* is a type of *dog*.

10. (C); Synonym. *Provocative* and *stimulating* have nearly the same meaning, as do *turbulent* and *stormy*.

Lesson 2

p. 127 | Analogies

1. (D); Synonym. *Brevity* and *shortness* have nearly the same meaning, as do *length* and *extent*.

2. (A); Function. The function of a *connotation*, an idea associated with a word or phrase, is to *suggest* something. In the same way, the function of an *implication* is to *indicate* something.

3. (E); Antonym. *Embellish*, which means decorate or improve by adding detail, means the opposite of *simplify*. *Agree* and *differ* are also opposite in meaning.

4. (C); Function. The function of an *epithet*, a descriptive name or title, is to *describe* someone, just as the function of a *solvent* is to *dissolve* something.

5. (A); Synonym. *Evoke*, which means call forth, has nearly the same meaning as *summon*. *Defy* and *resist* also have nearly the same meaning.

6. (B); Cause and Effect. To *foreshadow*, or hint at a story's outcome, can cause *anticipation*, just as to *exercise* can cause *strength*.

7. (E); Action and Related Object. You *imbibe*, or drink, a *beverage*, just as you *devour* a *pastry*.

8. (D); Characteristic Quality. *Virtue* is *laudable*, or praiseworthy, just as *gibberish* is *unintelligible*, or impossible to understand.

9. (B); Characteristic Quality. A *daydreamer* is characteristically *nostalgic*, or longing for the past, just as a *hero* is characteristically *brave*.

10. (A); Synonym. *Reiterate* and *repeat* have the same meaning, as do *dispense*, which means to hand out, or *distribute*.

Lesson 3

p. 128 | Analogies

1. (B); Characteristic Quality. An *anecdote*, or brief story, is characteristically *entertaining*, just as a *joke* is characteristically *amusing*.

2. (D); Synonym. *Assertion* and *claim* (as a noun) both have the same meaning, as do *beat* (as a noun) and *rhythm*.

3. (C); Characteristic Quality. The *finale*, or end of a show, is characteristically *climactic*, or most dramatic. In the same way, most people regard a *vacation* as characteristically *relaxing*.

4. (C); Antonym. *Coherent*, or clear, is opposite in meaning to *muddled*. *Fantastic* and *ordinary* also have opposite meanings.

5. (B); Antonym. A *forte*, someone's best skill or character strength, is opposite in meaning to *weakness*, just as *sturdiness* is opposite in meaning to *fragility*.

6. (A); Degree. *Fulminate*, which means denounce loudly, differs in degree but has a meaning similar to *disagree*, just as *enrage* and *annoy* have similar meanings but differ in degree.

7. (E); Antonym. *Goad*, which means urge on, is opposite in meaning to *restrain*, which means hold back. *Reward* and *punish* are also opposite in meaning.

8. (C); Characteristic Quality. A *mystery* is characteristically *inexplicable*, just as a *donor* is characteristically *generous*.

9. (B); Cause and Effect. A *stigma*, or mark of scorn, can cause *shame*, just as winning a *medal* can cause one to have *pride*.

10. (A); Synonym. *Surmise* and *guess* have nearly the same meaning, as do *disregard* and *ignore*.

Lesson 4

p. 129 | Analogies

1. (E); Part and Whole. A *consonant*, any letter that is not a vowel, is part of the *alphabet*, just as a *word* is part of a *sentence*.

2. (A); Cause and Effect. A *bad influence* can cause *decadence*, or moral decline, just as winning an *award* can be cause for *celebration*.

3. (D); Antonym. *Erroneous*, which means wrong, is opposite in meaning to *correct*. In the same way, *beautiful* and *ugly* are also opposites.

4. (B); Performer and Related Action. A *peacock flaunts*, or displays, its feathers, just as a *squirrel hoards* nuts.

5. (E); Synonym. *Gibe* and *jeer* have nearly the same meaning, as do *braid* and *interweave*.

6. (B); Degree. *Hypercritical* is a greater degree of *critical*, just as *loud* is a greater degree of *audible*.

7. (A); Synonym. *Irascible* and *irritable* have nearly the same meaning, as do *peaceful* and *harmonious*.

8. (D); Synonym. A *miscreant* is a *villain*, just as a *meddler* is a *busybody*.

9. (E); Degree. *Ostentatious* indicates a greater degree of showiness than *noticeable*. *Wrathful* indicates a greater degree of anger than *annoyed*.

10. (C); Antonym. *Pretentious* is opposite in meaning to *humble*, just as *generous* is opposite in meaning to *miserly*.

p. 130 | Analogies

1. (B); Action and Related Object. You *abridge*, or shorten, a *text*, just as you *shrink fabric*.

2. (B); Characteristic Quality. An *expletive*, or curse, is characteristically *profane*, just as a *tribute* is characteristically *complimentary*.

3. (C); Characteristic Quality. A *language* is characteristically *idiomatic*, just as *customs* are characteristically *traditional*.

4. (C); Synonym. *Impromptu* and *spontaneous* have nearly the same meaning, as do *contaminated* and *polluted*.

5. (E); Characteristic Quality. *Emotion* is characteristically *intangible*, or untouchable, and *light* is characteristically *luminous*, or radiant.

6. (B); Antonym. *Lucrative* and *unprofitable* are opposite in meaning, as are *skillful* and *awkward*.

7. (E); Characteristic Quality. A *shrew*, or irritable woman, is characteristically *bad-tempered*, just as a *miser* is characteristically *stingy*.

8. (D); Synonym. *Supercilious* and *haughty* both mean proud and scornful. *Superfluous* and *excessive* both mean more than is needed.

9. (E); Antonym. *Tawdry* and *tasteful* have opposite meanings, as do *customary* and *unusual*.

10. (C); Synonym. *Verbose* and *wordy* have the same meaning, as do *oral* and *spoken*.

p. 131 | Analogies

1. (D); Antonym. *Ambivalent* and *certain* are opposite in meaning, as are *absolute* and *conditional*.

2. (E); Location. *Documents* can be found in *archives*, just as *artwork* can be found in a *museum*.

3. (E); Classification. An *autocrat*, or dictator, is classified as a *ruler*, just as a *democracy* is classified as a *government*.

4. (C); Characteristic Quality. A *charity* is characteristically *beneficent*—that is, it does good. In the same way, a *sage* is a characteristically *wise* person.

5. (E); Degree. Being *betrothed* is a lesser degree of commitment than being *married*. Similarly, *groggy* is a lesser degree of relaxation than *asleep*.

6. (E); Synonym. *Congenital* and *inborn* have the same meaning, as do *temporary* and *impermanent*.

7. (C); Synonym. *Procrastinate* and *postpone* both mean to put off until another time. *Schedule* and *plan* also have the same meaning.

8. (E); Antonym. *Repugnant* and *attractive* are opposite in meaning, as are *reduced* and *enlarged*.

9. (A); Characteristic Quality. Someone who is *sick* is characteristically *sallow*, or grayish yellow, just as someone who is *healthy* is characteristically *bright-eyed*.

10. (B); Characteristic Quality. A *sortie*, or raid, is characteristically *sudden* and quick. An *attack* is characteristically *vigorous*.

Workshop Answer Key *(continued)*

Lesson 7

p. 132 | Analogies

1. (E); Synonym. *Blithe* and *happy* have nearly the same meaning, as do *thoughtful* and *considerate*.

2. (D); Antonym. *Cede*, which means surrender, means the opposite of *claim* (when *claim* is used as a noun), just as *agree* means the opposite of *dispute*.

3. (A); Performer and Related Action. A *jury exonerates*, or clears of blame, just as an *athlete competes*.

4. (B); Characteristic Quality. *Filial* behavior is characteristic of children, or *offspring*, just as a *father* is *paternal*, or fatherly.

5. (E); Synonym. *Interpose* and *interject* both mean to put in between. *Repose* and *recline* both mean to rest or lie back.

6. (A); Synonym. *Precipitate* (as an adjective) and *sudden* have nearly the same meaning, as do *profound* and *deep*.

7. (C); Antonym. *Proficient*, or competent, means the opposite of *unskilled*, just as *childish* means the opposite of *mature*.

8. (C); Cause and Effect. A *query*, or inquiry, can lead to a *response*, just as a *puncture* can lead to a *leak*.

9. (D); Cause and Effect. *Remission*, which can mean forgiveness of sins or lessening of pain or disease, can cause *relief*, just as a *fire* can cause *warmth*.

10. (C); Antonym. *Secular* and *religious* have opposite meanings, as do *passive* and *active*.

Lesson 8

p. 133 | Analogies

1. (A); Synonym. An *altercation* is the same thing as a *quarrel*, just as an *obligation* is the same thing as a *duty*.

2. (D); Degree. *Assail* suggests a greater degree of attack than *confront*, just as *demolish* suggests a greater degree of destruction than *damage*.

3. (B); Part and Whole. A *brunt*, or a heavy blow, is part of an *attack*, just as a *point* is part of an *argument*.

4. (A); Part and Whole or Location. A *bulwark*, or fortified wall, is part of a *fortress*, or can be found in one, just as a *seawall* is part of a *harbor* or can be found at one.

5. (B); Degree. *Heinous*, which means evil or wicked, has a meaning similar to *bad* but to a greater degree. In the same way, *sweltering*, which means very hot and sultry, has a meaning similar to *warm* but to a greater degree.

6. (D); Antonym. *Insidious*, or devious, is opposite in meaning to *straightforward*. *Attractive* and *repulsive* also have opposite meanings.

7. (B); Synonym. *Invidious*, which means giving offense, means the same as *offensive*. *Haughty* and *proud* also have the same meaning.

8. (C); Performer and Related Action. A *martyr suffers*, and a *poet writes*.

9. (D); Part and Whole. A *soldier* is part of a *phalanx*, or military formation, just as a *cow* is part of a *herd*.

10. (A); Antonym. *Repression*, to control or suppress, is the opposite in meaning to *freedom*. In the same way, *drought*, the absence of rain, is opposite to *moisture*.

Workshop Answer Key *(continued)*

Lesson 9

p. 134 | Analogies

1. **(B); Antonym.** *Affinity*, or attraction, is opposite in meaning to *repulsion*. *Virtue* and *vice* are also opposite in meaning.

2. **(B); Synonym.** *Array* (when it is used as a noun referring to clothing) and *finery* have nearly the same meaning, as do *act* and *deed*.

3. **(D); Characteristic Quality.** A *pirate* is characteristically *audacious*, or bold and daring. In the same way, a *rustler*, or thief of livestock, is characteristically *dishonest*.

4. **(C); Action and Related Object.** You *bandy*, or throw around, *words*, just as you *toss balls*.

5. **(C); Performer and Related Action.** A *queen* may *deign*, or condescend, to shake her subject's hand, just as a *governor* might *pardon* a criminal.

6. **(C); Characteristic Quality.** An *insult* is *derogatory*, or belittling, just as *praise* is *complimentary*.

7. **(A); Synonym.** *Efficacious* and *effective* have the same meaning, as do *beneficial* and *good*.

8. **(D); Performer and Related Object.** An *epicure* is someone who appreciates fine *food*, just as a *fashion designer* appreciates fine *clothing*.

9. **(A); Antonym.** *Imperious*, which means overbearing and arrogant, is opposite in meaning to *meek*. *Wild* and *tame* are also opposite in meaning.

10. **(E); Antonym.** *Ingratiate*, which means to win approval, is opposite in meaning to *offend*. *Resist* and *submit* are also opposite in meaning.

Lesson 10

p. 135 | Analogies

1. **(E); Synonym.** *Auspicious* and *favorable* have nearly the same meaning, as do *conspicuous* and *obvious*.

2. **(B); Part and Whole.** *Departments* are part of a *bureaucracy*, just as *stores* are part of a *mall*.

3. **(D); Synonym.** *Demeanor* and *behavior* have the same meaning, as do *faith* and *belief*.

4. **(A); Performer and Related Object.** An *impostor* uses a *guise* to disguise himself or herself, just as *troops* use *camouflage* to hide.

5. **(B); Antonym.** *Inane* and *meaningful* are opposite in meaning, as are *remote* (as an adjective) and *nearby*.

6. **(E); Synonym.** *Transient* and *temporary* are similar in meaning just as are *courageous* and *brave*.

7. **(B); Synonym.** *Politic* and *shrewd* both mean crafty or clever. *Transparent* has the same meaning as *clear*.

8. **(A); Antonym.** *Premeditated*, which means planned in advance, is opposite in meaning to *spontaneous*, which means unplanned. *Simple* and *sophisticated* are also opposite in meaning.

9. **(C); Synonym.** *Purport* and *claim* (when claim is a verb) have nearly the same meaning, as do *suppose* and *assume*.

10. **(C); Performer and Related Action.** One expects a *scapegoat* to *suffer*, just as one expects a *bodyguard* to *protect*.

Workshop Answer Key *(continued)*

Lesson 11

p. 136 | Analogies

1. (A); Action and Related Object. One can *augment*, or enlarge, a *plan*, just as legislators can *pass* a *law*.

2. (E); Synonym. *Dissipate* and *scatter* have nearly the same meaning, as do *change* (when *change* is a verb) and *alter*.

3. (D); Antonym. *Diverge* and *merge* have opposite meanings, as do *divorce* and *marry*.

4. (E); Classification. *Entomology*, the study of insects, is classified as a *science*. In the same way, *poetry* is classified as *literature*.

5. (D); Synonym. *Faction* and *group* have nearly the same meaning, as do *gathering* and *congregation*.

6. (A); Classification. A *fiord* is classified as an *inlet*, just as an *apple* is classified as a *fruit*.

7. (B); Characteristic Quality. *Bears* are characteristically *omnivorous*, which means that they eat both animals and plants, just as *zebras* are characteristically *striped*.

8. (C); Antonym. *Subside* and *increase* have opposite meanings, as do *shrink* and *swell*.

9. (C); Degree. *Tepid*, or lukewarm, is less hot than *hot*, just as *cool* is less cold than *cold*.

10. (C); Synonym. *Vogue* and *fashion* have nearly the same meaning, as do *hazard* and *danger*.

Lesson 12

p. 137 | Analogies

1. (C); Performer and Related Action. A *bully accosts*, just as a *security guard patrols*.

2. (E); Synonym. An *appraisal*, or estimate of value, is the same thing as a *valuation*. A *union* is the same thing as a *merger*.

3. (B); Synonym. *Correlate* and *relate* have similar meanings, as do *correct* and *rectify*.

4. (D); Antonym. *Exhaustive*, which means thorough, is opposite in meaning to *superficial*. *Full* and *partial* also have opposite meanings.

5. (B); Characteristic Quality. A *thief* is characteristically *furtive*, or secretive, just as a *clown* is characteristically *funny*.

6. (B); Synonym. *Permeate* and *penetrate* have similar meanings, as do *ooze* and *seep*.

7. (B); Degree. *Rapacious* is more extreme in degree than *selfish*, just as *violent* is more extreme in degree than *aggressive*.

8. (D); Degree. *Recalcitrant*, or uncooperative, suggests a greater degree of unwillingness than *reluctant*, just as *delighted* suggests a greater degree of pleasure than *satisfied*.

9. (A); Cause and Effect. *Recrimination*, or counteraccusation, can be the effect of an *accusation*, just as an *injury* can be the effect of an *accident*.

10. (E); Synonym. *Undermine*, or to remove underlying support, is similar in meaning to *erosion*. In the same way, *modest* and *humble* are similar in meaning.

Lesson 13

p. 138 | Analogies

1. (E); Part and Whole. An *acquisition*—something that is acquired—is part of a *collection*, just as a *member* is part of a *sorority*.

2. (E); Antonym. A *debacle*, or failure, is the opposite of a *success*, just as *contraction* is the opposite of *expansion*.

3. (C); Synonym. *Enthrall* and *spellbind* have the same meaning, as do *sway* and *influence*.

4. (E); Characteristic Quality. A *microcosm* is a small part that is characteristically *representative* of the whole. A *flag* is characteristically *symbolic*.

5. (E); Characteristic Quality. A *platitude* is a commonplace, or *trite*, remark, just as a *pet name* is an *affectionate* name.

6. (C); Synonym. *Rigorous* and *strict* have similar meanings, as do *crucial* and *important*.

7. (D); Synonym. *Synchronize* and *coordinate* have nearly the same meaning, as do *match* and *correspond*.

8. (B); Antonym. *Thwart*, which means prevent, is opposite in meaning to *assist*, just as *clasp* is opposite in meaning to *release*.

9. (A); Synonym. *Ulterior*, or hidden, means the same as *undisclosed*, just as *interior* means the same as *internal*.

10. (D); Characteristic Quality. A *trickster* is characteristically *wily*, or crafty, just as a *ball* is characteristically *round*.

Lesson 14

p. 139 | Analogies

1. (A); Synonym. *Abate* and *lessen* have nearly the same meaning, as do *swell* and *increase*.

2. (B); Synonym. *Contrition* and *remorse* both mean sorrow for doing wrong. *Sensation* and *feeling* (as a noun) also have the same meaning.

3. (D); Antonym. *Defile* and *purify* have opposite meanings, as do *pollute* and *cleanse*.

4. (A); Performer and Related Action. An *intruder* is someone who *encroaches*, or intrudes, just as a *thief* is someone who *steals*.

5. (A); Antonym. *Fallible* and *perfect* are opposite in meaning, as are *famous* and *unknown*.

6. (D); Antonym. *Innocuous*, or harmless, means the opposite of *lethal*, just as *tardy*, or late, means the opposite of *early*.

7. (D); Synonym. A *panacea* is a *cure-all*, just as an *antidote* is a *remedy*.

8. (B); Synonym. *Protract* and *lengthen* have the same meaning, as do *shorten* and *abbreviate*.

9. (A); Performer and Related Action. A *slanderer vilifies*, or uses defaming language, just as a *criminal victimizes*.

10. (D); Performer and Related Action. A *purse snatcher wrests* purses from their owners, just as a *batter swings*.

Workshop Answer Key *(continued)*

Lesson 15

p. 140 | Analogies

1. (E); Synonym. *Abut* and *adjoin* both have the same meaning, as do *liberate* and *release*.

2. (A); Characteristic Quality. A *garden* is characteristically *arable*, or able to support plants, just as a *quicksand* is characteristically *treacherous*.

3. (A); Characteristic Quality. A *gradation*, or gentle increase or incline, is *gradual*, just as an *aggravation* is *annoying*.

4. (C); Synonym. *Incise* and *carve* have nearly the same meaning, as do *snare* and *catch*.

5. (D); Antonym. *Indigenous*, or native, means the opposite of *exotic*. *Foreign* and *familiar* are also opposite in meaning.

6. (E); Performer and Related Action. One expects a *parent* to *nurture*, or care for children, just as one expects a *general* to *command* an army.

7. (E); Function. The function of a *map* is to *orient*, or guide a traveler, just as the function of an *oven* is to *bake*.

8. (D); Part and Whole. The *solstice* is a part of *summer*, just as *Tuesday* is part of the *week*.

9. (E); Characteristic Quality. A *stoic* is characteristically *unexcitable*, just as an *eccentric* is characteristically *unusual*.

10. (B); Performer and Related Action. *Conquerors vanquish*, or defeat their foes, just as *instigators initiate*, or begin, something.

Reading New Words in Context

Lesson 1

p. 145 | Exercise 1: Finding Synonyms

Answers will vary. The following are possible responses.

1. inconsistency
2. main character
3. emphasize
4. a story that has symbolic meaning
5. inclusive
6. vague
7. complex
8. appropriate
9. degenerate; depraved
10. concise
11. verbose (or longwinded)
12. preliminary reason
13. contemplative; deep-thinking
14. fierceness
15. overthrow
16. contemptible
17. a person who hates all people
18. dialect; spoken language
19. guesswork; inference
20. stimulating

p. 146 | Exercise 2: Reading Strategically

1. A
2. C
3. B
4. E
5. B
6. D
7. A
8. C
9. E
10. B
11. E
12. C
13. D
14. D
15. C
16. A
17. B
18. E
19. D
20. E

Workshop Answer Key *(continued)*

Lesson 2

p. 150 | Exercise 1: Finding Synonyms

Answers will vary. The following are possible responses.

1. conference or collection of essays
2. closely examine
3. elusive; slippery
4. clear
5. amateur; inexperienced
6. draw as a conclusion
7. salary
8. wealthy
9. briefness
10. a descriptive name
11. teasing
12. praiseworthy
13. adorn; decorate
14. suggest something beforehand
15. extend the presence of
16. something past or far away
17. drink; take in
18. a suggested meaning
19. call forth
20. restate

p. 151 | Exercise 2: Reading Strategically

1. C
2. A
3. B
4. E
5. A
6. D
7. B
8. E
9. B
10. C
11. C
12. A
13. C
14. B
15. B
16. A
17. D
18. C
19. C
20. A

Lesson 3

p. 157 | Exercise 1: Finding Synonyms

Answers will vary. The following are possible responses.

1. brief story
2. claim
3. strong point
4. prod
5. unexplainable
6. someone who complains about imaginary ills
7. neutral
8. firm
9. nose
10. culminating; most important
11. mark of shame
12. denounce; explode violently
13. in a logically connected way
14. conclusion; afterword
15. guess
16. improvised
17. rearrangement of letters in a to word make another word
18. faithfulness
19. highly gifted person
20. idealistic

p. 158 | Exercise 2: Reading Strategically

1. D
2. B
3. A
4. E
5. A
6. D
7. C
8. B
9. B
10. E
11. A
12. D
13. B
14. C
15. E
16. C
17. A
18. C
19. C
20. B

Workshop Answer Key (continued)

Lesson 4

p. 163 | Exercise 1: Finding Synonyms

Answers will vary. The following are possible responses.

1. incorrect
2. overly showy
3. overly generalized view
4. affected
5. show off
6. a first principle
7. moral decay
8. criminal
9. support
10. harmonious
11. irritable
12. inferior
13. attractive
14. pushy
15. lively
16. comebacks
17. satisfy
18. overly severe in judgment
19. quote
20. taunt

p. 164 | Exercise 2: Reading Strategically

1. C
2. B
3. E
4. C
5. A
6. D
7. B
8. E
9. A
10. C
11. B
12. D
13. B
14. E
15. A
16. C
17. D
18. C
19. D
20. B

Lesson 5

p. 168 | Exercise 1: Finding Synonyms

Answers will vary. The following are possible responses.

1. deception
2. uproar
3. profitable
4. haughty
5. reinforce
6. bad-tempered woman
7. condense
8. correction
9. gaudy; cheaply showy
10. abstract
11. friendly
12. returned
13. yearning
14. spontaneous
15. call upon
16. curse
17. decisiveness
18. characteristic of a particular language
19. wordy
20. talkative

p. 169 | Exercise 2: Reading Strategically

1. E
2. C
3. A
4. B
5. D
6. B
7. A
8. B
9. E
10. A
11. C
12. C
13. B
14. D
15. D
16. A
17. C
18. B
19. E
20. C

Lesson 6

p. 174 | Exercise 1: Finding Synonyms

Answers will vary. The following are possible responses.

1. discourage
2. generosity
3. humble request
4. inborn
5. arrogant; dictatorial
6. general agreement
7. dictatorial
8. unyielding
9. delay
10. courageous; determined
11. mixed; conflicting
12. dissenting; quarrelsome
13. unending
14. sickly pale; grayish yellow
15. disgusting
16. buoyant; springing back into shape
17. angered
18. place where historical records are kept
19. a raid on attackers
20. engaged

p. 175 | Exercise 2: Reading Strategically

1. C
2. C
3. B
4. C
5. A
6. D
7. E
8. A
9. A
10. C
11. D
12. B
13. A
14. B
15. B
16. A
17. C
18. D
19. D
20. C

Workshop Answer Key *(continued)*

Lesson 7

p. 180 | Exercise 1: Finding Synonyms

Answers will vary. The following are possible responses.

1. essential
2. skeptical; unbelieving
3. incitement
4. hasten
5. ask
6. do without
7. skillful; fully qualified
8. embarrassment
9. charming
10. intervene
11. password
12. common; vulgar; crude
13. lessening
14. cheerful
15. worldly
16. expected of a child
17. absolve
18. yield
19. hasten
20. unintelligible

p. 181 | Exercise 2: Reading Strategically

1. B
2. B
3. A
4. E
5. B
6. D
7. C
8. A
9. E
10. B
11. A
12. D
13. B
14. C
15. A
16. B
17. C
18. E
19. A
20. B

Lesson 8

p. 186 | Exercise 1: Finding Synonyms

Answers will vary. The following are possible responses.

1. mass departure
2. attack
3. vile; wicked
4. largest part
5. relinquish
6. outer; nonessential
7. offensive
8. hateful
9. disapprove of
10. person who precedes
11. surrounded
12. a united group of individuals
13. give in
14. remedy; rectify
15. protector; supporter
16. fight
17. one who dies for a cause
18. relieve; ease
19. suppression; constraint
20. alliance

p. 187 | Exercise 2: Reading Strategically

1. C
2. B
3. E
4. E
5. A
6. C
7. C
8. D
9. A
10. C
11. B
12. B
13. D
14. A
15. C
16. D
17. C
18. C
19. C
20. A

Lesson 9

p. 192 | Exercise 1: Finding Synonyms

Answers will vary. The following are possible responses.

1. bold; insolent
2. natural attraction
3. effective
4. explain away
5. dress
6. exchange jokes
7. bring into favor
8. overbearing
9. serious crime
10. criticize severely
11. belittling
12. give in
13. pertaining to horses
14. condescend
15. a lover of fine food and drink
16. malicious
17. depraved; corrupt
18. jovial; lively
19. particular; finicky
20. waver

p. 193 | Exercise 2: Reading Strategically

1. A
2. C
3. D
4. D
5. E
6. B
7. A
8. B
9. C
10. E
11. C
12. A
13. D
14. B
15. C
16. A
17. B
18. D
19. E
20. C

Lesson 10

p. 199 | Exercise 1: Finding Synonyms

Answers will vary. The following are possible responses.

1. bearing
2. someone who is blamed for another's crimes
3. smuggled goods
4. senseless; stupid
5. intimidate
6. false appearance
7. a group that bands together to carry on business
8. claim
9. to make ashamed
10. planned ahead
11. a person who stands in for another
12. temporary
13. whimsical
14. central; essential
15. shrewd
16. respect
17. attraction
18. promising
19. the administration of government through departments
20. before memory

p. 200 | Exercise 2: Reading Strategically

1. D
2. B
3. C
4. A
5. B
6. D
7. C
8. E
9. D
10. C
11. B
12. A
13. E
14. E
15. B
16. D
17. D
18. D
19. C
20. A

Lesson 11

p. 204 | Exercise 1: Finding Synonyms

Answers will vary. The following are possible responses.

1. fashion
2. model
3. a subgroup
4. a being
5. move away from
6. a person who studies insects
7. a narrow, steep-sided inlet
8. emotional purification
9. increase
10. believability
11. refrain
12. contaminate; stain
13. eating both plants and animals
14. abate
15. test
16. innate
17. a work about a pastoral scene
18. incessant
19. scattering
20. lukewarm

p. 205 | Exercise 2: Reading Strategically

1. B
2. C
3. E
4. B
5. B
6. D
7. C
8. A
9. D
10. C
11. A
12. E
13. E
14. C
15. B
16. C
17. E
18. D
19. A
20. D

Lesson 12

p. 211 | Exercise 1: Finding Synonyms

Answers will vary. The following are possible responses.

1. thorough
2. the masses
3. spread throughout
4. incapacitate; disable
5. inform
6. to show the relationship between
7. deadly
8. great wickedness
9. countercharge
10. to approach aggressively
11. careful; prudent
12. motivated by a desire for money
13. assessment
14. greedy
15. joy
16. plain; ascetic
17. working class
18. friendship
19. secretive
20. to present

p. 212 | Exercise 2: Reading Strategically

1. D
2. A
3. E
4. D
5. C
6. B
7. A
8. C
9. C
10. E
11. B
12. A
13. C
14. E
15. D
16. A
17. B
18. E
19. D
20. C

Workshop Answer Key *(continued)*

Lesson 13

p. 216 | Exercise 1: Finding Synonyms

Answers will vary. The following are possible responses.

1. sly; crafty
2. undisclosed
3. overused saying
4. miniature world
5. difficult; demanding
6. coordinate
7. total collapse
8. captivated
9. persistence
10. unquenchable
11. act of obtaining
12. difficult to do; steep
13. prophet
14. relieve
15. overly grand
16. furiously moving
17. heavy rainfall
18. channel
19. defeat
20. abrupt; blunt

p. 217 | Exercise 2: Reading Strategically

1. D
2. C
3. B
4. C
5. A
6. D
7. C
8. C
9. E
10. B
11. B
12. A
13. E
14. B
15. C
16. D
17. A
18. C
19. D
20. D

Lesson 14

p. 223 | Exercise 1: Finding Synonyms

Answers will vary. The following are possible responses.

1. intrude
2. remorse; regret
3. capable of mistakes
4. arrogant
5. without impact
6. pull; twist
7. combined
8. reproduce
9. island-like; isolated
10. lessen
11. lead an inactive life
12. job; task
13. horrid
14. long-term
15. lazy
16. sterile
17. cure-all
18. spoiled; fouled
19. accustomed
20. condemned

p. 224 | Exercise 2: Reading Strategically

1. C
2. A
3. D
4. E
5. B
6. E
7. C
8. A
9. C
10. C
11. D
12. E
13. B
14. A
15. B
16. D
17. C
18. A
19. B
20. E

Lesson 15

p. 228 | Exercise 1: Finding Synonyms

Answers will vary. The following are possible responses.

1. to adjust; to position
2. crooked
3. gaunt
4. sleepy
5. first day of summer
6. impassive
7. defeated
8. native to the region
9. border
10. cultivatable
11. surrounding
12. care for
13. attendants
14. gradual reduction
15. beating
16. freedom from punishment
17. cut
18. threatening
19. gradual change
20. mutually binding

p. 229 | Exercise 2: Reading Strategically

1. B
2. D
3. E
4. B
5. C
6. D
7. D
8. C
9. A
10. E
11. B
12. C
13. E
14. A
15. D
16. B
17. C
18. A
19. D
20. D

Fifth Course | *Vocabulary Workshop*

Tests Answer Key

Formative Assessment

p. 3 | Test 1

1. A	**6.** E
2. A	**7.** A
3. D	**8.** A
4. C	**9.** A
5. D	**10.** D

p. 4 | Test 2

1. A	**6.** A
2. D	**7.** B
3. C	**8.** D
4. B	**9.** B
5. A	**10.** E

p. 5 | Test 3

1. A	**6.** B
2. A	**7.** D
3. B	**8.** E
4. B	**9.** C
5. C	**10.** D

p. 6 | Test 4

1. E	**6.** A
2. C	**7.** B
3. B	**8.** C
4. B	**9.** C
5. E	**10.** D

p. 7 | Test 5

1. B	**6.** B
2. A	**7.** E
3. D	**8.** E
4. B	**9.** C
5. E	**10.** C

p. 8 | Test 6

1. D	**6.** C
2. D	**7.** A
3. D	**8.** A
4. C	**9.** D
5. B	**10.** B

p. 9 | Test 7

1. C	**6.** C
2. A	**7.** A
3. B	**8.** E
4. B	**9.** D
5. C	**10.** B

p. 10 | Test 8

1. A	**6.** E
2. C	**7.** E
3. D	**8.** D
4. C	**9.** A
5. B	**10.** B

p. 11 | Test 9

1. C	**6.** C
2. D	**7.** A
3. D	**8.** B
4. C	**9.** E
5. D	**10.** B

p. 12 | Test 10

1. B	**6.** D
2. B	**7.** C
3. A	**8.** E
4. A	**9.** C
5. A	**10.** A

p. 13 | Test 11

1. A	**6.** D
2. C	**7.** A
3. C	**8.** A
4. A	**9.** D
5. D	**10.** E

p. 14 | Test 12

1. E	**6.** A
2. C	**7.** E
3. B	**8.** B
4. B	**9.** E
5. D	**10.** C

Tests Answer Key *(continued)*

p. 15 | Test 13

1. D	6. B
2. B	7. C
3. B	8. E
4. E	9. A
5. D	10. D

p. 16 | Test 14

1. C	6. A
2. D	7. D
3. B	8. C
4. D	9. E
5. D	10. D

p. 17 | Test 15

1. A	6. A
2. B	7. E
3. D	8. C
4. E	9. A
5. D	10. A

p. 18 | Test 16

1. E	6. E
2. C	7. B
3. B	8. D
4. C	9. D
5. C	10. A

p. 19 | Test 17

1. B	6. E
2. B	7. C
3. D	8. B
4. A	9. A
5. C	10. C

p. 20 | Test 18

1. A	6. A
2. D	7. D
3. E	8. D
4. B	9. D
5. B	10. A

p. 21 | Test 19

1. C	6. B
2. A	7. C
3. B	8. B
4. E	9. A
5. C	10. A

p. 22 | Test 20

1. A	6. D
2. E	7. C
3. D	8. D
4. A	9. C
5. B	10. D

p. 23 | Test 21

1. D	6. B
2. C	7. C
3. C	8. D
4. C	9. D
5. B	10. B

p. 24 | Test 22

1. B	6. B
2. D	7. C
3. E	8. C
4. B	9. D
5. C	10. A

p. 25 | Test 23

1. A	6. B
2. C	7. E
3. B	8. B
4. C	9. A
5. B	10. B

p. 26 | Test 24

1. A	6. B
2. B	7. B
3. C	8. C
4. E	9. C
5. E	10. C

p. 27 | Test 25

1. B	6. B
2. D	7. A
3. A	8. D
4. B	9. C
5. C	10. E

p. 28 | Test 26

1. D	6. E
2. D	7. D
3. A	8. C
4. C	9. A
5. A	10. B

p. 29 | Test 27

1. A	6. C
2. C	7. E
3. D	8. B
4. E	9. C
5. C	10. A

p. 30 | Test 28

1. B	6. A
2. B	7. E
3. C	8. A
4. D	9. D
5. B	10. C

p. 31 | Test 29

1. C	6. A
2. E	7. B
3. C	8. A
4. E	9. B
5. D	10. B

p. 32 | Test 30

1. D	6. D
2. B	7. A
3. C	8. E
4. C	9. B
5. B	10. B

Summative Assessment

p. 35 | Test 1 Part A

1. C	14. C
2. A	15. A
3. D	16. B
4. E	17. D
5. B	18. C
6. D	19. A
7. A	20. D
8. C	21. A
9. C	22. C
10. A	23. B
11. D	24. B
12. E	25. E
13. D	

p. 39 | Test 1 Part B

26. C	49. E
27. E	50. D
28. E	51. A
29. E	52. D
30. C	53. C
31. E	54. E
32. B	55. A
33. D	56. B
34. A	57. A
35. C	58. B
36. C	59. C
37. A	60. B
38. C	61. D
39. C	62. D
40. A	63. C
41. D	64. E
42. C	65. B
43. B	66. D
44. E	67. C
45. C	68. C
46. E	69. A
47. E	70. B
48. B	

Tests Answer Key *(continued)*

p. 44 | Test 1 Part C

71. (C); Synonym. *Agree* and *consent* have similar meanings, as do *fulminate*, which means denounce loudly, and *scold*.

72. (C); Classification. An *allegory* is classified as a *story*, just as a *ballad* is classified as a *song*.

73. (B); Characteristic Quality. An *anecdote*, or brief story, is characteristically *entertaining*, just as a *joke* is characteristically *amusing*.

74. (E); Characteristic Quality. *Assurance* is characteristically *comforting*, just as a *shrew*, or irritable woman, is characteristically *bad-tempered*.

75. (B); Antonym. *Bolster*, or strengthen, means the opposite of *undermine*, or weaken. *Hinder* and *encourage* are also opposite in meaning.

76. (E); Synonym. *Braid* and *interweave* have nearly the same meaning, as do *gibe* and *jeer*.

77. (C); Cause and Effect. *Joy* can cause *celebration*, just as *corruption* can cause *decadence*.

78. (C); Characteristic Quality. A *peak* is characteristically *climactic*, just as a *conclusion* is characteristically *final*.

79. (C); Antonym. *Consonant* and *vowel* have opposite meanings, as do *capital* and *lowercase*.

80. (A); Synonym. *Defy* and *resist* have nearly the same meaning. *Evoke*, which means call forth, has nearly the same meaning as *summon*.

81. (D); Characteristic Quality. A *villain* is characteristically *despicable*, just as a *model* is characteristically *photogenic*.

82. (A); Synonym. *Disregard* and *ignore* have nearly the same meaning, as do *surmise* and *guess*.

83. (B); Characteristic Quality. An *expletive*, or curse, is characteristically *profane*, just as a *tribute* is characteristically *complimentary*.

84. (A); Characteristic Quality. A *lion* is characteristically *ferocious*, just as a *mouse* is characteristically *timid*.

85. (C); Action and Object. You can *goad*, or urge, *oxen*, just as you can *poke cattle*.

86. (E); Antonym. *Incongruous*, which means lacking in harmony or agreement, means the opposite of *harmonious*, just as *reluctant*, or unwilling, means the opposite of *enthusiastic*.

87. (D); Degree. *Jealous* means *envious* to a greater degree. *Ostentatious* suggests a greater degree of showiness than does *conspicuous*.

88. (D); Synonym. A *meddler* is the same as a *busybody*, just as a *miscreant* is the same as a *villain*.

89. (A); Synonym. *Peaceful* and *harmonious* have nearly the same meaning, as do *irascible* and *irritable*.

90. (C); Part and Whole. A *preamble* is the first part of a *constitution*, as a *prologue* is the first part of a *play*.

91. (C); Antonym. *Pretentious* is opposite in meaning to *humble*, just as *generous* is opposite in meaning to *miserly*.

92. (E); Synonym. *Prodigy* and *genius* have similar meanings, as do *disaster* and *devastation*.

93. (A); Part and Whole. A *protagonist* is part of a *novel*, just as a *dancer* is part of a *ballet*.

94. (C); Characteristic Quality. A *rhetorical* speech is characteristically *flowery*, just as *inclement* weather is characteristically *stormy*.

95. (C); Action and Object. You can *satiate*, or satisfy, an *appetite*, just as you can *quench* a *thirst*.

96. (D); Antonym. *Stereotypical* means the opposite of *original*, just as *despondent*, or hopeless, means the opposite of *joyful*.

97. (B); Cause and Effect. A *stigma*, or mark of scorn, can cause *shame*, just as a *medal* can cause *pride*.

98. (D); Synonym. *Superfluous* and *excessive* both mean more than is needed. *Supercilious* and *haughty* both mean proud and scornful.

99. (E); Antonym. *Tawdry* and *tasteful* have opposite meanings, as do *customary* and *unusual*.

100. (E); Synonym. *Usurp* and *seize* have similar meanings as do *subside* and *decrease*.

p. 47 | Test 2 Part A

1. D	**14.** D
2. B	**15.** A
3. C	**16.** C
4. A	**17.** E
5. B	**18.** B
6. D	**19.** D
7. A	**20.** B
8. E	**21.** B
9. C	**22.** A
10. E	**23.** B
11. C	**24.** C
12. B	**25.** C
13. B	

p. 51 | Test 2 Part B

26. D	**49.** C
27. E	**50.** C
28. A	**51.** B
29. B	**52.** A
30. A	**53.** E
31. C	**54.** E
32. D	**55.** A
33. D	**56.** A
34. B	**57.** B
35. D	**58.** D
36. D	**59.** B
37. E	**60.** D
38. D	**61.** B
39. C	**62.** C
40. A	**63.** A
41. E	**64.** E
42. B	**65.** E
43. C	**66.** B
44. D	**67.** A
45. C	**68.** D
46. B	**69.** B
47. B	**70.** A
48. A	

p. 56 | Test 2 Part C

71. (D); Degree. *Assail* suggests a greater degree of attack than *confront*, just as *demolish* suggests a greater degree of destruction than *damage*.

72. (E); Classification. An *autocrat*, or dictator, is classified as a *ruler*, just as *democracy* is classified as a *government*.

73. (A); Synonym. *Betrothed* and *engaged* have the same meaning, as do *finished* and *completed*.

74. (A); Part and Whole or Location. A *breakwater* is part of a *harbor* or can be found at one, just as a *bulwark*, or fortified wall, is part of a *fortress*, or can be found in one.

75. (B); Part and Whole. A *brunt* is part of a *blow*, just as a *thrust*, in the sense of a main point, is part of an *argument*.

76. (B); Part and Whole. *Departments* are part of a *bureaucracy*, just as *stores* are part of a *mall*.

77. (D); Antonym. *Cede*, which means surrender, means the opposite of *claim* (when claim is used as a verb), just as *agree* means the opposite of *dispute*.

78. (C); Characteristic Quality. *Praise* is *complimentary*, just as *insult* is *derogatory*, or belittling.

79. (E); Synonym. *Congenital* and *inherited* have the same meaning, as do *persuasive* and *convincing*.

80. (C); Synonym. *Deign* and *stoop* have the same meaning, as do *love* and *adore*.

81. (D); Synonym. *Demeanor* and *behavior* have the same meaning, as do *faith* and *belief*.

82. (D); Characteristic Quality. A *rustler*, or thief of livestock, is characteristically *dishonest*. In the same way, a *pirate* is characteristically *audacious*, or bold and daring.

83. (D); Performer and Related Action. A *jury* *exonerates*, or clears someone of blame, just as an *athlete* *competes*.

84. (D); Performer and Related Object. A *burglar* commits a *felony*, just as a *sculptor* creates *art*.

85. (D); Characteristic Quality. A *guise* is characteristically *superficial*, just as a *crime* is characteristically *offensive*.

86. (D); Antonym. *Insidious*, or devious, is opposite in meaning to *straightforward*. *Attractive* and *repulsive* also have opposite meanings.

87. (E); Performer and Related Action. One who was *sacrificed* may be a *martyr*, just as one who was *punished* may be a *convict*.

88. (A); Synonym. An *obligation* is the same thing as a *duty*, just as an *altercation* is the same thing as a *quarrel*.

89. (A); Antonym. *Peripheral*, or a nonessential matter, is the opposite of *essential*, just as *sinful* is the opposite of *religious*.

90. (D); Part and Whole. A *soldier* is part of a *phalanx*, or military formation, just as a *cow* is part of a *herd*.

91. (A); Synonym. *Profound* and *deep* have nearly the same meaning, as do *precipitate* (as an adjective) and *sudden*.

92. (E); Antonym. *Reduced* and *enlarged* are opposite in meaning, as are *repugnant* and *attractive*.

93. (E); Synonym. *Repression* and *control* have nearly the same meaning, as do *fairness* and *justice*.

94. (D); Characteristic Quality. Someone who is *sick* is characteristically *sallow*, or grayish yellow in color, just as someone who is *healthy* is characteristically *ruddy*.

95. (C); Synonym. *Schedule* and *plan* have the same meaning. *Procrastinate* and *postpone* both mean to put off until another time.

96. (B); Characteristic Quality. A *sortie*, or raid, is characteristically *sudden* and quick. An *attack* is characteristically *aggressive*.

97. (B); Degree. *Sweltering*, which means very hot and sultry, has a meaning similar to *warm* but to a greater degree. In the same way, *heinous*, which means evil or wicked, has a meaning similar to *bad* but to a greater degree.

98. (E); Synonym. *Thoughtful* and *considerate* have nearly the same meaning, as do *blithe* and *happy*.

99. (E); Performer and Related Action. You *hurt* a *victim*, just as you *blame* a *scapegoat*.

100. (C); Characteristic Quality. A *sage* is a characteristically *wise* person. In the same way, a *charity* is characteristically *beneficent*—that is, it does good.

p.59 | Test 3 Part A

1. E		**14.** B	
2. B		**15.** D	
3. D		**16.** C	
4. B		**17.** A	
5. C		**18.** C	
6. A		**19.** C	
7. D		**20.** B	
8. C		**21.** D	
9. C		**22.** E	
10. D		**23.** A	
11. E		**24.** D	
12. A		**25.** C	
13. C			

p. 63 | Test 3 Part B

26. B	49. C
27. C	50. C
28. C	51. A
29. C	52. C
30. A	53. D
31. C	54. A
32. E	55. C
33. D	56. A
34. D	57. B
35. B	58. D
36. D	59. D
37. C	60. E
38. B	61. E
39. C	62. B
40. A	63. B
41. D	64. D
42. B	65. D
43. B	66. B
44. E	67. C
45. B	68. A
46. E	69. C
47. C	70. E
48. A	

p. 68 | Test 3 Part C

71. (A); Synonym. *Appraisal, value, estimation,* and *worth* all have similar meanings.

72. (A); Synonym. To *correlate* can reveal a *relationship,* just as to *organize* can produce *order.*

73. (E); Antonym. A *debacle,* or failure, is the opposite of a *success,* just as *contraction* is the opposite of *expansion.*

74. (A); Performer and Related Action. An *intruder encroaches,* or trespasses, just as a *thief steals.*

75. (E); Classification. *Entomology,* the study of insects, is classified as a branch of *zoology.* In the same way, *poetry* is classified as a type of *literature.*

76. (D); Characteristic Quality. A *clown* is characteristically *funny,* just as a *thief* is characteristically *furtive,* or secretive.

77. (C); Synonym. *Hazard* and *danger* have nearly the same meaning, as do *vogue* and *fashion.*

78. (E); Synonym. *Inherent* and *basic* have nearly the same meaning, as do *broad* and *wide.*

79. (A); Synonym. *Interior* means the same as *inside,* just as *ulterior,* or hidden, means the same as *undisclosed.*

80. (E); Synonym. *Liberate* and *release* have the same meaning, as do *abut* and *adjoin.*

81. (E); Characteristic Quality. A *microcosm* is a small part that is characteristically *representative* of the whole. A *flag* is characteristically *symbolic.*

82. (E); Performer and Related Action. One expects a *parent* to *nurture,* or care for children, just as one expects a *general* to *command* an army.

83. (E); Synonym. *Obstinate* and *stubborn* have the same meaning, as do *recalcitrant* and *uncooperative.*

84. (B); Characteristic Quality. *Humans* are characteristically *omnivorous,* which means that they eat both animals and plants, just as *zebras* are characteristically *striped.*

85. (B); Synonym. *Ooze* and *seep* have similar meanings, as do *permeate* and *penetrate.*

86. (B); Synonym. *Sensation* and *feeling* (as a noun) have the same meaning. In the same way, *contrition* and *remorse* both mean sorrow for doing wrong.

87. (B); Classification. *Softball* may be classified as a *sport,* just as a *recrimination* may be classified as a *response.*

88. (E); Degree. *Stare* is stronger in degree than *glance,* just as *wrest* is stronger in degree than *tug.*

89. (B); Synonym. One meaning of *stint* is a set amount, as is *quota.* In the same way, *statute* and *law* are similar in meaning.

90. (E); Characteristic Quality. Someone who is *stoic* is characteristically *unexcitable*, just as someone who is *eccentric* is characteristically *strange*.

91. (C); Synonym. *Sway* and *influence* have the same meaning, as do *enthrall* and *spellbind*.

92. (C); Antonym. *Swell* and *shrink* have opposite meanings, as do *subside* and *increase*.

93. (A); Antonym. *Taint* can mean to contaminate and is opposite in meaning to *purify*. In the same way, to *scorn* someone would be the opposite of to *praise* her.

94. (B); Synonym. *Tenacity*, or holding firmly, has a meaning similar to *grip*, as do *firmness* and *hold*.

95. (C); Degree. *Tepid*, or lukewarm, is less hot than *hot*, just as *cool* is less cold than *cold*.

96. (C); Cause and Effect. To *undermine*, which can mean to dig beneath, could create a *tunnel*. In the same way, to *compose* could create a *song*.

97. (B); Performer and Related Action. *Conquerors vanquish*, or defeat, their foes, just as *instigators initiate*, or begin, something.

98. (D); Antonym. *Vilify* means the opposite of *admire*, just as *criticize* means the opposite of *praise*.

99. (B); Degree. *Violent* is more extreme in degree than *rough*, just as *rapacious* is stronger in degree than *greedy*.

100. (D); Characteristic Quality. A *fox* is characteristically *wily*, or crafty, just as an *owl* is characteristically *wise*.

Workshop Answer Key

Making New Words Your Own

Lesson 1

p. 3 | Exercise 1: Wordbusting

> **NOTES**
> - For each Vocabulary Word, students should fill in at least one of the **context, structure,** and **sound** boxes.
> - Check that students vary the boxes they use throughout the exercise.
> - Make sure students look up each word in the dictionary and fill in the dictionary box; answers will vary depending on the dictionary used.

p. 5 | Exercise 2: Context Clues

11. J	glib	16. D	banal
12. E	lugubrious	17. I	pseudonym
13. A	finesse	18. B	lampoon
14. H	nemesis	19. G	nefarious
15. C	purloin	20. F	bellicose

p. 6 | Exercise 3: Sentence Completion

21. E	26. C
22. B	27. A
23. A	28. E
24. A	29. A
25. B	30. A

Lesson 2

p. 7 | Exercise 1: Wordbusting

> **NOTES**
> - For each Vocabulary Word, students should fill in at least one of the **context, structure,** and **sound** boxes.
> - Check that students vary the boxes they use throughout the exercise.
> - Make sure students look up each word in the dictionary and fill in the dictionary box; answers will vary depending on the dictionary used.

p. 9 | Exercise 2: Context Clues

11. D	euphemism	17. G	admonish
12. J	nebulous	18. I	prosaic
13. F	abject	19. E	phlegmatic
14. A	propriety	20. H	commen-surate
15. C	revile		
16. B	distraught		

p. 10 | Exercise 3: Sentence Completion

21. A	26. D
22. D	27. B
23. C	28. C
24. E	29. E
25. A	30. C

Lesson 3

p. 11 | Exercise 1: Wordbusting

> **NOTES**
> - For each Vocabulary Word, students should fill in at least one of the **context, structure,** and **sound** boxes.
> - Check that students vary the boxes they use throughout the exercise.
> - Make sure students look up each word in the dictionary and fill in the dictionary box; answers will vary depending on the dictionary used.

p. 13 | Exercise 2: Context Clues

11. C	incognito	16. G	omniscient
12. E	cognizant	17. H	fortuitous
13. D	farcical	18. J	assimilate
14. F	discursive	19. I	ennui
15. A	hyperbole	20. B	mesmerism

p. 14 | Exercise 3: Sentence Completion

21. C	26. C
22. B	27. B
23. E	28. D
24. D	29. E
25. A	30. A

Workshop Answer Key *(continued)*

Lesson 4

p. 15 | Exercise 1: Wordbusting

NOTES

- For each Vocabulary Word, students should fill in at least one of the **context, structure,** and **sound** boxes.

- Check that students vary the boxes they use throughout the exercise.

- Make sure students look up each word in the dictionary and fill in the dictionary box; answers will vary depending on the dictionary used.

p. 17 | Exercise 2: Context Clues

11. J dirge	**16.** B feign
12. C despot	**17.** A blazon
13. G expatriate	**18.** F choleric
14. E colloquy	**19.** H adroit
15. I allay	**20.** D bravado

p. 18 | Exercise 3: Sentence Completion

21. C	**26.** B
22. C	**27.** D
23. D	**28.** B
24. E	**29.** C
25. E	**30.** A

Lesson 5

p. 19 | Exercise 1: Wordbusting

NOTES

- For each Vocabulary Word, students should fill in at least one of the **context, structure,** and **sound** boxes.

- Check that students vary the boxes they use throughout the exercise.

- Make sure students look up each word in the dictionary and fill in the dictionary box; answers will vary depending on the dictionary used.

p. 21 | Exercise 2: Context Clues

11. I guile	**16.** J protégé
12. G proffer	**17.** E sanguine
13. C seraphic	**18.** F doggerel
14. D amorphous	**19.** A ascetic
15. B decorum	**20.** H facile

p. 22 | Exercise 3: Sentence Completion

21. A	**26.** E
22. C	**27.** C
23. D	**28.** D
24. B	**29.** B
25. C	**30.** B

Lesson 6

p. 23 | Exercise 1: Wordbusting

NOTES

- For each Vocabulary Word, students should fill in at least one of the **context, structure,** and **sound** boxes.

- Check that students vary the boxes they use throughout the exercise.

- Make sure students look up each word in the dictionary and fill in the dictionary box; answers will vary depending on the dictionary used.

p. 25 | Exercise 2: Context Clues

11. G implicit	**17.** I parsimo-
12. D nondescript	nious
13. F sundry	**18.** B exhort
14. A inveigle	**19.** H nonentity
15. J dogma	**20.** C vociferous
16. E scurrilous	

p. 26 | Exercise 3: Sentence Completion

21. E	**26.** C
22. C	**27.** B
23. A	**28.** D
24. E	**29.** B
25. D	**30.** C

Workshop Answer Key (continued)

Lesson 7

p. 27 | Exercise 1: Wordbusting

NOTES
- For each Vocabulary Word, students should fill in at least one of the **context, structure,** and **sound** boxes.
- Check that students vary the boxes they use throughout the exercise.
- Make sure students look up each word in the dictionary and fill in the dictionary box; answers will vary depending on the dictionary used.

p. 29 | Exercise 2: Context Clues

11. D gratuitous
12. F etymology
13. C venerate
14. A truism
15. H erudite
16. J charlatan
17. I extol
18. E broach
19. B predispose
20. G immutable

p. 30 | Exercise 3: Sentence Completion

21. C
22. B
23. D
24. A
25. E
26. B
27. C
28. D
29. C
30. B

Lesson 8

p. 31 | Exercise 1: Wordbusting

NOTES
- For each Vocabulary Word, students should fill in at least one of the **context, structure,** and **sound** boxes.
- Check that students vary the boxes they use throughout the exercise.
- Make sure students look up each word in the dictionary and fill in the dictionary box; answers will vary depending on the dictionary used.

p. 33 | Exercise 2: Context Clues

11. G infringe
12. B specious
13. E ostensible
14. I absolve
15. F subjugate
16. A antipodes
17. C retroactive
18. H antipathy
19. D nettle
20. J indigent

p. 34 | Exercise 3: Sentence Completion

21. E
22. B
23. A
24. D
25. C
26. B
27. C
28. E
29. C
30. C

Lesson 9

p. 35 | Exercise 1: Wordbusting

NOTES
- For each Vocabulary Word, students should fill in at least one of the **context, structure,** and **sound** boxes.
- Check that students vary the boxes they use throughout the exercise.
- Make sure students look up each word in the dictionary and fill in the dictionary box; answers will vary depending on the dictionary used.

p. 37 | Exercise 2: Context Clues

11. C mundane
12. J eulogy
13. B progeny
14. D copious
15. H tenure
16. I euphony
17. E sonorous
18. F abnegation
19. A poignant
20. G extraneous

p. 38 | Exercise 3: Sentence Completion

21. D
22. B
23. C
24. E
25. A
26. D
27. D
28. E
29. C
30. B

ANSWER KEY

185

Lesson 10

p. 39 | Exercise 1: Wordbusting

> **NOTES**
> - For each Vocabulary Word, students should fill in at least one of the **context, structure,** and **sound** boxes.
> - Check that students vary the boxes they use throughout the exercise.
> - Make sure students look up each word in the dictionary and fill in the dictionary box; answers will vary depending on the dictionary used.

p. 41 | Exercise 2: Context Clues

11.	H hackneyed	17.	C idiosyn-
12.	I paragon		crasy
13.	F ascribe	18.	J elegy
14.	G inconse-	19.	B introvert
	quential	20.	E homily
15.	D humdrum		
16.	A engender		

p. 42 | Exercise 3: Sentence Completion

21.	D	26.	E
22.	E	27.	B
23.	D	28.	D
24.	A	29.	C
25.	C	30.	A

Lesson 11

p. 43 | Exercise 1: Wordbusting

> **NOTES**
> - For each Vocabulary Word, students should fill in at least one of the **context, structure,** and **sound** boxes.
> - Check that students vary the boxes they use throughout the exercise.
> - Make sure students look up each word in the dictionary and fill in the dictionary box; answers will vary depending on the dictionary used.

p. 45 | Exercise 2: Context Clues

11.	E corroborate	16.	H salient
12.	C aberration	17.	A adjudge
13.	D herculean	18.	F diurnal
14.	B retrospect	19.	J candor
15.	G dearth	20.	I ludicrous

p. 46 | Exercise 3: Sentence Completion

21.	D	26.	E
22.	C	27.	D
23.	E	28.	C
24.	A	29.	B
25.	E	30.	B

Lesson 12

p. 47 | Exercise 1: Wordbusting

> **NOTES**
> - For each Vocabulary Word, students should fill in at least one of the **context, structure,** and **sound** boxes.
> - Check that students vary the boxes they use throughout the exercise.
> - Make sure students look up each word in the dictionary and fill in the dictionary box; answers will vary depending on the dictionary used.

p. 49 | Exercise 2: Context Clues

11.	A artifice	16.	F captivate
12.	G configuration	17.	I proponent
13.	B scrupulous	18.	H extant
14.	D deduce	19.	C chicanery
15.	E refute	20.	J augury

p. 50 | Exercise 3: Sentence Completion

21.	E	26.	D
22.	C	27.	C
23.	D	28.	E
24.	B	29.	B
25.	A	30.	D

Workshop Answer Key (continued)

Lesson 13

p. 51 | Exercise 1: Wordbusting

> **NOTES**
> - For each Vocabulary Word, students should fill in at least one of the **context, structure,** and **sound** boxes.
> - Check that students vary the boxes they use throughout the exercise.
> - Make sure students look up each word in the dictionary and fill in the dictionary box; answers will vary depending on the dictionary used.

p. 53 | Exercise 2: Context Clues

11. H gregarious	16. E germane
12. G exhilaration	17. C punctilious
13. A patrimony	18. F foible
14. J obsequious	19. B connoisseur
15. I civility	20. D precocious

p. 54 | Exercise 3: Sentence Completion

21. E	26. C
22. C	27. B
23. B	28. E
24. D	29. D
25. A	30. A

Lesson 14

p. 55 | Exercise 1: Wordbusting

> **NOTES**
> - For each Vocabulary Word, students should fill in at least one of the **context, structure,** and **sound** boxes.
> - Check that students vary the boxes they use throughout the exercise.
> - Make sure students look up each word in the dictionary and fill in the dictionary box; answers will vary depending on the dictionary used.

p. 57 | Exercise 2: Context Clues

11. A effusion	17. G guffaw
12. F querulous	18. I capitulate
13. C indulgent	19. H incarcerate
14. D affront	20. E magnani-
15. B propitious	mous
16. J munificent	

p. 58 | Exercise 3: Sentence Completion

21. B	26. A
22. D	27. D
23. C	28. C
24. E	29. A
25. C	30. E

Lesson 15

p. 59 | Exercise 1: Wordbusting

> **NOTES**
> - For each Vocabulary Word, students should fill in at least one of the **context, structure,** and **sound** boxes.
> - Check that students vary the boxes they use throughout the exercise.
> - Make sure students look up each word in the dictionary and fill in the dictionary box; answers will vary depending on the dictionary used.

p. 61 | Exercise 2: Context Clues

11. I perfidious	17. G abeyance
12. F illicit	18. B primordial
13. H discrepancy	19. D homoge-
14. C inundate	neous
15. E sumptuous	20. J pervade
16. A inscrutable	

p. 62 | Exercise 3: Sentence Completion

21. C	26. C
22. E	27. C
23. B	28. E
24. D	29. B
25. A	30. D

Workshop Answer Key *(continued)*

SIXTH COURSE

Lesson 16

p. 63 | Exercise 1: Wordbusting

> **NOTES**
> - For each Vocabulary Word, students should fill in at least one of the **context, structure,** and **sound** boxes.
> - Check that students vary the boxes they use throughout the exercise.
> - Make sure students look up each word in the dictionary and fill in the dictionary box; answers will vary depending on the dictionary used.

p. 65 | Exercise 2: Context Clues

11. B harbinger
12. C emanate
13. A demagogue
14. I prevaricate
15. F detriment
16. E obnoxious
17. G chastise
18. J irrevocable
19. D deplore
20. H intercede

p. 66 | Exercise 3: Sentence Completion

21. E
22. A
23. B
24. D
25. C
26. E
27. E
28. D
29. C
30. B

Lesson 17

p. 67 | Exercise 1: Wordbusting

> **NOTES**
> - For each Vocabulary Word, students should fill in at least one of the **context, structure,** and **sound** boxes.
> - Check that students vary the boxes they use throughout the exercise.
> - Make sure students look up each word in the dictionary and fill in the dictionary box; answers will vary depending on the dictionary used.

p. 69 | Exercise 2: Context Clues

11. H extricate
12. E menial
13. B rampant
14. C cajole
15. F pestilence
16. D anarchy
17. J nadir
18. I ethnology
19. G impair
20. A commodious

p. 70 | Exercise 3: Sentence Completion

21. C
22. A
23. D
24. B
25. E
26. C
27. D
28. B
29. A
30. E

Lesson 18

p. 71 | Exercise 1: Wordbusting

> **NOTES**
> - For each Vocabulary Word, students should fill in at least one of the **context, structure,** and **sound** boxes.
> - Check that students vary the boxes they use throughout the exercise.
> - Make sure students look up each word in the dictionary and fill in the dictionary box; answers will vary depending on the dictionary used.

p. 73 | Exercise 2: Context Clues

11. E profuse
12. D virulent
13. I strident
14. F consign
15. C elocution
16. G subversion
17. A cadaverous
18. H incorrigible
19. J promulgation
20. B maim

p. 74 | Exercise 3: Sentence Completion

21. C
22. D
23. D
24. B
25. A
26. C
27. D
28. D
29. B
30. A

Sixth Course | *Vocabulary Workshop*

Workshop Answer Key *(continued)*

Lesson 19

p. 75 | Exercise 1: Wordbusting

> **NOTES**
> - For each Vocabulary Word, students should fill in at least one of the **context, structure,** and **sound** boxes.
> - Check that students vary the boxes they use throughout the exercise.
> - Make sure students look up each word in the dictionary and fill in the dictionary box; answers will vary depending on the dictionary used.

p. 77 | Exercise 2: Context Clues

11. E propensity
12. C recant
13. J contingency
14. A litigation
15. D retaliate
16. B calumny
17. I sedentary
18. H impassive
19. F repudiate
20. G mollify

p. 78 | Exercise 3: Sentence Completion

21. C
22. E
23. B
24. A
25. D
26. E
27. C
28. B
29. C
30. A

Lesson 20

p. 79 | Exercise 1: Wordbusting

> **NOTES**
> - For each Vocabulary Word, students should fill in at least one of the **context, structure,** and **sound** boxes.
> - Check that students vary the boxes they use throughout the exercise.
> - Make sure students look up each word in the dictionary and fill in the dictionary box; answers will vary depending on the dictionary used.

p. 81 | Exercise 2: Context Clues

11. E vindicate
12. F reticent
13. I temerity
14. B fervid
15. D foment
16. J solicitous
17. G auspices
18. A hiatus
19. C clandestine
20. H vestige

p. 82 | Exercise 3: Sentence Completion

21. A
22. B
23. E
24. D
25. C
26. C
27. E
28. B
29. A
30. C

Lesson 21

p. 83 | Exercise 1: Wordbusting

> **NOTES**
> - For each Vocabulary Word, students should fill in at least one of the **context, structure,** and **sound** boxes.
> - Check that students vary the boxes they use throughout the exercise.
> - Make sure students look up each word in the dictionary and fill in the dictionary box; answers will vary depending on the dictionary used.

p. 85 | Exercise 2: Context Clues

11. I disparity
12. A renounce
13. D officious
14. C scathing
15. G facetious
16. E empirical
17. J differentiate
18. B treatise
19. H quiescence
20. F testimonial

p. 86 | Exercise 3: Sentence Completion

21. A
22. B
23. B
24. D
25. D
26. B
27. A
28. A
29. C
30. C

Workshop Answer Key *(continued)*

Lesson 22

p. 87 | Exercise 1: Wordbusting

> **NOTES**
> - For each Vocabulary Word, students should fill in at least one of the **context, structure,** and **sound** boxes.
> - Check that students vary the boxes they use throughout the exercise.
> - Make sure students look up each word in the dictionary and fill in the dictionary box; answers will vary depending on the dictionary used.

p. 89 | Exercise 2: Context Clues

11. B	chauvinism	**16.** I	repository
12. A	epitome	**17.** D	regimen
13. C	inexorable	**18.** G	sagacity
14. E	cosmopolitan	**19.** H	tenuous
15. J	devoid	**20.** F	moot

p. 90 | Exercise 3: Sentence Completion

21. D	**26.** C
22. A	**27.** E
23. C	**28.** B
24. D	**29.** A
25. E	**30.** D

Lesson 23

p. 91 | Exercise 1: Wordbusting

> **NOTES**
> - For each Vocabulary Word, students should fill in at least one of the **context, structure,** and **sound** boxes.
> - Check that students vary the boxes they use throughout the exercise.
> - Make sure students look up each word in the dictionary and fill in the dictionary box; answers will vary depending on the dictionary used.

p. 93 | Exercise 2: Context Clues

11. D	vantage point	**16.** G	terra firma
12. E	bode	**17.** B	burnish
13. A	gauntlet	**18.** H	esoteric
14. F	mottled	**19.** I	mete
15. C	misnomer	**20.** J	coerce

p. 94 | Exercise 3: Sentence Completion

21. C	**26.** C
22. E	**27.** D
23. D	**28.** E
24. A	**29.** D
25. B	**30.** A

Lesson 24

p. 95 | Exercise 1: Wordbusting

> **NOTES**
> - For each Vocabulary Word, students should fill in at least one of the **context, structure,** and **sound** boxes.
> - Check that students vary the boxes they use throughout the exercise.
> - Make sure students look up each word in the dictionary and fill in the dictionary box; answers will vary depending on the dictionary used.

p. 97 | Exercise 2: Context Clues

11. C	enigma	**17.** A	expound
12. D	voluminous	**18.** J	anachronism
13. E	consternation		
14. B	acrimonious	**19.** F	desist
15. H	precursor	**20.** G	loquacious
16. I	atrophy		

p. 98 | Exercise 3: Sentence Completion

21. D	**26.** C
22. B	**27.** D
23. E	**28.** E
24. C	**29.** B
25. A	**30.** C

Lesson 25

p. 99 | Exercise 1: Wordbusting

> **NOTES**
> - For each Vocabulary Word, students should fill in at least one of the **context**, **structure**, and **sound** boxes.
> - Check that students vary the boxes they use throughout the exercise.
> - Make sure students look up each word in the dictionary and fill in the dictionary box; answers will vary depending on the dictionary used.

p. 101 | Exercise 2: Context Clues

11. I equanimity	**16.** A denizen
12. E tenable	**17.** G mercurial
13. C inordinate	**18.** B assiduous
14. D aver	**19.** J iniquity
15. H pecuniary	**20.** F cessation

p. 102 | Exercise 3: Sentence Completion

21. D	**26.** D
22. C	**27.** B
23. B	**28.** A
24. E	**29.** E
25. C	**30.** C

Lesson 26

p. 103 | Exercise 1: Wordbusting

> **NOTES**
> - For each Vocabulary Word, students should fill in at least one of the **context**, **structure**, and **sound** boxes.
> - Check that students vary the boxes they use throughout the exercise.
> - Make sure students look up each word in the dictionary and fill in the dictionary box; answers will vary depending on the dictionary used.

p. 105 | Exercise 2: Context Clues

11. C extenuate	**16.** B impeccable
12. H duress	**17.** D corollary
13. A quell	**18.** J avarice
14. G rancor	**19.** F fissure
15. I conciliate	**20.** E espouse

p. 106 | Exercise 3: Sentence Completion

21. B	**26.** C
22. D	**27.** B
23. C	**28.** E
24. E	**29.** B
25. A	**30.** D

Lesson 27

p. 107 | Exercise 1: Wordbusting

> **NOTES**
> - For each Vocabulary Word, students should fill in at least one of the **context**, **structure**, and **sound** boxes.
> - Check that students vary the boxes they use throughout the exercise.
> - Make sure students look up each word in the dictionary and fill in the dictionary box; answers will vary depending on the dictionary used.

p. 109 | Exercise 2: Context Clues

11. B gambol	**17.** A caricature
12. I remuneration	**18.** D festoon
13. H pallor	**19.** G commiserate
14. E burgeoning	
15. J venal	**20.** C evanescent
16. F maudlin	

p. 110 | Exercise 3: Sentence Completion

21. D	**26.** C
22. A	**27.** E
23. B	**28.** B
24. D	**29.** E
25. C	**30.** C

Workshop Answer Key *(continued)*

Lesson 28

p. 111 | Exercise 1: Wordbusting

NOTES
- For each Vocabulary Word, students should fill in at least one of the **context, structure,** and **sound** boxes.
- Check that students vary the boxes they use throughout the exercise.
- Make sure students look up each word in the dictionary and fill in the dictionary box; answers will vary depending on the dictionary used.

p. 113 | Exercise 2: Context Clues

11. D	promontory	**16.** B	apostasy
12. J	opulence	**17.** E	fresco
13. F	abstruse	**18.** C	bauble
14. I	frugal	**19.** G	iridescent
15. A	usury	**20.** H	bullion

p. 114 | Exercise 3: Sentence Completion

21. C		**26.** E	
22. E		**27.** D	
23. D		**28.** C	
24. D		**29.** A	
25. B		**30.** B	

Lesson 29

p. 115 | Exercise 1: Wordbusting

NOTES
- For each Vocabulary Word, students should fill in at least one of the **context, structure,** and **sound** boxes.
- Check that students vary the boxes they use throughout the exercise.
- Make sure students look up each word in the dictionary and fill in the dictionary box; answers will vary depending on the dictionary used.

p. 117 | Exercise 2: Context Clues

11. E	ignominy	**16.** H	prognosis
12. D	circumvent	**17.** A	adjure
13. J	malinger	**18.** I	abscond
14. F	aspersion	**19.** G	malign
15. B	remonstrate	**20.** C	ethereal

p. 118 | Exercise 3: Sentence Completion

21. B		**26.** D	
22. C		**27.** E	
23. D		**28.** C	
24. A		**29.** B	
25. B		**30.** A	

Lesson 30

p. 119 | Exercise 1: Wordbusting

NOTES
- For each Vocabulary Word, students should fill in at least one of the **context, structure,** and **sound** boxes.
- Check that students vary the boxes they use throughout the exercise.
- Make sure students look up each word in the dictionary and fill in the dictionary box; answers will vary depending on the dictionary used.

p. 121 | Exercise 2: Context Clues

11. J	extort	**16.** E	biennial
12. I	reprisal	**17.** D	emaciate
13. H	elicit	**18.** B	longevity
14. G	taciturn	**19.** C	capricious
15. A	fiasco	**20.** F	equivocal

p. 122 | Exercise 3: Sentence Completion

21. D		**26.** C	
22. C		**27.** D	
23. B		**28.** E	
24. E		**29.** C	
25. A		**30.** B	

Connecting New Words and Patterns

Lesson 1

p. 126 | Analogies

1. (C); Degree.   To *admonish* suggests a lesser degree of punishment than to *condemn*. When used as verbs, *glance* means to look briefly, while *stare* means to look for a long time.

2. (E); Synonym.   *Banal*, which means ordinary or insipid, has a meaning similar to *commonplace*. *Strange* and *unusual* have the same meaning.

3. (E); Degree.   *Lugubrious* has a meaning similar to *sad*, but it also means mournful to an exaggerated or ridiculous degree. *Jubilant* has a meaning similar to *pleased* but also implies greater joy.

4. (C); Characteristic Quality.   *Fog* is characteristically *nebulous*, or indefinite and vague, just as a *blanket* is characteristically *soft*.

5. (D); Characteristic Quality.   A *villain* is characteristically *nefarious*, or wicked, just as a *clown* is characteristically *amusing*.

6. (A); Performer and Related Action.   You expect a *nemesis*, someone who imposes retribution or punishment, to *punish* others, just as you expect a *savior* to *save* others.

7. (B); Characteristic Quality.   A *loafer* is characteristically *phlegmatic,* sluggish and hard to get moving, just as an *artist* is characteristically *creative.*

8. (E); Antonym.   *Prosaic,* which means ordinary, is opposite in meaning to *exceptional,* which means special and distinctive. *Fancy* and *plain* also have opposite meanings.

9. (A); Classification.   A *pseudonym*, a fictitious alias assumed by an author, is classified as a *name,* just as an *actor* is classified as a *performer.*

Lesson 2

10. (E); Performer and Related Action.   You expect a *thief* to *purloin*, or steal, money, just as you expect a *surveyor* to *measure* land.

p. 127 | Analogies

1. (D); Action and Related Object.   You *assimilate*, or absorb, *food*, just as you *join* an *organization*.

2. (B); Performer and Related Object.   A *knight* carries a *blazon*, which can be a coat of arms, a heraldic shield, or a banner, just as a *police officer* carries a *badge*.

3. (A); Characteristic Quality.   A *hothead* is characteristically *choleric*, or bad-tempered, just as a *genius* is characteristically *brilliant*.

4. (E); Degree.   A *colloquy*, a formal discussion or conference, is distinguished from a *chat*, which is an informal conversation, often on light topics. A *festival* is an organized celebration, usually involving a large number of people, while a *gathering* is an informal meeting or assemblage of people.

5. (B); Synonym.   *Despot*, which means tyrant, is similar in meaning to *oppressor*. In the same way, *discover* and *find* have similar meanings.

6. (D); Part and Whole.   A *dirge* is a mournful song that is often part of a *funeral*, just as *scenery* is often a part of a *play*.

7. (E); Cause and Effect.   *Inactivity* can result in *ennui*, or boredom, just as *labor* can result in *fatigue*, or tiredness.

8. (C); Degree.   Something that is *farcical* is amusing, while something that is *hilarious* is extremely funny. In the same way, *good* implies a lesser degree of quality than *excellent*.

9. (A); Performer and Related Action.   You expect a *trickster* to *feign*, or make a false show of something, just as you expect a *surgeon* to *operate* on a patient.

10. (E); Antonym. *Fortuitous,* which means accidental, is opposite in meaning to *planned. Unfortunate* and *lucky* are also opposite in meaning.

Lesson 3

p. 128 | Analogies

1. (E); Characteristic Quality. An *ascetic* is characteristically *self-denying,* just as an *athlete* is characteristically *active.*

2. (A); Classification. *Doggerel,* or bad poetry, can be classified as a kind of *verse,* just as a *van* can be classified as a kind of *motor vehicle.*

3. (B); Action and Related Object. You *preach dogma,* or a set of beliefs, just as you *teach social studies.*

4. (E); Performer and Related Action. You expect an *advisor* to *exhort,* or urge, someone to do something, just as you expect a *witness* to *testify* in court.

5. (B); Antonym. *Facile,* which can mean insincere or superficial, is opposite in meaning to *sincere. Guilty* and *innocent* also have opposite meanings.

6. (B); Performer and Related Action. You expect a *deceiver* to *inveigle* others by tricking them or leading them on with deception, just as you expect a *detective* to *investigate* a case.

7. (D); Synonym. *Proffer* and *submit* have the same meaning, as do *trade* and *exchange.*

8. (C); Characteristic Quality. An *optimist* is characteristically *sanguine,* or relaxed and hopeful, just as a *protestor* is characteristically *dissatisfied.*

9. (D); Antonym. *Scurrilous* language, which is coarse, indecent, and vulgar, is the opposite of *refined* language. *Flexible* and *rigid* also have opposite meanings.

10. (E); Synonym. *Seraphic* and *angelic* have the same meaning, as do *anxious* and *worried.*

Lesson 4

p. 129 | Analogies

1. (D); Performer and Related Action. You expect a *jury* to *absolve,* or forgive and release a defendant, when it renders a verdict of not guilty. In the same way, you expect the voices in a *choir* to *harmonize* when singing together.

2. (A); Cause and Effect. *Antipathy,* which means strong dislike or aversion, can result in *avoidance* of that which causes the negative feeling, just as *success* can result in *confidence.*

3. (C); Synonym. *Antipodes* and *opposites* have similar meanings, as do *friends* and *comrades.*

4. (E); Performer and Related Action. You expect a *charlatan,* one who makes false claims, to *deceive* others, just as you expect an *impostor* to *trick* others.

5. (B); Characteristic Quality. A *scholar* is characteristically *erudite,* or learned, just as a *wrestler* is characteristically *strong.*

6. (D); Antonym. *Immutable,* which means never changing, is opposite in meaning to *changeable. Steadfast,* which means reliable and dependable, is opposite in meaning to *fickle.*

7. (E); Antonym. *Indigent,* which means poor, means the opposite of *wealthy. Solemn* and *silly* also have opposite meanings.

8. (B); Performer and Related Action. You expect a *violator* to be someone who *infringes,* or trespasses on, the rights of others, just as you expect a *partner* to *cooperate.*

9. (C); Classification. A *nettle* can be classified as a stinging or spiny *plant.* In the same way, a *quarter* can be classified as a *coin.*

10. (A); Synonym. *Ostensible* and *apparent* have similar meanings, as do *fragile* and *delicate.*

Lesson 5

p. 130 | Analogies

1. (D); Classification. An *elegy*, or verse written to lament the dead, can be classified as a *poem*. A *jet* can be classified as an *airplane*.

2. (B); Function. The function of a *eulogy*, a formal speech written about a person who has died, is to *praise* its subject. In the same way, the function of a *cartoon* is to *amuse*.

3. (A); Characteristic Quality. A *euphony*, or combination of agreeable sounds, is characteristically *pleasant*, just as *lightning* is characteristically *bright*.

4. (E); Antonym. *Extraneous*, which means irrelevant or inessential, is opposite in meaning to *essential*. *Cautious* and *careless* also have opposite meanings.

5. (D); Performer and Related Object. You expect a *minister* to deliver a *homily*, or moralizing sermon, to a congregation, just as you expect a *doctor* to perform an *examination* of a patient.

6. (C); Performer and Related Action. You expect an *introvert*, or shy person, to *withdraw* from others, just as you expect an *entertainer* to *perform* before an audience.

7. (B); Antonym. *Mundane*, which means ordinary or commonplace, means the opposite of *exceptional*. *Simple* and *complex* also have opposite meanings.

8. (D); Synonym. *Paragon* and *model* have similar meanings, as do *narrative* and *story*.

9. (E); Synonym. *Progeny* and *descendants* have the same meaning, as do *kin* and *relatives*.

10. (A); Characteristic Quality. A *cello* is characteristically *sonorous*, with a deep and rich sound, just as a *typhoon* is characteristically *destructive*.

Lesson 6

p. 131 | Analogies

1. (B); Antonym. *Candor*, which means openness and honesty, means the opposite of *deceitfulness*. *Growth* and *decline* also have opposite meanings.

2. (B); Synonym. *Configuration* and *shape* have similar meanings. *Alteration* and *change* also have similar meanings.

3. (A); Action and Related Object. You *corroborate*, or confirm, *evidence*, just as you *confirm* a *fact*.

4. (D); Synonym. *Dearth* and *scarcity* have the same meaning, as do *exaggeration* and *overstatement*.

5. (B); Performer and Related Action. You expect a *thinker* to *deduce*, or reason things out, just as you expect a *contributor* to *give*.

6. (A); Antonym. *Diurnal*, which means occurring during the daytime, and *nocturnal*, which means occurring at night, have opposite meanings. *Urban* and *rural* also have opposite meanings.

7. (B); Antonym. *Extant*, which means still existing, is opposite in meaning to *extinct*. *Sheltered* and *exposed* are also opposite in meaning.

8. (E); Degree. A *herculean* task is extraordinarily *difficult*, just as something that is *fascinating* is extraordinarily *interesting*.

9. (D); Characteristic Quality. A *fool* is characteristically *ludicrous*, or absurd, just as a *comedian* is characteristically *funny*.

10. (E); Performer and Related Action. You expect a *proponent* to *support* something, just as you expect a *forerunner* to *precede* something else.

Lesson 7

p. 132 | Analogies

1. (C); Performer and Related Action. You expect a *loser* to *capitulate*, or give up, just as you expect a *chef* to *cook*.

2. (E); Antonym. *Civility*, which means politeness, is opposite in meaning to *rudeness*. *Acceptance* and *rejection* are also opposite in meaning.

3. (B); Performer and Related Action. You expect a *connoisseur*, someone with fine taste and expert knowledge, to *appreciate* fine things, just as you expect a *scholar* to *study*.

4. (E); Synonym. *Foible* and *weakness* have similar meanings, as do *division* and *separation*.

5. (D); Cause and Effect. A *joke* can result in a *guffaw*, or loud laugh, just as *carelessness* can result in an *error*.

6. (D); Performer and Related Action. You expect a *jailer* to *incarcerate* a prisoner just as you expect a *pilot* to *fly* an airplane.

7. (C); Synonym. *Indulgent*, which means kind to excess, and *lenient* have similar meanings, as do *fortified* and *strengthened*.

8. (A); Antonym. *Magnanimous*, which means generous, is opposite in meaning to *selfish*. *Divided* and *united* also have opposite meanings.

9. (B); Degree. Someone who is *obsequious* shows an exaggerated desire to please and obey, whereas someone who is *obedient* is merely willing to follow instructions. Similarly, something that is *gigantic* is bigger than something that is *large*.

10. (B); Degree. *Punctilious* means *careful* but to a much greater degree, implying scrupulousness and precise attention to detail. In the same way, *hostile* means *unfriendly* but to a much greater degree.

Lesson 8

p. 133 | Analogies

1. (B); Performer and Related Action. You expect a *disciplinarian* to *chastise*, or scold, someone, just as you expect a *student* to *learn*.

2. (D); Classification. A *demagogue*, someone who gains power by stirring up emotions, can be classified as a *leader*, just as a *banana* can be classified as a *fruit*.

3. (B); Synonym. When used as nouns, *detriment* and *harm* have similar meanings, as do *scheme* and *plot*.

4. (E); Synonym. *Discrepancy* and *inconsistency* have the same meaning, as do *resolution* and *determination*.

5. (D); Characteristic Quality. *Bribery* is characteristically *illicit*, or illegal, just as a *skyscraper* is characteristically *tall*.

6. (A); Synonym. *Inscrutable*, or obscure and difficult to understand, is similar in meaning to *mysterious*. *Scholarly* and *learned* also have similar meanings.

7. (E); Performer and Related Action. A *peacemaker* is someone who *intercedes*, or steps between two parties that disagree. An *antagonist* is someone who *opposes* something.

8. (D); Antonym. *Obnoxious*, which means rude, is opposite in meaning to *pleasant*. *Ornery* and *agreeable* are also opposite in meaning.

9. (A); Antonym. *Perfidious*, which means disloyal, means the opposite of *faithful*. *Cordial* and *unfriendly* also have opposite meanings.

10. (E); Characteristic Quality. A *palace* is characteristically *sumptuous*, or lavish, just as a *doubter* is characteristically *skeptical*.

Lesson 9

p. 134 | Analogies

1. (E); Cause and Effect. *Chaos* can result from *anarchy*, which is a lack of law and order, just as an *poverty* can result from a *deprivation*.

2. (D); Synonym. To *cajole* and to *coax* have the same meaning, as do to *start* and to *begin*.

3. (E); Antonym. *Commodious*, which means roomy and spacious, is opposite in meaning to *cramped*. *Boundless* and *limited* also have opposite meanings.

4. (B); Classification. *Ethnology*, the study of human behavior and development, is classified as a kind of *anthropology*. *Pediatrics*, the medical care of infants and children, is classified as a kind of *medicine*.

5. (D); Degree. To *impair* something means to break it or make it unusable, while to *destroy* something means to obliterate or ruin it completely. In the same way, to *nibble* means to take small bites, while to *devour* means to eat voraciously.

6. (C); Antonym. *Nadir*, which means lowest point, means the opposite of *high point*. *Failure* and *success* also have opposite meanings.

7. (B); Characteristic Quality. A *pestilence*, or widespread, contagious, and often fatal disease, is characteristically *destructive*. A *benefactor* is characteristically *kind*.

8. (D); Synonym. *Promulgate*, which means to make known in public, is similar in meaning to *proclaim*, just as *consideration* is similar in meaning to *thoughtfulness*.

9. (C); Antonym. *Subversion*, which means overthrow or ruin, is opposite in meaning to *establishment*. *Reduction* and *increase* also have opposite meanings.

10. (A); Synonym. *Virulent* and *deadly* have similar meanings. *Courageous* and *brave* have the same meaning.

Lesson 10

p. 135 | Analogies

1. (B); Synonym. *Calumny* and *slander* (used as a noun) both mean a false statement that hurts someone's reputation. *Thrill* (used as a noun) and *excitement* have similar meanings.

2. (D); Degree. *Fervid*, which means intensely hot, is more intense than *heat*. In the same way *starvation* is more extreme than *hunger*.

3. (C); Performer and Related Action. You expect an *instigator* to *foment*, or stir up, trouble, just as you expect a *teacher* to *instruct* students.

4. (D); Antonym. *Impassive* and *emotional* have opposite meanings, as do *maintained* and *neglected*.

5. (A); Performer and Related Object. You expect a *lawyer* to be involved in *litigation*, or lawsuits, just as you expect a *diplomat* to be involved in *negotiation*.

6. (E); Synonym. *Mollify*, which means to appease or make less severe, has a meaning similar to *soothe*. *Scramble* and *mix* have the same meaning.

7. (E); Synonym. One meaning of *repudiate* is to *disown*, and therefore the two are similar in meaning in the same way as *coarse* and *rough*.

8. (C); Antonym. *Reticent*, which can mean reserved, is opposite in meaning to *unreserved*. *Agitated*, or excited, and *calm* also have opposite meanings.

9. (D); Characteristic Quality. A *typist*, who stays seated much of the time, is characteristically *sedentary*, just as a *snob* is characteristically *conceited*.

10. (A); Degree. *Temerity* means rash or foolish boldness, while *nerve* means boldness without the added degree of recklessness. *Absurdity* is an extreme degree of *silliness*.

Lesson 11

p. 136 | Analogies

1. (D); Degree. *Chauvinism* is an extreme degree of *devotion* to one's group, implying militancy and boastfulness. *Reverence* implies an extreme degree of *respect*.

2. (E); Antonym. *Facetious*, which means witty and joking, means the opposite of *serious*. *Caring* and *indifferent* also have opposite meanings.

3. (B); Synonym. *Inexorable*, which means unable to be moved or influenced by persuasion, has a meaning similar to *unrelenting*. *Intricate* and *complex* also have similar meanings.

4. (E); Characteristic Quality. A *controversy* is characteristically *moot*, or debatable, just as a *crime* is characteristically *illegal*.

5. (E); Characteristic Quality. A *meddler* is characteristically *officious*, or interfering, just as a *model* is characteristically *photogenic*.

6. (B); Synonym. *Quiescent* and *inactive* have the same meaning, as do *skeptical* and *doubting*.

7. (E); Performer and Related Object. A *soldier* follows a *regimen*, or a strict routine of diet and exercise, just as a *student* follows a *curriculum*, or prescribed course of study.

8. (B); Antonym. To *renounce*, or give up something, means the opposite of to *adopt*. *Withhold* and *give* also have opposite meanings.

9. (A); Function. The function of a *repository*, or container where things are kept, is to *contain*, just as the function of a *sieve* is to *strain*.

10. (E); Performer and Related Object. A *treatise* is a formal, systematic book or article composed by a *scholar*, just as a *memorandum* is an informative document composed by an *administrator*.

Lesson 12

p. 137 | Analogies

1. (E); Synonym. *Acrimonious* and *bitter* have similar meanings, as do *perpetual* and *continuous*.

2. (E); Synonym. *Atrophy*, or a wasting away, is similar in meaning to *deterioration*, just as *courage* and *bravery* are similar in meaning.

3. (C); Performer and Related Action. You expect a *tyrant* to *coerce*, or threaten or use force against his or her subjects, just as you expect a *mourner* to *grieve* a loss.

4. (A); Cause and Effect. A *tragedy* can cause *consternation*, a bewildering fear or shock, just as a *victory* can cause *celebration*.

5. (C); Antonym. *Desist* and *persist* have opposite meanings, as do *occupy* and *vacate*.

6. (D); Characteristic Quality. An *enigma*, or riddle, is characteristically *mysterious*, just as *honey* is characteristically *sweet*.

7. (D); Part and Whole. A *gauntlet*, which is a metal-plated glove, is part of a suit of *armor*, just as a *bristle* is part of a *brush*.

8. (B); Synonym. *Loquacious* and *talkative* have the same meaning, as do *venomous* and *poisonous*.

9. (E); Classification. A *misnomer*, that is, a misleading or inappropriate name, can be classified as an *error*, just as a *dime* can be classified as a *coin*.

10. (C); Degree. *Mottled* means marked with spots, blotches, or streaks of different colors, and is more extreme than simply *spotted*. In the same way, *vivid* and *colorful* have similar meanings but *vivid* is more extreme.

Workshop Answer Key *(continued)*

Lesson 13

p. 138 | Analogies

1. (B); Antonym. *Assiduous,* which means careful and diligent, is opposite in meaning to *careless. Prompt* and *tardy* are also opposite in meaning.

2. (D); Synonym. *Avarice* and *greed* have similar meanings, as do *vice* and *fault.*

3. (E); Performer and Related Action. You expect a *negotiator* to *conciliate,* or smooth over conflicts between opposing parties, just as you expect an *heir* to *inherit* an estate.

4. (B); Performer and Related Action. You expect a *denizen* to *inhabit* a place, just as you expect a *batter* to *swing* a bat.

5. (A); Synonym. *Duress,* which means the use of force or threats, is similar in meaning to *force. Perfection* and *flawlessness* have the same meaning.

6. (D); Antonym. *Equanimity,* which means calm and composure, is opposite in meaning to *excitability. Order* and *chaos* are also opposite in meaning.

7. (C); Cause and Effect. *Iniquity,* which means wickedness, can result in *punishment,* just as *experimentation* can result in *discovery.*

8. (B); Synonym. *Inordinate* and *excessive* have similar meanings, as do *foolhardy* and *reckless.*

9. (B); Antonym. *Mercurial,* which means volatile and changeable, is opposite in meaning to *constant. Virtuous* and *evil* also have opposite meanings.

10. (D); Cause and Effect. *Rancor,* which means hatred, can result in *mistreatment.* In the same way, *suffering* can result in *compassion.*

Lesson 14

p. 139 | Analogies

1. (E); Characteristic Quality. A *bauble,* or trinket, is characteristically *showy,* just as *lace* is characteristically *delicate.*

2. (D); Performer and Related Action. You expect a *sympathizer* to *commiserate,* or express sympathy, just as you expect a *debater* to *disagree.*

3. (B); Characteristic Quality. A *festoon,* a wreath or garland made of flowers or other materials, is characteristically *decorative,* just as a *ring* is characteristically *round.*

4. (A); Performer and Related Object. A *fresco,* a painting made on wet plaster, is created by a *painter,* just as a *blueprint,* or a design for a building, is created by an *architect.*

5. (E); Synonym. *Frugal* and *thrifty* have the same meaning, as do *evident* and *obvious.*

6. (B); Degree. *Maudlin* means excessively, often foolishly or tearfully, *sentimental.* In the same way, something that is *priceless* is *valuable* but to such a degree that a price cannot be put on it.

7. (C); Antonym. *Opulence,* or wealth, is opposite in meaning to *poverty. Simplicity* and *complexity* also have opposite meanings.

8. (C); Cause and Effect. An *illness* can result in *pallor,* or paleness, just as *insomnia,* or a lack of sleep, can result in *tiredness.*

9. (B); Location. A *promontory,* which is a peak of land that extends into a body of water, can be found along the *seacoast.* An *alligator* can be found in a *swamp.*

10. (D); Synonym. *Remuneration* and *compensation* have the same meaning, that of reward or pay. *Comprehension* and *understanding* have the same meaning.

ANSWER KEY

199

Workshop Answer Key *(continued)*

Lesson 15

p. 140 | Analogies

1. (B); Performer and Related Action. You expect a *criminal* to *abscond*, or run away to escape the law, just as you expect a *miser* to *hoard* money.

2. (D); Synonym. *Adjure* and *command* have the same meaning, as do *plead* and *beg*.

3. (C); Synonym. *Capricious*, which means erratic and inconstant, is similar in meaning to *fickle*, which means unstable and changeable. *Nonsensical* and *silly* also have similar meanings.

4. (B); Action and Related Object. A *body* can become *emaciated*, or abnormally lean, just as a *blade* can become *sharpened*.

5. (A); Antonym. One of the definitions of *ethereal* is heavenly, which is opposite in meaning to *worldly*. *Required* and *optional* also have opposite meanings.

6. (E); Characteristic Quality. A *fiasco*, which is a project that fails, is characteristically *unsuccessful*, just as a *disagreement* is characteristically *unpleasant*.

7. (E); Cause and Effect. *Wrongdoing* can result in *ignominy*, or shame and dishonor, just as *training* can result in *skill*.

8. (D); Cause and Effect. *Healthfulness* can result in *longevity*, or a long life, just as *exercise* can result in *fitness*.

9. (B); Performer and Related Action. You expect a *slanderer* to *malign*, or make damaging, false statements about another person, just as you expect a *mayor* to *govern* a city.

10. (B); Performer and Related Object. A *physician* makes a *prognosis*, or a prediction about the course of a patient's disease, just as a *judge* makes a *sentencing* about a defendant.

Reading New Words in Context

Lesson 1

p. 145 | Exercise 1: Finding Synonyms

Answers will vary. The following are possible responses.

1. stale from overuse
2. satirize
3. pen name
4. vague
5. acceptable behavior
6. commonplace
7. stole
8. a polite term for something unpleasant
9. wicked
10. warlike
11. avenger
12. deeply sad
13. agitated
14. warn
15. delicate skill
16. miserable
17. attacks with cruel language
18. indifferent
19. insincerely
20. equal

p. 146 | Exercise 2: Reading Strategically

1. D
2. C
3. B
4. D
5. A
6. A
7. A
8. E
9. D
10. C
11. C
12. E
13. D
14. B
15. A
16. E
17. C
18. B
19. B
20. C

200

Sixth Course | *Vocabulary Workshop*

Workshop Answer Key (continued)

Lesson 2

p. 150 | Exercise 1: Finding Synonyms

Answers will vary. The following are possible responses.

1. aware
2. absorbed
3. conference
4. obvious exaggeration
5. lessen
6. accidental
7. skillfully
8. tyrant
9. hypnotism
10. comical
11. bad-tempered
12. all-knowing
13. rambling
14. coats of arms
15. boredom
16. funeral hymns
17. people exiled from their native lands
18. in disguise
19. pretends
20. show of false bravery

p. 151 | Exercise 2: Reading Strategically

1. B
2. B
3. E
4. D
5. C
6. C
7. A
8. B
9. B
10. C
11. C
12. D
13. E
14. A
15. B
16. D
17. A
18. C
19. E
20. D

Lesson 3

p. 157 | Exercise 1: Finding Synonyms

Answers will vary. The following are possible responses.

1. implied
2. varied
3. craftiness
4. urge
5. loud and demanding
6. foulmouthed
7. coax
8. stingy
9. offers
10. hopeful
11. without recognizable qualities
12. angelic
13. unreal beings
14. badly written verse
15. easy
16. disorganized; shapeless
17. teachings
18. one who practices disciplined self-denial
19. polite behavior
20. someone helped by an influential person

p. 158 | Exercise 2: Reading Strategically

1. C
2. E
3. B
4. D
5. A
6. D
7. E
8. C
9. B
10. B
11. D
12. C
13. A
14. A
15. C
16. B
17. C
18. A
19. E
20. C

Workshop Answer Key (continued)

Lesson 4

p. 162 | Exercise 1: Finding Synonyms

Answers will vary. The following are possible responses.

1. revered
2. aversion
3. opposites
4. statement of obvious truth
5. free from blame
6. irritated
7. pertaining to word origins
8. unchangeable
9. poor
10. conquer
11. trespassing
12. apparent
13. made susceptible to
14. praise highly
15. without justification
16. introduced
17. scholarly
18. impostor
19. seemingly true but actually false
20. applying to a date in the past

p. 163 | Exercise 2: Reading Strategically

1. E
2. B
3. A
4. D
5. B
6. E
7. E
8. A
9. D
10. C
11. D
12. B
13. C
14. E
15. C
16. A
17. B
18. C
19. D
20. A

Lesson 5

p. 169 | Exercise 1: Finding Synonyms

Answers will vary. The following are possible responses.

1. produce
2. a shy, quiet person
3. self-denial
4. full of information
5. commonplace
6. having a deep, rich tone
7. offspring
8. dull
9. trite
10. unimportant
11. a long, moralizing sermon
12. tribute
13. emotionally touching
14. peculiarities
15. attributed
16. agreeableness of sound
17. irrelevant; unnecessary
18. perfect example
19. mournful poems
20. length of time in a position

p. 170 | Exercise 2: Reading Strategically

1. C
2. D
3. E
4. C
5. E
6. D
7. B
8. A
9. D
10. B
11. E
12. D
13. D
14. D
15. B
16. C
17. A
18. D
19. B
20. B

Lesson 6

p. 175 | Exercise 1: Finding Synonyms

Answers will vary. The following are possible responses.

1. outline; arrangement
2. noticeable
3. still existing
4. requiring great strength
5. ridiculous
6. concluded
7. confirmed
8. lack
9. exacting; precise
10. daily
11. frankness
12. fascinated
13. deviations
14. advocates
15. omens
16. an artful trick
17. disprove
18. trickery
19. decided
20. examination of the past

p. 176 | Exercise 2: Reading Strategically

1. D
2. A
3. C
4. E
5. A
6. B
7. D
8. C
9. C
10. D
11. E
12. B
13. B
14. A
15. C
16. D
17. E
18. B
19. A
20. C

Lesson 7

p. 180 | Exercise 1: Finding Synonyms

Answers will vary. The following are possible responses.

1. an expert in art or taste
2. pouring forth
3. excitement
4. sociable
5. loud laughter
6. shortcomings
7. fawning
8. exact and careful
9. mature for one's age
10. pertinent
11. politeness
12. noble in spirit
13. inheritance
14. complaining
15. favorable
16. extremely generous
17. lenient
18. confined
19. intentional insults
20. yielded

p. 181 | Exercise 2: Reading Strategically

1. B
2. C
3. A
4. D
5. A
6. E
7. C
8. D
9. B
10. A
11. A
12. E
13. C
14. A
15. C
16. B
17. A
18. D
19. C
20. E

Lesson 8

p. 187 | Exercise 1: Finding Synonyms

Answers will vary. The following are possible responses.

1. primitive
2. mysterious
3. highly offensive
4. luxurious
5. disapproved strongly
6. damage
7. overwhelmed
8. composed of similar parts; uniform
9. a leader who stirs up people's emotions
10. forerunner
11. illegal
12. spread throughout
13. originated from
14. treacherous
15. contradiction
16. lie
17. criticized severely
18. temporary suspension
19. irreversible
20. pleaded on another's behalf

p. 188 | Exercise 2: Reading Strategically

1. D
2. C
3. B
4. B
5. E
6. B
7. D
8. A
9. C
10. D
11. A
12. B
13. E
14. C
15. D
16. A
17. E
18. B
19. C
20. C

Lesson 9

p. 193 | Exercise 1: Finding Synonyms

Answers will vary. The following are possible responses.

1. release
2. declare
3. lowest possible point
4. art of public speaking
5. abundantly
6. harsh
7. spacious
8. crippled
9. corpselike
10. very contagious, often fatal diseases
11. widespread
12. deadly
13. weakened
14. state of disorder
15. overthrow of something or someone
16. of or suited to a servant
17. assigned
18. coaxed
19. incapable of being reformed
20. branch of anthropology that compares the cultures of recent societies

p. 194 | Exercise 2: Reading Strategically

1. C
2. D
3. D
4. B
5. C
6. C
7. E
8. D
9. A
10. E
11. B
12. A
13. D
14. C
15. C
16. E
17. A
18. D
19. B
20. E

Lesson 10

p. 198 | Exercise 1: Finding Synonyms

Answers will vary. The following are possible responses.

1. avoid
2. inclination
3. rashness
4. lawsuits
5. an interruption
6. hesitant
7. justified
8. incited
9. retracted
10. approval and support
11. get even with
12. possibility
13. not showing emotion
14. eagerly
15. unmoving
16. concerned with others
17. disagreed
18. secret
19. soothe
20. trace

p. 199 | Exercise 2: Reading Strategically

1. E
2. D
3. B
4. C
5. B
6. E
7. D
8. E
9. A
10. C
11. B
12. B
13. B
14. C
15. D
16. B
17. A
18. B
19. D
20. A

Lesson 11

p. 205 | Exercise 1: Finding Synonyms

Answers will vary. The following are possible responses.

1. overbearing
2. difference
3. harsh
4. essence
5. debatable
6. quiet
7. based on direct experience
8. routine
9. distinguish
10. international
11. a place of safekeeping
12. disagree with
13. unalterable
14. a supporting statement
15. devotion to one thing and contempt for its opposite
16. flimsy
17. a formal writing
18. insightfulness
19. poking fun at
20. lacking

p. 206 | Exercise 2: Reading Strategically

1. A
2. C
3. D
4. C
5. A
6. D
7. D
8. D
9. C
10. B
11. C
12. A
13. A
14. B
15. A
16. D
17. A
18. C
19. B
20. A

Workshop Answer Key *(continued)*

SIXTH COURSE

Lesson 12

p. 210 | Exercise 1: Finding Synonyms

Answers will vary. The following are possible responses.

1. forced
2. solid earth
3. talkative
4. give out
5. metal-plated glove
6. bitter
7. shock and resulting confusion
8. stop
9. spotted with different colors
10. polish
11. something out of its proper time
12. riddle
13. understood by few
14. foretell
15. waste away
16. extensive, filling many volumes
17. forerunner
18. explains
19. advantageous position
20. wrong name

p. 211 | Exercise 2: Reading Strategically

1. B
2. D
3. A
4. B
5. E
6. C
7. D
8. C
9. C
10. A
11. B
12. D
13. E
14. A
15. C
16. D
17. B
18. B
19. E
20. D

Lesson 13

p. 217 | Exercise 1: Finding Synonyms

Answers will vary. The following are possible responses.

1. unpredictably changeable
2. inhabitants
3. diligently
4. declare
5. reasonable
6. deep cracks
7. composure
8. ending
9. faultless
10. serving as an excuse
11. greed
12. financial
13. supported
14. result
15. excessive
16. evils
17. suppressed
18. use of threats or force
19. appease
20. bitterness

p. 218 | Exercise 2: Reading Strategically

1. E
2. C
3. A
4. D
5. B
6. E
7. B
8. B
9. C
10. B
11. A
12. C
13. E
14. D
15. C
16. B
17. A
18. E
19. B
20. B

Sixth Course | *Vocabulary Workshop*

Workshop Answer Key *(continued)*

SIXTH COURSE

Lesson 14

p. 223 | Exercise 1: Finding Synonyms

Answers will vary. The following are possible responses.

1. paintings made on wet plaster
2. fleeting
3. high point of land extending into water
4. swirling rainbow colors
5. paleness
6. developed rapidly
7. forsaking of beliefs
8. luxury
9. trinkets
10. decorated
11. complex
12. gold or silver bars, ingots
13. pay
14. an exaggerated portrait
15. economy or thrift
16. excessively sentimental
17. sympathy
18. charging high interest on loans
19. dishonest
20. frolicking

p. 224 | Exercise 2: Reading Strategically

1. C
2. D
3. A
4. E
5. A
6. B
7. C
8. C
9. B
10. E
11. B
12. D
13. B
14. C
15. E
16. B
17. D
18. B
19. C
20. A

Lesson 15

p. 229 | Exercise 1: Finding Synonyms

Answers will vary. The following are possible responses.

1. threaten
2. length of life
3. wasted away
4. pretending to be sick
5. bring forth
6. ran away
7. forecast
8. uncommunicative
9. avoid
10. unearthly
11. living or lasting for two years
12. protested
13. undecided
14. erratic
15. command
16. slander
17. injury done for injury received
18. complete failure
19. public disgrace
20. defamed

p. 230 | Exercise 2: Reading Strategically

1. A
2. E
3. D
4. C
5. A
6. B
7. B
8. E
9. A
10. C
11. C
12. E
13. D
14. B
15. C
16. A
17. C
18. D
19. B
20. E

ANSWER KEY

207

Tests Answer Key

Formative Assessment

p. 3 | Test 1

1. C	6. C
2. B	7. A
3. D	8. E
4. E	9. B
5. C	10. B

p. 4 | Test 2

1. C	6. A
2. D	7. A
3. D	8. D
4. C	9. C
5. B	10. E

p. 5 | Test 3

1. A	6. C
2. C	7. D
3. D	8. B
4. D	9. E
5. D	10. E

p. 6 | Test 4

1. B	6. B
2. E	7. C
3. D	8. D
4. B	9. C
5. D	10. A

p. 7 | Test 5

1. C	6. B
2. A	7. E
3. B	8. E
4. A	9. D
5. C	10. C

p. 8 | Test 6

1. D	6. B
2. C	7. B
3. A	8. B
4. A	9. A
5. E	10. C

p. 9 | Test 7

1. D	6. C
2. C	7. E
3. A	8. B
4. C	9. D
5. A	10. A

p. 10 | Test 8

1. B	6. C
2. B	7. B
3. A	8. C
4. E	9. E
5. C	10. D

p. 11 | Test 9

1. B	6. E
2. A	7. D
3. A	8. D
4. B	9. D
5. A	10. B

p. 12 | Test 10

1. D	6. E
2. B	7. D
3. E	8. A
4. E	9. C
5. C	10. D

p. 13 | Test 11

1. B	6. B
2. A	7. B
3. C	8. D
4. C	9. B
5. A	10. E

p. 14 | Test 12

1. B	6. A
2. B	7. A
3. D	8. E
4. C	9. C
5. D	10. D

p. 15 | Test 13

1. A	6. A
2. E	7. D
3. D	8. D
4. C	9. B
5. C	10. E

p. 16 | Test 14

1. C	6. A
2. B	7. E
3. C	8. D
4. A	9. A
5. C	10. B

p. 17 | Test 15

1. A	6. D
2. B	7. C
3. A	8. D
4. A	9. E
5. B	10. B

p. 18 | Test 16

1. D	6. E
2. B	7. E
3. D	8. B
4. C	9. A
5. C	10. A

p. 19 | Test 17

1. C	6. C
2. A	7. B
3. A	8. D
4. E	9. D
5. D	10. A

p. 20 | Test 18

1. B	6. D
2. E	7. A
3. D	8. B
4. C	9. C
5. B	10. A

p. 21 | Test 19

1. E	6. B
2. E	7. C
3. D	8. D
4. D	9. C
5. A	10. D

p. 22 | Test 20

1. B	6. B
2. A	7. B
3. D	8. D
4. A	9. C
5. D	10. E

p. 23 | Test 21

1. A	6. C
2. A	7. E
3. D	8. A
4. E	9. B
5. A	10. C

p. 24 | Test 22

1. A	6. E
2. E	7. B
3. D	8. C
4. B	9. B
5. C	10. C

p. 25 | Test 23

1. E	6. A
2. D	7. B
3. C	8. C
4. B	9. D
5. C	10. E

p. 26 | Test 24

1. D	6. C
2. A	7. E
3. D	8. E
4. C	9. B
5. A	10. D

p. 27 | Test 25

1. C	6. D
2. B	7. E
3. C	8. B
4. D	9. B
5. E	10. A

p. 28 | Test 26

1. B	6. D
2. C	7. A
3. D	8. C
4. B	9. C
5. E	10. B

p. 29 | Test 27

1. C	6. D
2. B	7. E
3. C	8. B
4. D	9. A
5. E	10. A

p. 30 | Test 28

1. B	6. B
2. C	7. D
3. D	8. E
4. A	9. A
5. C	10. C

p. 31 | Test 29

1. E	6. E
2. D	7. C
3. A	8. B
4. B	9. D
5. C	10. A

p. 32 | Test 30

1. D	6. B
2. A	7. A
3. A	8. B
4. D	9. D
5. C	10. E

Summative Assessment

p. 35 | Test 1 Part A

1. E	14. D
2. C	15. C
3. D	16. D
4. B	17. D
5. B	18. D
6. A	19. E
7. D	20. D
8. E	21. C
9. B	22. C
10. A	23. E
11. C	24. B
12. B	25. C
13. A	

p. 39 | Test 1 Part B

26. D	49. C
27. B	50. D
28. D	51. C
29. D	52. C
30. C	53. B
31. D	54. C
32. C	55. C
33. A	56. C
34. B	57. A
35. E	58. E
36. C	59. C
37. D	60. D
38. E	61. C
39. E	62. E
40. A	63. D
41. D	64. E
42. A	65. B
43. B	66. E
44. B	67. D
45. C	68. D
46. E	69. B
47. C	70. A
48. A	

p. 44 | Test 1 Part C

71. (A); Synonym. *Abject* and *miserable* have similar meanings, as do *tired* and *weary*.

72. (C); Degree. To *admonish* suggests a lesser degree of punishment than to *condemn*. *Look* suggests a lesser degree of severity than *glare*, which means to look angrily.

73. (D); Characteristic Quality. *Mist* is characteristically *amorphous*, or shapeless, just as a *jackhammer* is characteristically *loud*.

74. (B); Performer and Related Object. A *police officer* carries a *badge*, just as a *knight* carries a *blazon*, which can be a coat of arms, a heraldic shield, or a banner.

75. (D); Antonym. *Bravado*, which means excessive confidence, is opposite in meaning to *humility*, which means humbleness. *Bravery* and *cowardice* also have opposite meanings.

76. (A); Characteristic Quality. A *genius* is characteristically *brilliant*, just as a *hothead* is characteristically *choleric*, or bad-tempered and apt to explode in anger.

77. (E); Performer and Related Action. You expect a *charlatan*, one who makes false claims, to *deceive* others, just as you expect an *impostor* to *trick*.

78. (B); Characteristic Quality. A *despot*, or tyrant, is characteristically *oppressive* in the same way that a *thief* is characteristically *furtive*.

79. (B); Synonym. *Distraught* and *agitated* have similar meanings, as do *fashionable* and *stylish*.

80. (D); Synonym. *Etymology*, or the tracing of a word's origin, is similar in meaning to *source*. In the same way, *altercation* and *quarrel* are similar in meaning.

81. (C); Characteristic Quality. A *euphemism* is characteristically *inoffensive*, just as a *diamond* is characteristically *hard*.

82. (E); Degree. An *acquaintance* is a more formal relationship than a *friendship*, just as a *colloquy* is more formal than a *chat*.

83. (C); Synonym. *Glib* is similar in meaning to *insincere*, just as *evasive* is similar in meaning to *dishonest*.

84. (D); Synonym. *Guile* and *slyness* have the same meaning, as do *clamor* and *uproar*.

85. (B); Classification. A *hyperbole* can be classified as a *figure of speech*, just as a *novel* can be classified as a type of *literature*.

86. (D); Classification. A *jet* can be classified as a type of *airplane*. An *elegy*, or verse written to lament the dead, can be classified as a type of *poem*.

87. (E); Synonym. *Kin* and *relatives* have the same meaning, as do *progeny* and *descendants*.

88. (D); Antonym. *Nondescript* is opposite in meaning to *colorful*. *Stubborn* means the opposite of *yielding*.

89. (C); Degree. *Omniscient*, which means all-knowing, is greater in degree than *knowledgeable*. *Infinite*, which means endless, is greater in degree than *large*.

90. (A); Performer and Related Action. You expect a *surgeon* to *operate* on a patient, just as you expect a *trickster* to *feign*, or make a false showing of something.

91. (A); Synonym. *Ostensible* and *apparent* have the same meaning, as do *fragile* and *delicate*.

92. (D); Antonym. *Poignant*, or emotionally moving, is opposite in meaning to *dull*, just as *exciting* and *boring* are opposite in meaning.

93. (C); Performer and Related Action. You expect a *thief* to *purloin*, or steal, things, just as you expect a *surveyor* to *measure* land.

Tests Answer Key *(continued)*

94. (D); Antonym. *Retroactive,* or having an effect on things in the past, is opposite in meaning to *anticipatory* in the same way as *hospitable* and *unfriendly* are opposite in meaning.

95. (C); Performer and Related Action. You expect a *slanderer* to *revile,* or scold, someone, just as you expect an *admirer* to *praise* someone.

96. (B); Performer and Related Action. You expect a *savior* to attempt to *save* someone, just as you expect a *nemesis,* someone who imposes retribution or punishment, to *punish* another.

97. (E); Antonym. *Solemn* means the opposite of *silly,* just as *indigent,* or poor, means the opposite of *wealthy.*

98. (E); Characteristic Quality. *Propaganda* is characteristically *specious,* or misleading, just as a *busybody* is characteristically *meddlesome.*

99. (B); Synonym. *Subjugate* and *conquer* have the same meaning. *Lose* and *misplace* have similar meanings.

100. (A); Degree. *Vociferous,* which means clamorous, is greater in degree than *cheering,* just as *ecstatic* is greater in degree than *happiness.*

p. 47 | Test 2 Part A

1. D	**14.** E
2. B	**15.** A
3. A	**16.** B
4. C	**17.** D
5. E	**18.** B
6. C	**19.** A
7. B	**20.** D
8. E	**21.** C
9. A	**22.** A
10. B	**23.** C
11. D	**24.** D
12. C	**25.** C
13. C	

p. 51 | Test 2 Part B

26. D	**49.** A
27. D	**50.** C
28. C	**51.** B
29. A	**52.** E
30. A	**53.** D
31. D	**54.** E
32. B	**55.** C
33. D	**56.** B
34. C	**57.** C
35. E	**58.** A
36. D	**59.** B
37. C	**60.** D
38. D	**61.** C
39. B	**62.** E
40. D	**63.** D
41. B	**64.** C
42. D	**65.** B
43. C	**66.** A
44. E	**67.** C
45. E	**68.** C
46. A	**69.** C
47. A	**70.** E
48. D	

p. 56 | Test 2 Part C

71. (C); Synonym. *Aberration* and *abnormality* have the same meaning. *Evolution* and *development* have similar meanings.

72. (C); Antonym. *Acknowledge* means the opposite of *deny. Repudiate,* or *reject,* is the opposite of *accept.*

73. (B); Synonym. *Alteration* and *change* have the same meaning. *Configuration* and *shape* have similar meanings.

74. (E); Performer and Related Object. You expect a *prophet* to interpret an *augury,* just as you expect a *mathematician* to solve an *equation.*

75. (D); Classification. A *banana* can be classified as a *fruit,* just as a *demagogue,* or someone who gains power by stirring up people's emotions, can be classified as a *leader.*

212   Sixth Course | *Vocabulary Workshop*

76. (D); Synonym. *Considerate* and *thoughtful* have similar meanings. *Profuse*, which means in great amount, is similar in meaning to *abundant*.

77. (C); Synonym. *Contingency* and *possibility* have similar meanings, as do *opportunity* and *chance*.

78. (A); Antonym. *Cordial* and *unfriendly* have opposite meanings. *Perfidious*, which means disloyal, means the opposite of *faithful*.

79. (E); Synonym. *Elocution* and *public speaking* have similar meanings, as do *quarrel* and *dispute*.

80. (B); Degree. Something that is *gigantic* is considered to be bigger than something that is *large*. Someone who is *obsequious* shows an excessive desire to please and obey, whereas someone who is *obedient* is merely willing to follow instructions.

81. (E); Antonym. *Gregarious*, which means friendly, is opposite in meaning to *unfriendly*. *Comical* and *tragic* also have opposite meanings.

82. (B); Antonym. *Growth* and *decline* have opposite meanings. *Candor*, which means openness and honesty, means the opposite of *deceitfulness*.

83. (A); Characteristic Quality. A *harbinger*, or herald, is characteristically *informative*, just as a *vacation* is characteristically *refreshing*.

84. (B); Synonym. *Hiatus*, which means gap, and *interruption* have similar meanings, as do *silliness* and *foolishness*.

85. (D); Characteristic Quality. *Twins* are characteristically *homogeneous*, or similar, just as *ice* is characteristically *slippery*.

86. (B); Synonym. *Inundate* and *overwhelm* have similar meanings, just as do *complete* and *finish*.

87. (D); Characteristic Quality. A *fool* is characteristically *ludicrous*, or absurd, just as a *comedian* is characteristically *funny*.

88. (A); Antonym. *Magnanimous*, which means generous, is opposite in meaning to *selfish*. *Divided* and *united* also have opposite meanings.

89. (D); Degree. *Munificent* is more extreme in degree than *generous*, just as *infuriating* is more extreme in degree than *annoying*.

90. (E); Performer and Related Object. An *heir* receives a *patrimony*, just as an *employee* receives a *salary*.

91. (B); Classification. *Pediatrics*, the medical care of infants and children, is classified as a kind of *medicine*. *Ethnology*, the study of human behavior and development, is classified as a type of *anthropology*.

92. (E); Degree. *Primordial*, which means primitive, suggests a greater degree of antiquity than does *early*, just as *ancient* suggests a greater degree of age than does *old*.

93. (A); Synonym. *Procedure* and *method* have similar meanings, as do *foible* and *weakness*.

94. (A); Performer and Related Action. You expect a *proofreader* to be *accurate*, just as you expect an *orator* to be *fervid*, or enthusiastic.

95. (B); Characteristic Quality. A *complainer* is characteristically *querulous*, just as a *trickster* is characteristically *mischievous*.

96. (B); Synonym. *Salient* and *prominent* have similar meanings, as do *alone* and *solitary*.

97. (D); Characteristic Quality. A *typist*, who stays seated much of the time, is characteristically *sedentary*, just as a *snob* is characteristically *conceited*.

98. (E); Characteristic Quality. A *doubter* is characteristically *skeptical*, just as a *palace* is characteristically *sumptuous*.

99. (D); Synonym. *Start* and *begin* have the same meaning, as do *cajole* and *coax*.

100. (B); Performer and Related Action. A *jury* may *vindicate* someone, just as the *police* may *protect* someone.

1. B	**14.** E
2. C	**15.** B
3. D	**16.** B
4. C	**17.** C
5. E	**18.** A
6. A	**19.** A
7. D	**20.** C
8. C	**21.** B
9. B	**22.** C
10. A	**23.** D
11. E	**24.** B
12. C	**25.** E
13. D	

p. 63 | **Test 3 Part B**

26. C	**49.** A
27. D	**50.** E
28. A	**51.** B
29. E	**52.** A
30. D	**53.** D
31. C	**54.** C
32. D	**55.** B
33. B	**56.** A
34. E	**57.** B
35. C	**58.** A
36. D	**59.** E
37. B	**60.** B
38. C	**61.** C
39. D	**62.** D
40. A	**63.** A
41. E	**64.** D
42. C	**65.** C
43. A	**66.** C
44. E	**67.** D
45. D	**68.** D
46. A	**69.** E
47. E	**70.** C
48. E	

p. 68 | **Test 3 Part C**

71. (D); Antonym. *Apostasy* and *allegiance* have opposite meanings, as do *freedom* and *captivity*.

72. (C); Cause and Effect. An *aspersion* can cause a *bad reputation*, just as *practice* can cause *mastery*.

73. (B); Antonym. *Aver*, which means affirm, means the opposite of *deny*. *Allow* and *forbid* are also opposite in meaning.

74. (D); Part and Whole. A *bristle* is part of a *brush*, just as a *gauntlet*, a metal-plated glove, is part of a suit of *armor*.

75. (D); Action and Object. You *burnish*, or polish, *silverware*, just as you *baste* a *turkey*.

76. (B); Synonym. *Corollary* and *deduction* have similar meanings, as do *verification* and *proof*.

77. (C); Synonym. *Differentiate* and *distinguish* have similar meanings, just as do *practice* and *rehearse*.

78. (A); Antonym. *Disparity*, which means difference, means the opposite of *similarity*, just as *reunion* means the opposite of *separation*.

79. (D); Synonym. *Espouse* and *support* have similar meanings, as do *inspect* and *examine*.

80. (C); Performer and Related Action. You expect a *commentator* to *expound*, or explain, just as you could expect a *gymnast* to *somersault*.

81. (B); Performer and Related Action. You expect a *blackmailer* to *extort*, just as you expect a *deer* to *run*.

82. (D); Synonym. *Fashionable* and *stylish* have similar meanings, as do *burgeoning* and *expanding*.

83. (C); Performer and Related Action. You expect a *mourner* to *grieve*, just as you expect a *tyrant* to *coerce*.

84. (B); Performer and Related Action. You expect a *miser* to *hoard* money, just as you expect a *criminal* to *abscond*, or run away.

85. (B); Synonym. *Inexorable*, which means unable to be moved or influenced by persuasion, has a meaning similar to *unrelenting*. *Intricate* and *complex* also have similar meanings.

86. (E); Performer and Related Action. You expect an *heir* to *inherit* an estate, just as you expect a *negotiator* to *conciliate*, or smooth over, conflicts between opposing parties.

87. (C); Characteristic Quality. A *rainbow* is characteristically *iridescent*, which means having rainbowlike colors, just as a *mountain* is characteristically *high*.

88. (E); Characteristic Quality. *Lace* is characteristically *delicate*, just as a *bauble* is characteristically *showy*.

89. (E); Performer and Related Action. A *memorandum* is an informative document composed by an *administrator*, just as a *treatise* is a formal, systematic book or article composed by a *scholar*.

90. (A); Synonym. *Mete* and *distribute* have the same meaning, as do *surround* and *enclose*.

91. (D); Synonym. *Mottled* and *splotchy* have the same meaning, as do *slim* and *slender*.

92. (C); Characteristic Quality. A *model* is characteristically *photogenic*, just as a *meddler* is characteristically *officious*, or interfering.

93. (B); Location. A *promontory*, which is a peak of land that extends into a body of water, can be found along the *seacoast*. An *alligator* can be found in a *swamp*.

94. (D); Antonym. *Remonstrate*, which means to plead in protest, is opposite in meaning to *accept*. *Organize* and *confuse* are also opposite in meaning.

95. (D); Synonym. *Reprisal* and *revenge* can both mean retaliation. *Satisfaction* and *contentment* also have the same meaning.

96. (B); Cause and Effect. *Learning* can be the result of *study*, just as *rancor* can be the result of a *dispute*.

97. (A); Antonym. *Taciturn*, or habitually silent, is opposite in meaning to *talkative*, just as *courteous* is opposite in meaning to *impolite*.

98. (C); Cause and Effect. *Insomnia*, the inability to sleep, can cause *tiredness*, just as *illness* can cause *pallor*, or paleness associated with poor health.

99. (C); Characteristic Quality. *Usury*, or lending money at an excessive rate of interest, is characteristically *unfair*. In the same way, *smuggling* is characteristically *illegal*.

100. (B); Synonym. *Venal* and *corrupt* have similar meanings, as do *temporary* and *short-lived*.

Notes